D1277564

PERSONALITY ASSESSMENT IN ORGANIZATIONS

PERSONALITY ASSESSMENT IN ORGANIZATIONS

Edited by
H. John Bernardin
and David A. Bownas

PRAEGER

PRAEGER SPECIAL STUDIES • PRAEGER SCIENTIFIC

New York • Philadelphia • Eastbourne, UK
Toronto • Hong Kong • Tokyo • Sydney

Library of Congress Cataloging in Publication Data
Main entry under title:

Personality assessment in organizations.

Includes index.
1. Psychology, Industrial—Addresses, essays,
lectures. 2. Personality assessment—Addresses,
essays, lectures. I. Bernardin, H. John.
II. Bownas, David A.
HF5548.8.P3995   1985   158.7   84-26355
ISBN 0-03-072023-0   (alk. paper)

Published in 1985 by Praeger Publishers
CBS Educational and Professional Publishing, a Division of CBS Inc.
521 Fifth Avenue, New York, NY 10175 USA

© 1985 by Praeger Publishers

Printed in the United States of America on acid-free paper

INTERNATIONAL OFFICES

Orders from outside the United States should be sent to the appropriate address listed below. Orders from areas not listed below should be placed through CBS International Publishing, 383 Madison Ave., New York, NY 10175 USA

Australia, New Zealand
Holt Saunders, Pty, Ltd., 9 Waltham St., Artarmon, N.S.W. 2064, Sydney, Australia

Canada
Holt, Rinehart & Winston of Canada, 55 Horner Ave., Toronto, Ontario, Canada M8Z 4X6

Europe, the Middle East, & Africa
Holt Saunders, Ltd., 1 St. Anne's Road, Eastbourne, East Sussex, England BN21 3UN

Japan
Holt Saunders, Ltd., Ichibancho Central Building, 22-1 Ichibancho, 3rd Floor, Chiyodaku, Tokyo, Japan

Hong Kong, Southeast Asia
Holt Saunders Asia, Ltd., 10 Fl, Intercontinental Plaza, 94 Granville Road, Tsim Sha Tsui East, Kowloon, Hong Kong

Manuscript submissions should be sent to the Editorial Director, Praeger Publishers, 521 Fifth Avenue, New York, NY 10175 USA

Introduction

The general feeling among academic psychologists is that personality measurement has little or no validity for the selection and placement of personnel. In the most recent review of alternatives to cognitive ability testing, Reilly and Chao (1982) did not even include a section on standardized personality tests. Two early reviews on the subject are probably most responsible for the lack of academic attention to personality measurement applied to organizational decision making. Both Ghiselli and Barthol (1953) and Guion and Gottier (1965) concluded that little empirical support could be found for personality testing. Guion (1965) later stated, "One cannot survey the literature on the use of personality tests in industry without becoming thoroughly disenchanted" (1965, p. 353). Most contemporary textbooks in industrial/organizational psychology have little discussion of personality testing. There are no texts devoted to personality assessment in organizations.

Despite the lack of attention to this research area in the academic journals and texts, virtually every organization with which we are familiar makes personnel decisions on the basis of some type of personality assessment. Be it through a standardized testing program, an employment interview for selection/placement, or a trait-based performance appraisal system, personality assessment plays an important part in personnel decisions. Professional interviewers and performance appraisers describe personnel with phrases like "he seemed to lack the drive for this type of work" or "she certainly is likable; perfect for a sales job" or "his lack of self-esteem will create problems if he is promoted". Real-life personnel decision makers are well aware of the relationship between these personality variables and employee performance, so personality assessment of one form or another is an important component of personnel decision making.

Managers are, however, generally unaware of how inaccurately they measure these constructs. Evidence is clear that most assessors cannot even define such concepts consistently, let alone measure them reliably or validly. Bass and Barrett (1981) asked 50 executives to define the word "dependability"; they received 47 distinctly different definitions. Thus, the true issue becomes not whether personality variables *will* be assessed in organization but *which* characteristics should be measured and *how* they can be assessed most validly.

v

While there is a paucity of published research on personality assessment in organizations, the business of personality testing applied to industry is flourishing. As organizational decision makers struggle with ways to affect the "bottom line," low-cost personnel selection devices are appealing. Unfortunately, many of these practitioners do not know how to interpret research evidence regarding particular personality measures. The typical adoption scenario is for the practitioner first to be influenced by a slick brochure from the publisher of "Snake Oil Extraordinaire (SOE)." The brochure probably has guarded and ambiguous statements of support for the use of SOE. Testimonials may make such claims as "my productivity went up 20% after I started to select my managers using the SOE" or "preliminary evidence shows the SOE increases productivity, decreases turnover and absenteeism, and reverses male pattern baldness." The probability that the practitioner will purchase the test may be more a function of the slickness of the brochure and the fast-talking sales representative than of the actual validity of the instrument being peddled. One common marketing strategy in this area is to publish related articles in magazines and soft trade journals that are read by organizational decision makers. These outlets often lack the expertise to critically assess the veracity of claims regarding the instrument. Airline magazines are a great target for this strategy. For example, three articles appeared in airline magazines in 1983 extolling the virtues of handwriting analysis for predicting sales and managerial success. All were by the same author, who happens to have a consulting firm specializing in graphology. In fact, there is virtually no evidence to support the use of handwriting analysis to predict work performance (e.g., Rafaeli & Klimoski, 1983).

"Let the buyer beware" is really the key point here. In an earnest attempt to solve some of the company's personnel or productivity problems (and for only $18 a copy, plus scoring) the decision maker may fail to carefully examine, or more commonly does not know how to examine, the scientific evidence regarding the instrument. At a recent presentation for the American Society of Personnel Administrators, one of the authors found that 98 percent of practitioners thought personality/motivational constructs should be measured in selection/placement systems and 75 percent were doing it in one form or another. Only 2 percent had even heard of *Buros Mental Measurements Yearbook*.

The purpose of this volume is to propose an academic revival of sorts: a revival that, we hope, will stimulate research in this area, and ultimately help the practitioner make better personnel decisions. Inspired by the great void in published technical writing on the subject, we organized a symposium at Virginia Polytechnic Institute and State University, and invited some of the experts closely associated with the use of personality assessment in organizations. The chapters of this volume are refinements of the 1983 presentations. We believe they are a start in rekindling academic interest on the subject.

REFERENCES

Bass, B.M., & Barrett, G.V. *People, work, and organizations.* Boston: Allyn & Bacon, 1981.

Ghiselli, E.E., & Barthol, R.P. The validity of personality inventories in the selection of employees. *Journal of Applied Psychology,* 1953, *38,* 18–20.

Guion, R.M. *Personnel testing.* New York: McGraw-Hill, 1965.

Guion, R.M. & Gottier, R.F. Validity of personality measures in personnel selection. *Personnel Psychology,* 1965, *18,* 135–164.

Rafaeli, A., & Klimoski, R.J. Predicting sales success through handwriting analysis: An evaluation of the effects of training and handwriting sample content. *Journal of Applied Psychology,* 1983, *68,* 212–217.

Reilly, R.R., & Chao, G.T. Validity and fairness of some alternative employee selection procedures. *Personnel Psychology,* 1982, *35,* 1–62.

Contents

1

The Use of Personal Assessment in Industry: Methodological and Interpretive Problems
Anne Anastasi

The use of personality tests in industry is beset with methodological and interpretive problems of both a practical and a theoretical nature. Personality tests share all the major problems and pitfalls encountered in ability testing, and they present several additional problems peculiar to themselves. They have been a target for the principal criticisms directed at ability tests, plus special criticisms designed just for personality tests. It is these special problems and special criticisms that I want to address in this chapter.

EARLY HISTORY OF PERSONALITY ASSESSMENT IN INDUSTRY

Some of the practical testing problems encountered today can be better understood if viewed against the historical background of personality assessment in industry (Anastasi 1979, ch. 1; Hale 1980, 1982). Industrial personnel testing in the United States was introduced on a regular operational basis during the third and fourth decades of the twentieth century, although its use in civil service dates from the late nineteenth century. The 1920s and 1930s witnessed an upsurge in the use of personality inventories in industry. Special interest centered on the personality assessment of sales personnel. Another, more general use was in predicting who would function most harmoniously with fellow workers and supervisors. The assessment of managerial personnel was a still later development in personality testing. Personnel testing in general rose to a peak in the early 1960s and then began to wane for various reasons, both technical and societal.

The early industrial use of personnel tests was closely linked to the rapid growth of large-scale industry. The increasing need for workers with specialized skills and training, the high rates of labor turnover, the low productivity, and the high frequency of accidents in the workplace stimulated a demand for more effective and systematic techniques for selecting employees and for assigning them to appropriate jobs. In the 1910s and 1920s a few authentic tests that could be useful in industry were beginning to appear, but they offered meager fare to the practical businessman. Charlatans rushed in to fill the gap with their alluring promises of short-cuts and confident solutions. An example was the Blackford Plan of character analysis, with its assertions about the characteristic traits of blonds and brunets and its system for reading physiognomy and handwriting (Blackford & Newcomb 1919). That such systems flourished early in the century is not too surprising. What is noteworthy, however, is the persistence of charlatanism (see Stryker 1953). Even today it is not difficult to find evidence of charlatans having a significant impact on personnel assessment—some in the continuing practice of ancient pseudosciences, such as astrology; others in more sober modern dress, with degrees from diploma mills.

There is another, more disturbing aspect to the problem of charlatanism. Charlatans may come and go, but the public demand for the magic formulas they offer goes on. The desire for quick solutions that yield clear-cut, unqualified answers is extremely viable. The early applied psychologists had to compete with the charlatans in meeting these demands. When psychology expanded into the public arena and psychological tests achieved wide recognition, it was the psychologists who were expected to produce the magic.

The persistence of this demand for magic formulas accounts for many of the prevalent misuses and misinterpretations of tests among such groups as educators and personnel workers. It is clearly illustrated by the well-nigh indestructible belief that intelligence and aptitude tests measure innate capacity, and that if they don't, then psychologists should invent a test that does. For personality testing, about which general knowledge is even more fuzzy, expectations are even more bizarre.

Most current criticisms of testing are essentially directed not to the tests themselves, but to misuses of tests and misinterpretations of test results. This conclusion has been reached so often by blue ribbon panels, commissions, task forces, and other specially appointed groups that it has become almost a cliché. To be sure, some of these misuses may be assumed or exaggerated by the critics; they may not actually occur, or at least not occur so frequently as claimed. Nevertheless, test scores *are* sometimes misinterpreted and test results misused by persons who are inadequately informed about tests or psychology, or both. The latest edition of the *Standards for Educational and Psychological Testing* (1985) recommends that test authors and publishers make special efforts to caution test users against common misconceptions about tests and misinterpretations of test scores. Such efforts are also the responsibility of professionals who serve as consultants or supervisors of test users.

PRACTICAL PROBLEMS AND PITFALLS

Turning to practical problems and pitfalls encountered in personality assessment, I shall cite three examples of special relevance to industry. The first, stereotype accuracy, represents a pitfall that both test constructor and test user can easily fall into in their efforts to establish the validity of the instrument. The second, faking, relates to the confidence that can be placed in test responses when examinees are motivated to create a particular impression. The third, invasion of privacy, pertains to questions of professional ethics and societal concerns that the test user must face and resolve in ways appropriate to particular situations.

Stereotype Accuracy

The first problem, that of stereotype accuracy, is closely associated with the previously mentioned role of charlatanism in industrial testing. A favorite sales appeal of charlatans and borderline "consultants" is to invite business executives to undergo their particular brand of personality assessment so that they may "judge it for themselves." Then they provide a personality description overloaded with vague generalities applicable to most people. When confronted with such a description, the executives are usually impressed with its apparent accuracy and insight, and they conclude that the method will work equally well with their employees. This apparent self-validation has been called the "Barnum effect" (Dunnette 1957, p. 223; Meehl 1956, p. 266). It was named after Phineas T. Barnum, the famous showman and acknowledged master of the art of humbug.

That such generalized personality descriptions are readily accepted as true of oneself has been repeatedly demonstrated—with personnel managers and miscellaneous adult workers, as well as with the ever-ready population of college students. As early as 1933, two German researchers (Krüger & Zietz 1933) gave each of 39 subjects a single, uniform personality description allegedly based on an analysis of the subject's handwriting and horoscope. Each accepted the description as a good analysis of his or her own personality. Some participants expressed amazement at its accuracy, and no one rejected the analysis as a whole.

More recently, Ross Stagner (1958) conducted his well-known investigation of the same problem with personnel managers attending a conference. A standard personality inventory was administered to the group, and the papers were then collected for scoring. Before getting the actual scores, each participant received an identical copy of a personality analysis allegedly derived from his test responses. This analysis consisted of a list of descriptive statements in which the same 13 had been marked for each person. After examining his own report, each participant was asked to rate its accuracy on a five-step scale. Of the 68 respondents, 50 percent rated the report "amazingly accurate," 40 percent, "rather good," and the remaining 10 percent, "about half and half." None chose the two lowest ratings, which were "more wrong than right" and "almost entirely wrong." When the hoax was explained to them, it was apparent that none of the participants had doubted the authenticity of the reports.

These findings have been repeatedly corroborated in other studies (Diamond & Bond 1974; Donceel, Alimena, & Birch 1949; Forer 1949; Halperin, Snyder, Shenkel, & Houston 1976; Merrens & Richards 1970; Snyder & Larson 1972; Sundberg 1955; Ulrich, Stachnik, & Stainton 1963). Although the personality reports are more frequently accepted as accurate when they are stated in favorable terms, even unflattering descriptions are widely perceived as correct when offered by someone with recognized professional prestige.

The "Barnum effect" refers to the deliberate attempt to capitalize on the fallacy of stereotype accuracy. At a more subtle level, the bona fide investigator may succumb to this fallacy unwittingly. Suppose, for example, that in the validation of a projective technique, each individual protocol derived from test responses is described in terms of Q-sort statements, and the same Q sort is applied independently to each person's case history to provide a criterion measure. The degree of congruence between the descriptive statements chosen for each individual by the two methods is then taken as an indication of the validity of the test. Some control for this type of error can be obtained by measuring the congruence between the test evaluation of each person and the criterion evaluation of another person within the validation sample (see Silverman 1959, p. 9).

Faking

Approaching testing from a different viewpoint, we can look at the problem of faking by the examinee. Because falsification of responses is easier and more likely on self-report inventories, it has been more fully investigated with that type of instrument. In most industrial situations, whether for selection of applicants or for evaluation of job incumbents, the examinee is motivated to create a favorable impression. Under these circumstances, the faking of personality test responses, either deliberately or through more subtle, unrecognized response sets, is a possibility that cannot be ignored.

There is considerable experimental evidence that examinees can choose personality inventory responses to produce a given effect (Jacobs & Barron 1968; Radcliffe 1966; Stricker 1969; Wiggins 1966). This can be demonstrated by giving two comparable groups the directions to respond as a happy, well-adjusted person in one case and as a severely maladjusted person in the other. Or the same individuals can be given these two sets of directions at different times. The mean scores obtained under the two conditions have proved to be both significantly and conspicuously different. Specific simulation for particular jobs also can be successfully achieved. For example, on an inventory designed to measure self-confidence, subjects were instructed on one occasion to respond as though applying for a selling job; on the second occasion, the inventory was readministered with similar instructions except that the job was that of librarian (Wesman 1952). The mean self-confidence scores were much higher with the salesperson than with the librarian instructions. That job applicants do in fact fake personality test responses was demonstrated in still another study, in which the scores obtained by a group of applicants were compared with the scores of a comparable group of jobholders who were tested "for research purposes only" (R.F. Green 1951). Under these contrasting motivating conditions, the scores of the two groups differed in the expected direction.

Several procedures have been followed in the effort to meet the problem of faking. The construction of relatively subtle or neutral-sounding items may reduce the frequency of faking (Block 1965). There is some evidence, however, to suggest that so-called subtle items may in fact be items of low validity for the trait to be measured or the criterion to be predicted (Jackson 1971). A second, well-known solution utilizes specially developed verification scales, either to detect faking or to provide a correction term applied to the scores as a suppressor variable. Both are illustrated in the MMPI: the L and F scales for detection and the K scale for correction. Verification scales are now commonly included in self-report inventories, but at best they provide only partial solutions.

Still another procedure, the use of forced-choice items, is directed not to the detection but to the prevention of faking. Essentially, the forced-choice technique requires the respondent to choose between self-descriptive terms or phrases that are equated in social desirability but differ sharply in validity. The social desirability of each item is estimated either by having the items rated for this variable by a representative group of raters or by finding the number of people who endorse each item in self-descriptions. The two methods yield social desirability indexes that are highly correlated (Edwards 1957). Although the forced-choice technique appeared quite promising at the outset, it presents certain technical difficulties, and it does not work as well in practice as had been anticipated (Anastasi 1982b, pp. 522–524). For one thing, items that are equated for general social desirability may still differ in desirability for particular occupations, and can be identified as such by the respondents (Dunnette, McCartney, Carlson, & Kirchner 1962).

From another angle, efforts can be made through test instructions and the establishment of rapport to motivate examinees to respond frankly on self-report inventories. It is certainly not in the individual's best interests to be placed in a job that is incompatible with his or her personality characteristics. Proper orientation of examinees regarding the nature and purposes of testing should be of some help in eliciting accurate self-reports, but we cannot expect it to be effective in all situations or for all persons.

Finally, faking on personality tests should be viewed within the broader setting of façade effects and response sets. The tendency to choose socially desirable responses is only one of several response sets that have been identified (Anastasi 1982b, pp. 524–526; Jackson 1973). Another is acquiescence, the tendency to answer "Yes" or "True." When first identified, such response sets were considered solely as a source of irrelevant or error variance, and efforts were made to rule out their influence through special item types, verification keys, or correction terms. Later they came to be regarded as indicators of broad and durable personality characteristics that were worth measuring in their own right (Jackson & Messick 1958, 1962; Wiggins 1962). At that stage they were commonly designated "response styles." For example, the tendency to give socially desirable responses could indicate a pervasive personality need for conformity and social approval. It should be noted, however, that the assessment of such a stylistic trait still requires a specially constructed and separately scored scale, so as not to confound this trait with other, content-related traits such as dominance, sociability, or emotional stability.

The role of response sets and of content versus style in personality assessment is far from settled. It is likely that some stylistic scales will eventually prove to be valid predictors of important personality traits, but it is unlikely that they will generally replace content-related scales in personality inventories. Thus far, the voluminous research and the lively debate regarding the interrelated problems of faking, response sets, and stylistic traits have at least served to sharpen our awareness of what self-report inventories are measuring and what they may ultimately be able to measure.

Confidentiality and Privacy

The ethical responsibility to meet the need for confidentiality and privacy in the use of tests poses a complex and many-sided problem. It calls for protecting the validity and meaningfulness of the tests, on the one hand, and protecting the well-being and rights of the examinee, on the other. The problem has been fully and widely debated from a variety of angles over several decades (see American Psychological Association 1970, 1981; Anastasi 1980, 1982b, pp. 49–56; *Privacy and behavioral research* 1967). Popular concern about this problem rose to a peak in the mid-1960s. Its most conspicuous public display was provided by the Congressional inquiry into testing reported in the special issue of the *American Psychologist,* Testing and Public Policy (1965; see also Testimony 1966).

How, specifically, does the protection of privacy relate to personality testing? In a report entitled *Privacy and Behavioral Research* (1967), prepared for the Office of Science and Technology, the right to privacy was defined as "the right of the individual to decide for himself how much he will share with others his thoughts, his feelings, and the facts of his personal life" (p. 2). If we apply this definition to personality testing, we can identify at least three distinct facets of the problem. The first—and probably the most obvious—pertains to the possible invasion of privacy by the testing process itself. This is a question of what information the test should try to obtain in the first place. The second facet is that of confidentiality: To whom may test results be revealed? The third relates to the person's right to know his or her own test results. Here the question centers on what should be communicated to the examinee and in what form. Basically, the three facets involve disclosure to the examiner, to third parties, and to the examinee. I shall say no more about the last two facets, since they apply just as fully to ability tests as to personality tests; and they have been widely and meticulously examined in discussions of testing in general. Let me comment a bit further on the first facet, which underlies many popular objections to personality testing.

For purposes of testing effectiveness, it may be necessary to keep the examinee in ignorance of the specific ways in which individual responses on a personality test are to be interpreted. It follows that the examinee may, in the course of such a test, reveal characteristics without realizing that he or she is doing so. Logically, however, the possibility of invading privacy is not limited to personality tests. Any intelligence, aptitude, or achievement test may reveal limitations in skills and knowledge that an individual would rather not disclose. Moreover, any observation of an individual's behavior—as in an interview, a casual conversation, or other personal encounter—may yield information that the individual would prefer to conceal and that he or she may reveal unwittingly. The fact that personality tests have been singled out in discussions of the invasion of privacy probably reflects prevalent misconceptions about tests. If all tests were recognized as measures of behavior samples, with no mysterious powers to penetrate beyond behavior, popular fears and suspicions would be lessened.

In all psychological testing, the protection of privacy involves two key concepts: relevance and informed consent. The information that the individual is asked to reveal must be relevant to the stated purposes of the testing. An important implication of this principle is that all practicable efforts should be made to ascertain the validity of tests for the particular diagnostic or predictive purpose for which they are used. An instrument that is demonstrably valid for a given purpose is one that provides relevant information. It also behooves the test user to make sure that test scores are correctly interpreted.

The concept of informed consent also requires clarification, and its application in individual cases may call for the exercise of considerable professional judgment. The examinee should certainly be informed about the purpose of the testing, the kinds of data sought, and the use that will be made of the scores. It is not implied, however, that he or she should be shown the test items in advance or be told how specific responses will be scored. Such information would probably tend to distort responses on many personality tests. For example, if an examinee is told in advance that a self-report inventory will be scored with a dominance scale, his or her responses are likely to be influenced by stereotyped (and often erroneous) ideas he or she may have about this trait, or by a false or distorted self-concept.

In some self-report personality inventories, respondents may find particular items objectionable. This can be illustrated with the Minnestoa Multiphasic Personality Inventory (MMPI), which has probably been cited most often as an example of the invasion of privacy (see Testing and public policy 1965, especially pp. 923–926). A survey of the most common objections suggests that they usually stem from a literal interpretation of item content. It has been argued, for example, that job applicants who take the MMPI are examined in such areas as family relations, social life, and sexual and religious attitudes, which are considered both too personal and irrelevant to the testing purpose. The critics evidently overlook the fact that the items are not grouped, scored, or interpreted in terms of these apparent content areas, but in terms of empirically established behavioral correlates. Nor do they realize that individual item responses are not part of the examinee's record and cannot be identified in the total score reported for each scale.

One way to meet individual objections to such personality test items is to inform respondents that they may omit any items that they find too personal or otherwise unacceptable. But this is not a very satisfactory solution, because it tends to lower score reliability and may affect different scales unevenly (Butcher & Tellegen 1966; Walker 1967; Walker & Ward 1969). Moreover, it has not been demonstrated that the option to omit items makes the test more acceptable to examinees, who have no way of knowing how the omission of certain items may affect the interpretation of their performance (Fink & Butcher 1972).

A different solution is to include in the test instructions a simple explanation of the basic procedures followed in selecting items and in computing individual scores. The purpose of such an explanation is essentially to correct prevalent misconceptions about the construction and use of personality tests. Its potential effectiveness was demonstrated in an exploratory study conducted with college students at the University of Minnesota (Fink & Butcher 1972). While the control subjects took the MMPI with the standard instructions, the experimental subjects were given modified instructions, which provided simple information on how the test was constructed. Following the completion of the test, all subjects answered a brief questionnaire in which they reported how they would feel about the test if they had been asked to take it as part of the selection procedure in applying for a job. The results showed that the explanatory instructions significantly reduced the number of respondents who felt that the test represented an invasion of privacy or who considered some of the items offensive. At the same time, the mean score profile was not affected by the modified instructions.

This study suggests a promising avenue of research that merits further exploration. Test constructors and researchers could profitably investigate the use of similar explanatory instructions with other types of examinees, other tests, and other testing contexts. Of course, altering standard test instructions is not a procedure that a test user can initiate. It must first be established that the expanded instructions do not reduce the validity of a particular test or alter the meaning of the scores. With appropriate methodological safeguards, however, this procedure offers an open and forthright approach to the dilemma of informed consent while promoting a clearer understanding of testing procedures.

THEORETICAL PROBLEMS AND CONCEPTS

Let me turn now from practical to theoretical problems presented by personality assessment in industry. These problems impinge not so much on test use as on test construction, the choice of tests for specific purposes, and the interpretation of test results. Personality testing is both more recent and more complex than ability testing. As such, it has not yet attained the technical standards met by some of the best ability tests.

To be sure, the 1970s witnessed significant efforts in the application of psychometric standards to personality test development (Exner 1974, 1978; Jackson 1970, 1973, 1978). Nevertheless, when the majority of available personality tests are evaluated as psychometric instruments, they are found wanting in one or more respects. Personality tests, more often than other types of tests, have fallen short of providing adequate norms, that is, norms for clearly defined populations derived from truly representative samples of those populations. Similarly, empirical data on test reliability may either be lacking or be limited to a single type of error variance. For industrial uses of tests, temporal stability is especially relevant because of the need to predict subsequent behavior (Schuerger, Tait, & Tavernelli 1982). For certain instruments, such as projective techniques, the assessment of examiner variance is usually desirable, as is the variance attributable to scorer (or score interpreter). For the purposes of this chapter, however, I shall focus on two areas that are theoretically more basic and also broader in their implications for test development: the concept of validation and the nature of personality traits.

Validation of Personality Tests

Essentially, the purpose of test validation is to provide an understanding of what a test measures. All procedures for assessing test validity are concerned with relationships between performance on the test and other, independently observable facts about the behavior variables under consideration. The specific methods employed for investigating these relationships are numerous and have been designated by various names. The first edition of the *Technical Recommendations for Psychological Tests and Diagnostic Techniques,* published in 1954 by the American Psychological Association, formally introduced the now familiar classification into content, predictive, concurrent, and construct validity. In subsequent editions of these standards, predictive and concurrent validity were combined under criterion-related validity. This tripartite division has survived to the present, albeit in a more flexible form, as categories of validity evidence (*Standards for educational and psychological testing,* 1985).

Gradually, the concept of different *kinds* of validity has been giving way to a recognition of construct validation as an all-encompassing approach. This approach utilizes all available validation procedures to delineate the interpretive meaningfulness of scores on a given test. Construct validation centers attention on the role of psychological theory in test construction and on the need to formulate hypotheses that can be confirmed or disconfirmed in the validation process. Both the development of newly published personality tests and the research conducted with well-established earlier tests, such as the MMPI, reflect this increasing focus on the assessment of personality constructs rather than the prediction of particular criteria. This trend away from the blind empiricism of an earlier era and toward an increasing concern with theory in test development parallels a similar movement occurring in American psychology as a whole.

In the use of personality tests in industry, construct validation offers several special advantages over the earlier, more limited criterion-related approach. First, there are certain technical difficulties in the way of conducting a satisfactory criterion-related validation study in industrial settings. Principal among these difficulties are inadequate sample size, reduction of range through selective loss of cases, and criterion unreliability. A second problem is that most real-life criteria are complex. Tests can more effectively measure identifiable constructs than they can measure a heterogeneous and ill-defined criterion composite. A third, and most important, advantage of construct validation stems from the greater generalizability of its findings. Broad trait constructs are more likely to be transportable to different contexts and to different jobs. In contrast, the results obtained against composite criteria may be narrowly limited by the unknown effects of the purely local and idiosyncratic aspects of particular criterion measures. If we follow this thinking a bit further, we can see that all test use and all interpretation of test scores imply construct validity, a fact that is being increasingly recognized (Guion 1977; Messick 1980; Tenopyr 1977). Since tests are rarely, if ever, used under conditions that are identical with those under which validation data were gathered, some degree of generalizability of results is inevitably involved. Thus the interpretive meaning of test scores is always based on constructs, although these constructs may vary widely in breadth of generalizability with regard to behavior domains, populations, and situations.

A word of caution is in order. Construct validation is a sophisticated psychometric concept that has not always been clearly understood by test users or even by some test constructors. Superficial adoption of this approach to validation presents certain hazards. If loosely applied, it may open the way for subjective, unverified assertions about the validity of a test. Under the label "construct validity," some test manuals provide what looks like a description of test content in terms of psychological trait names. Thus they offer as construct validity purely subjective accounts of what the test authors believe (or hope) their test measures. When properly conducted, however, construct validation is solidly based on empirical data and on clearly specified, reproducible operations. It is noteworthy that, in their original presentation of the concept of construct validity, Cronbach and Meehl (1955) pointed out that the nomological network of relationships, through which construct validation is established, must make "contact with observations" and that psychological constructs "must be behavior-relevant." They also cautioned against tests for which "a finespun network of rationalizations has been offered as if it were validation" (p. 291).

Procedurally, current applications of construct validation are characterized not only by trait constructs derived from personality theory but also by multiple validation procedures (Comrey 1970; Jackson 1970, 1973, 1978; Millon 1977). These procedures are employed sequentially, at different stages of test construction. Validity is thus built into the test from the outset, rather than being limited to the last stage of test construction, as in traditional, criterion-related validation.

Typically, the validation process begins with the formulation of detailed trait definitions derived from both personality theory and prior research. Test items are then written to fit these trait definitions. Item analysis follows, yielding data on such item characteristics as endorsement frequencies, correlations with total trait scores, and correlations with total scores on *other* traits covered by the test. To be retained, an item must be both theoretically and empirically relevant, that is, it must correlate higher with the trait for which it was written than it correlates with any other trait. This requirement will be recognized as just one more application of what Campbell and Fiske (1959) described as convergent and discriminant validation. The fourth stage involves the intercorrelation and factor analysis of item clusters or scales designed to measure each of the initially defined traits. The final stage covers the validation and cross-validation of scale scores through criterion-related analyses. At this stage the investigator may utilize contrasted groups, behavior ratings by appropriate observers, peer ratings, self-ratings, or any other basis for validation against external data.

Nature of Personality Traits

Finally, let us look at the nature of personality traits, as viewed from the vantage point of the 1980s. A long-standing controversy regarding the generalizability of traits versus the situational specificity of behavior reached a peak in the late 1960s and the 1970s. Several developments of the 1960s focused attention on narrowly defined "behaviors of interest" and away from broadly defined traits. In the noncognitive or personality domain, the strongest impetus toward behavioral specificity came from psychologists identified with social learning theory and with the general orientation characterizing behavior modification and behavior therapy (Bandura 1969; Bandura & Walters 1963; Goldfried & Kent 1972; Mischel 1968, 1969, 1973).

Criticism was directed especially toward the early view of traits as fixed, unchanging, and underlying causal entities. Few psychometricians today would argue for such a concept of traits (Anastasi 1983). The scarcity of this type of "trait theorist" was eloquently characterized by Jackson and Paunonen in their chapter in the 1980 *Annual Review of Psychology*. They wrote, "Like witches of 300 years ago, there is confidence about their existence, and even possibly their sinister properties, although one is hard pressed to find one in the flesh or even meet someone who has" (p. 523). It seems to be a popular sport to fabricate an account of what psychometricians allegedly believe and then to demonstrate the obvious falsity of that belief. This is the familiar technique of setting up a straw man and then demolishing it. The psychometric barn is littered with a superabundance of loose straw!

Turning to the other side of the controversy, we find that situational specificity is much more characteristic of personality traits than it is of abilities. For example, a person may be quite sociable at the office but shy and reserved at social gatherings. Or a student who cheats on examinations may be scrupulously honest in money matters. An extensive body of empirical evidence has been assembled by social learning theorists (Mischel 1968; Peterson 1968) showing that individuals exhibit considerable situational specificity in many nonintellective dimensions, such as aggression, social conformity, dependency, rigidity, honesty, and attitudes toward authority.

Part of the explanation for the higher cross-situational consistency of cognitive than of noncognitive functions may be found in the greater standardization of one's reactional biography in the intellectual than in the personality domain (Anastasi 1958, ch. 11; 1982a, ch. 6). The formal school curriculum, for example, fosters the development of broadly applicable cognitive skills in the verbal and numerical areas. In contrast, personality development occurs under far less uniform conditions. In the personality domain, moreover, the same response may lead to social consequences that are positively reinforcing in one situation and negatively reinforcing in another. The individual may thus learn to respond in quite different ways in different contexts.

Both the theoretical discussions and the research on traits-versus-situations have undoubtedly enriched our understanding of the many conditions that determine individual behavior. Concurrently, there has been a growing consensus among the adherents of contrasting views. This rapprochement was especially evident in several well-balanced and thoughtful discussions of the problem appearing in the 1970s (Bem & Allen 1974; Bem & Funder 1978; Bowers 1973; Endler & Magnusson 1976; Epstein 1979, 1980; Hogan, DeSoto, & Solano 1977; Mischel 1977, 1979). A number of noteworthy points emerged from these discussions. When random samples of persons and situations are investigated, individual differences contribute more to total behavior variance than do situational differences. Interaction between persons and situations contributes as much as do individual differences, or slightly more. To identify broad personality traits, we must measure individuals across many situations and aggregate the results (Epstein 1980). Whether we aggregate items, tests, or criterion measures, the combining serves to cancel out situational aspects, leaving an index of behavioral consistency at the trait level (B.F. Green 1978).

The degree of behavioral specificity among situations varies from person to person. In this connection, Mischel (1979) refers to individual differences in the discriminativeness of social behavior. Persons differ in the extent to which they alter their behavior to meet the demands of each situation. In this respect, moderate inconsistency indicates effective and adaptive flexibility, while excessive consistency indicates maladaptive rigidity. Moreover, the particular situations across which behavior is consistent may vary among persons. Intersituational consistency is influenced by the way individuals perceive and categorize situations (Lord 1982; Mischel & Peake 1982). And such grouping of situations in turn depends on the individual's goals and on his or her prior experience with similar situations. This conception of behavioral consistencies derives from the early idiographic approach to personality assessment formulated by Gordon Allport (1937) and by George Kelly (1955, 1963), among others (see Landfield & Leitner 1980).

While contributing to our understanding of individual differences, the proponents of situational specificity have come to recognize the need for trait categories, for both theoretical and practical reasons. If a person's behavior exhibited no significant consistencies across situations, both science and society would be in a state of chaos. To meet different assessment needs, behavioral observations can be aggregated in different ways and with appropriate degrees of generality or specificity (Mischel & Peake 1982). The focus may be on intraindividual consistencies or on situational categories of broad or narrow scope.

For particular assessment purposes, we have to ascertain whether there is a situationally linked trait construct, reasonably stable over time and extending over an identifiable class of similar situations of practical usefulness within the given culture. An example of such a class of situations is provided by self-report inventories designed to assess test anxiety (Sarason 1980; Spielberger 1980; Tryon 1980). Persons high in test anxiety tend to perceive evaluative situations as personally threatening. Besides a total score indicative of anxiety proneness in test situations, such inventories may provide subscores on two major components identified through factor analysis: worry and emotionality. In this context, worry has been defined as "cognitive concerns about the consequences of failure" and emotionality as "reactions of the autonomic nervous system that are evoked by evaluative stress" (Spielberger 1980, p. 1). The general instructions may be modified to define the anxiety-provoking situations even more specifically, by asking examinees to respond, for example, with reference to mathematics tests or essay tests.

Role of the Test User

From this examination of some of the practical and theoretical problems of personality assessment in industry, the picture that emerges is certainly not simple. But then, the complexities we have encountered serve to illustrate the fact that personality tests—even more so than other types of tests—require a knowledgeable and psychologically sophisticated test user. Such tests cannot be employed routinely and automatically without serious danger of misinterpreting results. The important part played by the professionally trained test user in all testing is being recognized increasingly. Both the testing *Standards* (1985) and the more specialized *Princi-*

ples prepared by the APA Division of Industrial-Organizational Psychology (1980) contain evidence of the growing emphasis placed on the professional expertise and judgment of the test user.

The properly qualified test user is aware not only of common pitfalls and limitations but also of the myriad positive ways that tests can serve to provide cues and leads for further exploration and verification. The skilled professional follows a cycle of successive hypothesis formation and hypothesis testing (see Anastasi 1982b, pp. 488–494). This use of trained professional judgment is often called the clinical method, although it is not restricted to clinical practice or to the assessment of pathology. Essentially, it means the intensive study of the individual by a highly qualified professional through a multiplicity of mutually corroborative procedures. It is admittedly costly, in both time and personnel. If the situation is such as to render this approach cost-effective, then it is the method of choice. In contrast, mass assessment procedures are appropriate when large, heterogeneous groups are to be screened. Even in such situations, however, a trained professional is needed to direct and supervise the process.

REFERENCES

Allport, G.W. *Personality: A psychological interpretation.* New York: Holt, 1937.

American Psychological Association. Psychological assessment and public policy. *American Psychologist,* 1970, *25,* 264–266.

_____. *Ethical principles of psychologists.* Washington, D.C.: APA, 1981. (Also published in *American Psychologist,* 1981, *36,* 633–638.)

American Psychological Association, Division of Industrial-Organizational Psychology. *Principles for the validation and use of personnel selection procedures:* Second Edition. Berkely, Calif.: The Industrial-Organizational Psychologist, 1980.

Anastasi, A. *Differential psychology* (3rd ed.). New York: Macmillan, 1958.

_____. *Fields of applied psychology* (2nd ed.). New York: McGraw-Hill, 1979.

_____. *Psychological testing and privacy.* In W.C. Bier (ed.), *Privacy: A vanishing value?* New York: Fordham University Press, 1980.

_____. *Contributions to differential psychology: Selected papers.* New York: Praeger, 1982. (a)

_____. *Psychological testing* (5th ed.). New York: Macmillan, 1982. (b)

_____. Evolving trait concepts. *American Psychologist,* 1983, *38,* 175–184.

Bandura, A. *Principles of behavior modification.* New York: Holt, Rinehart & Winston, 1969.

Bandura, A., & Walters, R.H. *Social learning and personality development.* New York: Holt, Rinehart & Winston, 1963.

Bem, D.J., & Allen, A. On predicting some of the people some of the time: The search for cross-situational consistencies in behavior. *Psychological Review,* 1974, *81,* 506–520.

Bem, D.J., & Funder, D.C. Predicting more of the people more of the time: Assessing the personality of situations. *Psychological Review,* 1978, *85,* 485–501.

Blackford, K.M.H., & Newcomb, A. *The job, the man, the boss.* Garden City, N.Y.: Doubleday, 1919.

Block, J. *The challenge of response sets: Unconfounding meaning, acquiescence, and social desirability in the MMPI.* New York: Irvington, 1965.

Bowers, K. Situationism in psychology: An analysis and a critique. *Psychological Review,* 1973, *80,* 307–336.

Butcher, J.N., & Tellegen, A.T. Objections to MMPI items. *Journal of Consulting Psychology,* 1966, *30,* 527–534.

Campbell, D.T., & Fiske, D.W. Convergent and discriminant validation by the multitrait-multimethod matrix. *Psychological Bulletin,* 1959, *56,* 81–105.

Comrey, A.L. *Comrey Personality Scales: Manual.* San Diego, Calif.: Educational and Industrial Testing Service, 1970.

Cronbach, L.J., & Meehl, P.E. Construct validity in psychological testing. *Psychological Bulletin,* 1955, *52,* 281–302.

Diamond, M.J., & Bond, M.H. The acceptance of "Barnum" personality interpretation by Japanese, Japanese-American, and Caucasian-American college students. *Journal of Cross-cultural Psychology,* 1974, *5,* 228–235.

Donceel, J.F., Alimena, B.S., & Birch, C.M. Influence of prestige suggestion on the answers of a personality inventory. *Journal of Applied Psychology,* 1949, *33,* 352–355.

Dunnette, M.D. Use of the sugar pill by industrial psychologists. *American Psychologist,* 1957, *12,* 223–225.

Dunnette, M.D., McCartney, J., Carlson, H.C., & Kirchner, W.K. A study of faking behavior on a forced-choice self-description checklist. *Personnel Psychology,* 1962, *15,* 13–24.

Edwards, A.L. *The social desirability variable in personality assessment and research.* New York: Dryden, 1957.

Endler, N.S., & Magnusson, D. Toward an interactional psychology of personality. *Psychological Bulletin,* 1976, *83,* 956–974.

Epstein, S. The stability of behavior: I. On predicting most of the people much of the time. *Journal of Personality and Social Psychology,* 1979, *37,* 1097–1121.

_____. The stability of behavior: II. Implications for psychological research. *American Psychologist,* 1980, *35,* 790–806.

Exner, J.E., Jr. *The Rorschach: A comprehensive system.* New York: Wiley, 1974.

_____. *The Rorschach: A comprehensive system,* vol. 2: *Current research and advanced interpretations.* New York: Wiley-Interscience, 1978.

Fink, A., & Butcher, J.N. Reducing objections to personality inventories with special instructions. *Educational and Psychological Measurements*, 1972, *32*, 631–639.

Forer, B. The fallacy of personal validation: A classroom demonstration of gullibility. *Journal of Abnormal and Social Psychology*, 1949, *44*, 118–123.

Goldfried, M.R., & Kent, R.N. Traditional versus behavioral personality assessment: A comparison of methodological and theoretical assumptions. *Psychological Bulletin*, 1972, *77*, 409–420.

Green, B.F., Jr. In defense of measurement. *American Psychologist*, 1978, *33*, 664–670.

Green, R.F. Does a selection situation induce testees to bias their answers on interest and temperament tests? *Educational and Psychological Measurement*, 1951, *11*, 503–515.

Guion, R.M. Content validity: Three years of talk—What's the action? *Public Personnel Management*, 1977, *6*, 407–414.

Hale, M. *Human science and the social order: Hugo Münsterberg and the origins of applied psychology*. Philadelphia: Temple University Press, 1980.

_____. History of employment testing. In A.K. Wigdor & W.R. Garner (eds.), *Ability testing: Uses, consequences, and controversies, Part II: Documentation Section*. Washington, D.C.: National Academy Press, 1982.

Halperin, K., Snyder, C.R., Shenkel, R.J., & Houston, B.K. Effects of source status and message favorability on acceptance of personality feedback. *Journal of Applied Psychology*, 1976, *61*, 85–88.

Hogan, R., DeSoto, C.B., & Solano, C. Traits, tests, and personality research. *American Psychologist*, 1977, *32*, 255–264.

Jackson, D.N. A sequential system for personality scale development. In C.D. Spielberger (ed.), *Current topics in clinical and community psychology*, vol. 2. New York: Academic Press, 1970.

_____. The dynamics of structured personality tests. *Psychological Review*, 1971, *78*, 229–248.

_____. Structured personality assessment. In B.B. Wolman (ed.), *Handbook of general psychology*. Englewood Cliffs, N.J.: Prentice-Hall, 1973.

_____. Interpreter's guide to the Jackson Personality Inventory. In P. McReynolds (ed.), *Advances in psychological assessment*, vol. 4. San Francisco: Jossey-Bass, 1978.

Jackson, D.N., & Messick, S. Content and style in personality assessment. *Psychological Bulletin*, 1958, *55*, 243–252.

_____. Response styles and the assessment of psychopathology. In S. Messick & J. Ross (eds.), *Measurement in personality and cognition*. New York: Wiley, 1962.

Jackson, D.N. & Paunonen, S.V. Personality structure and assessment. *Annual Review of Psychology*, 1980, *31*, 503–551.

Jacobs, A., & Barron, R. Falsification of the Guilford-Zimmerman Temperament Survey: II. Making a poor impression. *Psychological Reports*, 1968, *23*, 1271–1277.

Kelly, G.A. *The psychology of personal constructs*. New York: Norton, 1955.
———. *A theory of personality*. New York: Norton, 1963.

Krüger, H., & Zietz, K. Das Verifikationsproblem: Experimentelle Untersuchungen über die psychologischen Grundlagen der Bestätigung von Charactergutachten. *Zeitschrift für angewande Psychologie*, 1933, *45*, 140–171.

Landfield, A.W., & Leitner, L.M. (eds.). *Personal construct psychology: Psychotherapy and personality*. New York: Wiley, 1980.

Lord, C.G. Predicting behavioral consistency from an individual's perception of situational similarities. *Journal of Personality and Social Psychology*, 1982, *42*, 1076–1088.

Meehl, P.E. Wanted—a good cookbook. *American Psychologist*, 1956, *11*, 263–272.

Merrens, M.R., & Richards, W.S. Acceptance of generalized versus "bona fide" personality interpretations. *Psychological Reports*, 1970, *27*, 691–694.

Messick, S. Test validity and the ethics of assessment. *American Psychologist*, 1980, *35*, 1012–1027.

Millon, T. *Millon Clinical Multiaxial Inventory: Manual*. Minneapolis: NCS Interpretive Scoring Systems, 1977.

Mischel, W. *Personality and assessment*. New York: Wiley, 1968.
———. Continuity and change in personality. *American Psychologist*, 1969, *24*, 1012–1018.
———. Toward a cognitive social learning reconceptualization of personality. *Psychological Review*, 1973, *80*, 252–283.
———. On the future of personality measurement. *American Psychologist*, 1977, *32*, 246–254.
———. On the interface of cognition and personality: Beyond the person-situation debate. *American Psychologist*, 1979, *34*, 740–754.

Mischel, W., & Peake, P.K. Beyond déjà vu in the search for cross-situational consistency. *Psychological Review*, 1982, *89*, 730–755.

Peterson, D. *The clinical study of social behavior*. New York: Appleton-Century-Crofts, 1968.

Privacy and behavioral research. Washington, D.C.: U.S. Government Printing Office, 1967.

Radcliffe, J.A. A note on questionnaire faking with 16PFQ and MPI. *Australian Journal of Psychology*, 1966, *18*, 154–157.

Sarason, I.G. (ed.). *Test anxiety: Theory, research, and applications*. Hillsdale, N.J.: Erlbaum, 1980.

Schuerger, J.M., Tait, E., & Tavernelli, M. Temporal stability of personality by questionnaire. *Journal of Personality and Social Psychology,* 1982, *43,* 176–182.

Silverman, L.H. A Q-sort study of the validity of evaluations made from projective techniques. *Psychological Monographs,* 1959, *73* (7, whole no. 477).

Snyder, C.R., & Larson, G.R. A further look at student acceptance of general personality interpretations. *Journal of Consulting and Clinical Psychology,* 1972, *38,* 384–388.

Spielberger, C.D. *Test Anxiety Inventory: Preliminary manual.* Palo Alto, Calif.: Consulting Psychologists Press, 1980.

Stagner, R. The gullibility of personnel managers. *Personnel Psychology,* 1958, *11,* 347–352.

Standards for educational and psychological testing. Washington, D.C.: American Psychological Association, 1985.

Stricker, L.J. "Test-wiseness" on personality scales. *Journal of Applied Psychology Monograph,* 1969, *53* (3, part 2).

Stryker, P. Is there an executive face? *Fortune,* 1953, *48,* 145–147, 162–168.

Sundberg, N.D. The acceptability of "fake" versus "bona fide" personality test interpretations. *Journal of Abnormal and Social Psychology,* 1955, *50,* 145–147.

Technical recommendations for psychological tests and diagnostic techniques. Washington, D.C.: American Psychological Association, 1954.

Tenopyr, M.L. Content-construct confusion. *Personnel Psychology,* 1977, *30,* 47–54.

Testimony before House special subcommittee on invasion of privacy of the committee on government operations. *American Psychologist,* 1966, *21,* 404–422.

Testing and public policy. *American Psychologist,* 1965, *20,* 857–992. (Special issue.)

Tryon, G.S. The measurement and treatment of test anxiety. *Review of Educational Research,* 1980, *50,* 343–372.

Ulrich, R., Stachnik, T., & Stainton, R. Student acceptance of generalized personality interpretations. *Psychological Reports,* 1963, *13,* 831–834.

Walker, C.E. The effect of eliminating offensive items on the reliability and validity of the MMPI. *Journal of Clinical Psychology,* 1967, *23,* 363–366.

Walker, C.E., & Ward, J. Identification and elimination of offensive items from the MMPI. *Journal of Projective and Personality Assessment,* 1969, *33,* 385–388.

Wesman, A.G. Faking personality test scores in a simulated employment situation. *Journal of Applied Psychology,* 1952, *36,* 112–113.

Wiggins, J.S. Strategic, method, and stylistic variance in the MMPI. *Psychological Bulletin,* 1962, *59,* 224–242.

———. Social desirability estimation and "faking good" well. *Educational and Psychological Measurement,* 1966, *26,* 329–341.

2

Personality Assessment and Personnel Selection
Robert Hogan, Bruce N. Carpenter,
Stephen R. Briggs, and Robert O. Hansson

INTRODUCTION

The use of personality tests in personnel decisions began very early in the century. By 1909, for example, Parsons and Munsterberg were doing vocational assessments for industry (Hale 1982). In 1915 the Carnegie Institute of Technology hired Walter V. Bingham to head its Division of Applied Psychology. Bingham (1923) reports that the greatest demand for his services came from sales managers who wanted to ". . . select salesmen whose traits of mind and personality most suited them to the job."

The history of personality testing in industry since 1915 has numerous milestones. The massive Army recruit screening program during World War I legitimized personality measurement in the public consciousness. In 1921 James McKeen Cattell organized the Psychological Corporation, which subsequently published personality tests for a profit. Woodword's World War I psychiatric screening battery turned into the Thurstone Personality Scale and then the Allport Ascendance-Submission Test; these tests were widely used during the economically troubled 1930s to identify "stable" and cooperative employees. During the late 1930s and early 1940s the Bernreuter Personality Inventory and the Humm-Wadsworth Temperament Scale were used extensively to identify employees who would ". . . enter into working relationships cooperatively." World War II brought the OSS selection program as well as increased and generalized military psychiatric screening. The post-World War II period saw a virtual explosion in personality inventory construction—the MMPI, the CPI, the Guilford-Zimmerman Temperament Survey, the 16-PF, and so on. In 1948 the Institute of Personality Assessment Research (IPAR) was founded at the University of California at Berkeley. Sparked by the example of Bray at AT&T, the use of assessment centers began growing rapidly in the 1950s, and the process continues to the present (see Thornton & Byham 1982). Finally, the climate of the 1960s and early 1970s brought great enthusiasm for all matters psychological and a corresponding wave of tests to assess various aspects of human potential (such as the FIRO-B, the Myers-Briggs Type Indicator, the POI). In the 1980s it has become a full-time job to stay well informed about the personality testing enterprise.

Despite an almost feverish enthusiasm for personality testing in certain areas of government and industry, many authorities in industrial/organizational psychology are skeptical of its value. Most textbooks cite the well-known reviews by Guion and Gottier (1965) and Ghiselli (1973) as demonstrating the limited validity of personality measurement. Critics focus in particular on such conclusions as the following: "In brief, it is difficult in the face of this summary to advocate, with a clear conscience, the use of personality measures in most situations as a basis for making employment decisions about people" (Guion & Gottier 1965, p. 162).

In view of the seeming consensus among experts regarding the limited utility of personality assessment, we feel compelled to explain why we continue to advocate this approach to selection. Our first point concerns the notion that earlier reviews repudiate personality measurement. Consider the Guion and Gottier paper, for example. Although they point out that in pre-1963 research the meager findings seem normative, they also point out that in many studies the research design was inadequate—studies often used criteria that were inappropriate for the tests in question; conceptual ambiguities abound—in many cases the research was badly conceived and conceptualized; personality measures in fact worked more often than could be explained simply by chance, so that no blanket indictment is justified or sensible; and "homemade" measures often work better than standard measures. They then ask, "Is it possible that serious, concerted effort might yield more generalized systems of prediction using personality measures. The present workers [Guion & Gottier] lean toward the latter possibility" (Guion & Gottier 1965). So, obviously, do we.

A second major review (Ghiselli 1973) examined the validity of 5 categories of tests (intellectual, spatial and mechanical, perceptual, motor abilities, and personality) across 21 types of jobs (from executives to laborers) for two criteria—training success and job proficiency. Table 2.1 shows validity coefficients averaged across a diverse group of personality measures and occupational categories. With one exception, these validity coefficients are respectable both absolutely and relative to other kinds of tests. In fact, these results are remarkable, considering that they emerge from an indiscriminate lumping of different tests designed for varying purposes and of widely differing quality. As Ghiselli notes, ". . . the validity coefficients reported for the tests almost invariably are underestimates of their true predictive power" (1973, p. 1973). Our first point, then, is that the classic reviews of the validity of personality measures are less damaging than is typically believed.

TABLE 2.1
Validity Coefficients for Personality Trait Measures
Across Broad Occupational Categories

Occupation	Training Success	Job Proficiency
Managerial	.53	.22
Clerical	.17	.22
Sales	—	.32
Protective	-.11	.21
Service	—	.16
Vehicle operators	—	.26
Trades and crafts	.16	.24

Source: E.E. Ghiselli, The validity of aptitude tests in personnel selection, *Personnel Psychology,* 1973, *26,* 461–477. Reprinted with permission.

Our second point concerning the validity of personality measurement is that, historically, there has been no agreement among various test authors concerning what they are measuring. Personality is almost never defined in the various test manuals. Do differing test authors mean the same thing by the term "personality?" It is difficult to know, because such conceptual and definitional issues rarely come up. In the absence of consensus it also becomes impossible to say what should or should not be included on a typical inventory. Moreover, test authors disagree regarding the goals of inventory construction—some are concerned with external validity, some with response sets, some with internal consistency, and some with replicable factor structures.

What we have, then, is a diverse group of testing devices, each designed to accomplish a different goal but all called personality inventories. The various tests are *not* equivalent in their construction, their measurement goals, or their underlying theoretical bases. Although they were designed with different purposes in mind, they are nonetheless used in the same way. Consequently, research using similar populations but different inventories often yields different, incompatible, or even conflicting results. Consequently, the outsider confronts a topic area the results of which appear to be in total disarray. The problem, of course, is that a personality inventory is not a personality inventory—what it is, depends on the measurement goals of the test's author. The accumulation of knowledge is possible only within the literature surrounding a single test.

Our third point regarding the practical validity of personality measures concerns the fact that a great deal of early personality research in applied settings was oriented to detecting psychopathology. For example, during the 1940s Sears, with the help of L.L. Thurstone, developed a comprehensive managerial selection battery that was eventually administered to over 10,000 employees; it was designed, among other things, to detect ". . . a basic instability or a deep-seated temperamental maladjustment that might not become evident except in periods of stress" (Worthy 1951, p. 16). This emphasis on detecting latent psychopathology has two consequences. On the one hand, it suggests that a large number of people equate personality with psychopathological structures (a serious error). On the other hand, it may account for earlier meager validity coefficients—for the obvious reason that the absence of psychopathology does not guarantee the presence of competence. For example, we all know people who are both well-adjusted and hopelessly mediocre.

We can summarize this overview of the history of personality assessment in industry in terms of three points. First, personality measures have been an integral part of applied psychology since 1909. Second, in the applied context, personality measures have their enthusiasts and their critics, and both groups may be right for the wrong reasons and wrong for the right reasons (that is, practitioners are sometimes incompetent, but critics overgeneralize from such cases). Third, the core problem in the application of personality measures to real world selection is conceptual. Key terms are seldom defined; the goals of measurement are often unspecified; the meaning of test scores is rarely examined; and validity issues are often ignored.

In the midst of all this confusion, it is a testimonial to the robustness of the enterprise that significant empirical results are ever reported. In the remainder of this chapter we define our key terms, evaluate the utility of traditional clinical measures for selection purposes, review the results of selection research using nonclinical measures, and then discuss the implications of some recent work in personality psychology. In the final section we attempt to identify some important future directions for this research.

DEFINITIONS AND DISTINCTIONS

Assume that personality influences organizational or occupational performance; assume further that one decides to capitalize on this information by "measuring personality." What is it that one would measure when measuring personality? The answer depends on how you define personality and what you think personality test scores mean. With regard to both points there are four perspectives to be distinguished.

Defining Personality

Psychoanalytic Theory

Personality theory originated in nineteenth-century European psychiatry. When most educated people think about personality, they think about it in terms borrowed from psychoanalysis or a derivative theory. When people adopt this perspective on personality, either deliberately or *faute de mieux,* they automatically assume that at the core each person is in some way neurotic, and that adult personality is built on the residue of childhood trauma and unconscious defenses against antisocial impulses. Because job performance is adversely affected by eruptions of psychopathology, the task of assessment is to screen out those persons whose psychopathology is closest to the surface and/or most likely to erupt. According to this approach, vocational performance is simply related to the absence of psychopathology. This is, of course, the viewpoint underlying the use of the MMPI and other clinical measures in government and industry.

Humanistic Theory

Among the various humanistic psychologists, Gordon Allport is the one most closely identified with scientific psychology. According to Allport, each person's personality is composed of indwelling, neuropsychic structures called traits. These traits may or may not be pathological, although Allport strongly deemphasized the importance of psychopathology in normal career development. Allport believed that each person has a distinctive set of traits that must be assessed uniquely. Taken seriously, Allport's position makes the comparison of individuals impossible. He did, however, allow for the possibility that certain "common traits" (such as dominance-submission) might be important for everyday performance and could, therefore, be assessed by conventional means.

Allport stressed the importance of long-range goals as organizing forces in adult personality; in this way he anticipated important trends in applied measurement—especially in vocational preference testing. But his view of personality as the expression of fixed, indwelling, neuropsychic structures seems simplistic, and his emphasis on ipsative or idiographic measurement is inimical to the accumulation of an empirical data base for selection research.

Social Learning Theory

Perhaps the most influential application of behaviorism to personality psychology can be found in the writings of Albert Bandura and Walter Mischel. One aspect of their theoretical perspective seems indisputable—that most people can learn from experience and that what they learn probably affects their day-to-day performance. Beyond this, however, social learning theory has little to say that is relevant to our purposes. This is so for three reasons. First, it is little concerned with individual differences—it is principally directed toward finding general laws regarding the acquisition of behavior. Second, by emphasizing the role of "situational variables" in the determination of everyday conduct, social learning theory minimizes the importance of personal characteristics. At its best it regards people's actions as a function of person-by-situation interactions (but because the number of such interactions is potentially infinite, no coherent research agenda has been developed); at its worst social learning theory seems to imply that there is no stable core to personality (which means there is nothing in personality to study).

The third reason that social learning theory is largely irrelevant for our purposes is that the key writings in this tradition are implicitly and sometimes explicitly hostile to measurement. Although these writers presumably would endorse behavior samples as a selection method, they are pessimistic regarding the utility of personality assessment.

Trait Theory

Traditional Trait Theory. The master exponents of traditional trait theory are Raymond Cattell and Hans Eysenck. At bottom both men agree that personality can be described, and everyday behavior explained, in terms of a fixed set of traits. These traits are generic and universal, found to some degree in all human cultures. Cattell and Eysenck differ primarily in terms of the number of traits they think necessary adequately to explain human action: Cattell postulates about 16, whereas Eysenck believes that 3 very large general factors or traits are sufficient for describing the structure of personality. Cattell and Eysenck seem to disagree not about content but about level of analysis. Both men developed measurement models that parallel their conceptual systems. Evidence regarding the merits of these models is presented in the next two sections.

These traditional trait theories have two shortcomings that limit their utility as fully adequate accounts of everyday performance. On the one hand, the trait lists proposed are somehow *sui generis;* we are never told why just these traits (whatever they might be) are important and others are not. On the other hand, the research associated with these theories consists largely of showing the importance of these traits across samples. The relevance of the traits for everyday performance comes up only rarely.

Revisionist Trait Theory. Socioanalytic theory (Hogan 1982; Hogan, Jones, & Cheek 1983) is a competency-based theory that can be summarized as follows. Although there are always individual differences, people need attention and approval; status; and predictibility. These needs are largely satisfied through social interaction. The key to attaining status and approval is interpersonal competence. As observers, we think and talk about other people by using trait words. At a very general level, we use trait words to evaluate others in terms of their usefulness for our social groups; trait terms mark individual differences in social competence.

From this perspective, the goal of personality measurement is to assess factors that are associated with status and popularity in one's social groups. Six broad factors seem especially crucial for success in any group: intelligence (good judgment, accurate reasoning); adjustment (self-confidence, stable moods); prudence (honesty, self-control); ambition (leadership, energy level); sociability (affiliativeness); and likability (tolerance, warmth, tact). There is a measurement model associated with socioanalytic theory, and evidence regarding its utility will be presented in a later section.

The point of this brief review of personality psychology, once again, is to dramatize the fact that one's view regarding the nature of personality will determine what one looks for when doing personality assessment. Traditional depth psychology looks for psychopathology. Humanistic psychologists (such as Allport) attempt to characterize each person's uniqueness. Social learning theory focuses on very specific factors that are tied to situational variables. Traditional trait theory examines a limited number of trait dimensions, the number and content of which differ from theorist to theorist. Socioanalytic theory emphasizes characteristics that are associated with status and popularity in one's social groups and organizations. The literature on selection, when reviewing and evaluating the application of personality measures for personnel selection, never distinguishes among these perspectives.

The Meaning of Test Scores

Assuming that one is clear about what is meant by the term "personality," the next question concerns the meaning of scores on personality measures. Because scores are aggregations of individual item responses, we are necessarily concerned with the meaning of the individual responses. Although this subject has been discussed in the technical literature (see, for example, Wiggins 1973, ch. 9), it is typically ignored in the day-to-day use and interpretation of tests.

Two extreme positions can be identified. At one pole, item responses are considered to be, quite simply, veridical self-reports. They are assumed to reflect directly the internal states and external behavior of the respondent. In our judgment, to regard item responses as veridical self-reports—Buchwald (1961) calls this the correspondence approach—is to take a pretheoretical view of the data base. Such a perspective makes some questionable assumptions: that individuals understand each item; that they can answer objectively; and that they will report honestly. It should be clear, however, that the literal truth or falsity of such self-reports is impossible to ascertain. Recent thinking concerning the psychology of memory (Kihlstrom 1981), suggests that it is selective, and that what is "recalled" often says as much about what one thinks about oneself as it does about the events in question. There are, we believe, good logical reasons for rejecting the self-report theory of item responses.

At the other extreme of item response theory is the positivist model identified with the empirical approach to test construction (Meehl 1945). Textbook writers and test critics often seem unaware that this view of test construction contains a theory of item responses that is substantially more sophisticated and defensible, from an epistemological perspective, than the correspondence (or self-report) approach. Consistent with Wittgenstein's theory of meaning, the empirical tradition (Gough 1965; Meehl 1945) maintains that the meaning of an item response can be defined only in terms of how an item functions—what it predicts. The empirical approach to test construction has the unfortunate consequence of not deepening our understanding of the phenomena we can predict with these tests—how much, for example, has the Stanford-Binet contributed to or enhanced a theory of intelligence (Hogan 1980)? Nonetheless, this approach does contain an internally consistent, sophisticated, and self-conscious way of thinking about item responses.

Two further approaches, termed substantive and self-presentational, can be located somewhere between the extremes of the correspondence and the empirical approaches. The substantive approach (Loevinger 1957; Wiggins 1973) assumes the reality of traits in people. These underlying traits—along with situational factors, fluctuations in mood, and other influences—affect behavior. They also affect in a parallel fashion the way one responds to test items. Thus, item responses and nontest behaviors should be related because both are produced by or reflect an underlying trait, not because item responses correspond exactly to the trait or the nontest behavior.

In this approach, then, the content of the item is important because it presumably reflects the substance of the underlying trait, although this relationship cannot be assessed directly because traits are hypothetical entities. Interitem correlations and external validity are equally important because they provide evidence as to whether items do in fact measure a particular trait. It is also worth noting that, because some people are more perceptive about themselves than others, there should be systematic differences in the correlations between test scores and nontest behavior for persons high and low on self-knowledge. Research on self-consciousness suggests that this is so (Buss 1980; Cheek 1982; Scheier, Buss, & Buss 1978; Underwood & Moore 1981).

The self-presentational approach to item responses assumes that there is no difference in principle between responding to items on a personality inventory and participating in any other kind of social interaction. In test taking, as in life, people try, through unconscious and habitual forms of self-presentation, to manage and control the impressions that others form of them. When responding to items on a questionnaire, therefore, the literal truth or falsity of responses is irrelevant; what matters is the respondent's self-image and his or her typified ways of projecting that image. Because item-response dynamics are formal (that is, item responses are always a kind of self-presentation), the format of items on a questionnaire becomes largely irrelevant. This means that no valid distinction can be drawn between personality items and items from biographical or vocational preference measures. In each case, the respondent's goals are the same—to tell us how he or she wants to be regarded. Because some people are more skilled at self-presentation than others, there should be systematic differences in the correlations between test scores and peer ratings for those who are high and low on self-presentational skills. This prediction has been verified several times (see Cheek 1982; Johnson 1981; Mills & Hogan 1978).

The similarities and differences between the self-presentational and substantive approaches are worth noting. Both approaches are demonstrably more valid than the simple self-report view. Both approaches can be combined with empirical verification in order to capitalize on a well-kept secret in the empirical tradition of test development—that the best items (from an empirical perspective) tend to be the ones with good (but subtle) face validity (see Hase & Goldberg 1967), remembering, however, that a good item cannot be determined *a priori*. Also common to both approaches is the utility of moderator variables—self-presentational or acting skills on the one hand, and self-knowledge on the other. The approaches differ in terms of their assumptions. Although both positions assume that people exhibit consistent patterns of behavior (traits), one assumes the reality of underlying traits as well (presumably neuropsychic structures of some sort that organize behavior), whereas the other assumes that individuals do self-presentation (behave) in accordance with enduring self-images.

TRADITIONAL CLINICAL MEASURES IN SELECTION

When applied psychologists think of personality, they typically think of it in terms borrowed from clinical psychology. When they do personality measurement, they often use clinical measures, and this use has been quite extensive. For example, in a survey of 203 state and local police departments, Murphy (1972) found that 39 percent of the departments used "psychological examinations." Of these, 49 percent used the MMPI, 41 percent used a psychiatric interview, and 11 percent used the Rorschach. Other measures included sentence-completion tests, the draw-a-person or house-tree-person, and the TAT. More recently Parisher, Rios, and Reilley (1979) reported that, in a national sample of 130 police departments, most police psychologists or consultants were clinical psychologists and their primary duty was applicant screening. Fifty-four percent of the departments said they used tests for selection; of these, 79 percent used the MMPI.

Although much of the research using clinical measures has been with police, other groups can be mentioned. For example, Eiduson (1974) used the Rorschach to study research scientists, and Olson (1973) used it to select applicants to law school. Gyorgy (1979) compared Rorschach procedures for assessing top-level managers, and Moser (1981) used the Rorschach to select airplane pilots. Michaelis and Eysenck (1971) studied applicants to a motor manufacturing apprentice training program with an unpublished test having scales of "neurotocism" and "psychotocism." Psychiatric aides have been assessed with the MMPI (Butterfield & Warren 1962, 1963), as have security guards (Bernstein 1980) and child care workers (Saunders & Pappanikou 1970). There is even a report of an (unsuccessful) attempt to select life insurance salesmen by using handwriting analysis (Zdep & Weaver 1967). Thus, clinical measures are widely used for personnel selection. What can we learn about personality and personnel selection from these studies?

An Example from Police Selection

Police selection is often thought to be an area where clinical assessment is particularly appropriate. Many people feel not only that police work attracts a high proportion of maladjusted individuals, but also that the safety of the public makes it crucial that such individuals be identified. Using this common line of reasoning, it follows that clinical measures may more readily predict performance for this group than for others.

In a study of Chicago policemen, Baehr, Furcon, and Froemel (1968) found clinical personality measures to be unrelated to performance ratings. They used a scale of 30 MMPI items, a projective test in which the subject interpreted the meaning of 9 hand positions, and the arrow-dot test, a projective drawing measure.

In a series of studies, Schoenfeld and his colleagues (Merian, Stephan, Schoenfeld, & Kobos 1980; Costello, Schoenfeld, & Kobos 1982; Bernstein, Schoenfeld, & Costello 1982) compared policemen rated by superiors as unacceptable with commended and average policemen. Two experienced clinical psychologists could not distinguish the unacceptable from the commended officers by using blind analysis of MMPI profiles. Using the Goldberg Index, an MMPI composite developed for detecting psychotic profiles, an optimal cutoff yielded a hit rate above chance. However, the index still detected only 26 percent of the unacceptable officers, and when average policemen were added to the sample to lower the base rate to a more realistic level, the hit rate was no longer significant.

Hooke and Krauss (1971) compared patrolmen who had passed written and oral examinations for sergeant with a matched group of average patrolmen. They found three MMPI scales that significantly distinguished the groups, but the differences were so small that prediction was not greatly enhanced. With prescreened applicants, Mills and Stratton (1982) found several significant differences on the MMPI between successful and unsuccessful groups at several stages in a policeman's early career. They concluded, however, that the differences were too small to be useful. Bartol (1982) found a number of significant differences among small town policemen rated as above-average, average, or below-average, but the differences were relatively small.

An MMPI study by Saxe and Reiser (1976) was somewhat more successful in predicting performance. More scale comparisons were significant and the differences tended to be larger than in other studies, although their procedure does not suggest reasons for the greater success.

This sample of studies, which is typical of the literature, suggests that clinical measures in general, and the MMPI in particular, are not very useful for predicting police performance; although some relationships exist, in most studies they are too modest to be of much practical utility. In addition, because studies generally show that police have healthy MMPI profiles (for instance, Matarazzo, Allen, Saslow, & Wiens 1964), the focus on pathology becomes questionable for all but a few, probably very often obvious, cases. Moser (1981) reached a similar conclusion, using the Rorschach to select pilots. He emphasized that although his method might detect a few deviant individuals who should be deselected, it was not useful for selecting the best candidates.

Conclusions Based on Clinical Measures

Although clinical measures typically show validity coefficients only slightly above chance, they nonetheless often yield significant findings; that is, employee performance seems to be slightly predictable from these measures. It is helpful to ask, then, what conclusions emerge from this research.

First, there is a general trend for better employee performance to be associated with higher scores on some measures of deviance. For example, in the MMPI research there is a slight tendency for elevated scores on K, Hs, and Ma to be related to good job performance. Consequently, the clinical interpretation of the MMPI scores might actually result in hiring less qualified applicants, because deselection relies primarily on scale elevations.

In the same general vein, there is a modestly consistent finding that indices termed "social desirability," "lie," or "motivational distortion" are also associated with better performance; that is, higher scores on social desirability scales are associated with better on-the-job ratings. Thus, applicants who have the good sense to present themselves in a favorable light on personality measures also seem able to do so on the job—a conclusion consistent with socioanalytic theory.

A third general conclusion concerning clinical measures is that, when viewed from an appropriate theory base, a limited number of personality variables appear to be related in fairly direct, logical ways to success on the job. The work of McClelland and his colleagues with the Thematic Apperception Test (TAT) is an example of this, as is the research utilizing Eysenck's dimensions of personality. Because of the empirical usefulness of their work, each deserves mention in its own right.

McClelland and others might not agree that the TAT is a clinical measure; nonetheless, it has been most widely used in clinical applications. McClelland (1981) also argues that the assessment of motives in fantasy often taps information different from that reflected in questionnaires, although this assertion apparently has not been tested. It seems equally plausible that much of the same information could be obtained from appropriately constructed, theory-based questionnaires and biographical data sheets, without the usual difficulties of projective measures. This only points up the fact that McClelland's research is quite distinctive in its theory-driven quality.

The TAT work has focused on motives. Earlier, McClelland (1961) found a consistent relationship between successful entrepreneurship and the need to achieve. McClelland (1977) now regards this earlier work as greatly oversimplified. He has been able to improve the prediction of success by adding the construct of need for power to the need for achievement; at the same time he has included a small number of other motives that act much like moderator variables. Thus, his new, complex model of entrepreneurship and management uses two major personality constructs (McClelland 1975; McClelland & Burnham 1976). Other studies find that a more complete picture of successful managers includes a lower need for affiliation and a greater level of self-control or inhibition of activity (for instance, McClelland 1977). This basic pattern of needs in the managerial personality has been replicated in a number of groups; other variables come up, but they seem to be specific to the needs of localized populations.

This use of a relatively straightforward model with few variables has been rather successful in predicting employment success for key groups of leaders. Admittedly, the constructs that emerge from the TAT work are broad and complex, but their usefulness points to the underlying cohesiveness of the clusters of characteristics forming the constructs.

Research with the Eysenck Personality Questionnaire (EPQ) (Eysenck & Eysenck 1969) focuses on two broad and complex personality constructs, though they stem from a vastly different theoretical orientation. According to Eysenck's model of personality (1967, 1981), extraversion and neuroticism are key dimensions along which individuals differ. The EPQ measures both dimensions, and thus could be correctly described as a cross between a clinical and a normal personality measure. The model assumes the existence of stable traits rooted in genetics and physiology that demonstrably affect social behavior.

In general, extraverts perform best in jobs that involve dealing with other people (such as sales and personnel work, service occupations), whereas introverts are better able to resist boredom and are more dependable and conscientious (Eysenck 1971). In a test of driving performance (Fagerstrom & Lister 1977), extraverts showed a sharper deterioration over four hours than did introverts but also benefited more strikingly from stimulation (such as a car radio). Extraverts also seem to prefer and to work better in noisy environments than do introverts (Hockey 1972).

Several studies, however, point to the importance of examining both neuroticism and extraversion simultaneously. For example, in a study of South African bus drivers (Shaw & Sichel 1970), drivers with bad records were clustered primarily in the neurotic-extravert quadrant, whereas the best drivers were in the stable-introvert quadrant. Another study using "quadrant analysis" (Jessup & Jessup 1971) found that failure rates in a training program for pilots were lowest for stable-introverts (14 percent) and greatest for neurotic-introverts (60 percent). Failure rates among stable and neurotic extraverts were 32 percent and 37 percent, respectively.

Many personality theorists disagree with Eysenck's conceptualization of the trait universe in terms of two or three superfactors. Nevertheless, these findings demonstrate that such broad, overarching constructs are related to work performance.

NONCLINICAL MEASURES

In research that is sensibly designed and competently conducted, measures of normal personality have worked reasonably well. As we pointed out earlier, Ghiselli (1973) averaged validity coefficients across a varied group of personality measures; nonetheless, coefficients for predicting job proficiency ranged from .16 for service occupations to .32 for sales occupations (see Table 2.1). Campbell, Dunnette, Lawler, and Weick (1970) review a number of other studies in chapters 8 and 9 of their classic work on managers. Their review includes information not typically cited because it was gleaned from technical reports on major research programs conducted by large corporations. The following nonexhaustive review gives the flavor of the literature since these earlier reviews.

The Comrey Personality Scales (Comrey 1970) have been used successfully to predict the performance of Navy personnel (Hoiberg & Pugh 1978; Webster, Booth, Graham & Alf 1978). For example, Hoiberg and Pugh classified personnel as noneffective, satisfactory, or effective on the basis of their pay grade and rates of turnover, absenteeism, and confinement. Three of the Comrey scales—Orderliness, Social Conformity, and Extraversion (weighted negatively)—were related significantly to classification level. Together they correlated .24 with the criterion in a sample of almost 4,000 sailors from 6 broad occupational groups; in a cross-validation sample of equal size, the correlation was .17. These validity coefficients surpassed those obtained with aptitude, expectation, and motivational measures.

Saul B. Sells used the 16 P-F (Cattell, Eber, & Tatsuoka 1970) in his research with airline personnel (Murdy, Sells, Gavin, & Toole 1973; Toole, Gavin, Murdy, & Sells 1972). In the study by Toole et al., supervisors' ratings of semiskilled, unionized airline employees ($N = 520$) were correlated with scores on the 16 P-F scales. Good ratings were associated with a number of scales, including those for conscientiousness, humility, trust, and practicality. The particular set of scales that best predicted performance, however, depended on the race and age of the employees. Personality predictors had a validity coefficient of .28 in the sample of young Caucasians, .41 for young minority workers, and .31 for older Caucasians.

In another study, Porter and Steers (1973) identified a number of personality attributes associated with turnover and absenteeism. Bernardin (1977) then used the 16 P-F to examine further these relationships in two samples of male employees involved in telephone sales work. He found that factors C, G, Q3, and Q4 were related to turnover, and factors C, G, H, and Q4 to absenteeism. Multiple correlation coefficients were computed for both samples, and the regression equation for each sample was also applied to the other sample for a double cross-validation. Results for turnover and absenteeism are reported in Table 2.2. Further analyses indicated that conscientiousness and anxiety (factors G and Q4, respectively) accounted for most of the variance.

TABLE 2.2
Using the 16 P-F to Predict Employee Turnover and Absenteeism

	Sample A (N = 51)	Sample B (N = 48)
Turnover		
Validation	.39	.47
Cross-Validation	.38	.31
Absenteeism		
Validation	.35	.32
Cross-validation	.30	.27

Source: Adapted from Bernardin 1977.

Since its publication in 1949, the Guilford-Zimmerman Temperament Survey (GZTS) (Guilford & Zimmerman 1949) has been widely used in applied contexts. The most recent GZTS manual (Guilford, Zimmerman, & Guilford 1976), for example, reports 23 separate studies of managerial performance alone. Of this group, three studies are particularly noteworthy. The first, by Harrell and Harrell (1973), compared high- and low-achieving MBAs. Subjects in the study had completed a battery of personality tests as students at Stanford University. In a ten-year follow-up, several hundred MBAs were identified as high or low earners relative to their classmates. High achievers were found, relative to low achievers, to be higher in ascendance and social boldness, and, in large companies, to be more active and more extraverted. In a second study Sparks (1983) studied 2,478 men in a large oil company and found steady relationships between GZTS scores and indices of success, effectiveness, and managerial potential. In a third study Hobert and Dunnette (1967) studied 443 managers at

Standard Oil in an effort to identify moderator variables that would augment the prediction of managerial success. They found that those who performed better than predicted (the "underpredicted") were more emotionally stable, whereas those who did worse than predicted (the "overpredicted") were less emotionally stable and more hostile and hypersensitive.

The foregoing inventories, although showing greater practical validity than many people might realize, share some common shortcomings: they are not theory-based; they endorse the self-report model of item responses; and, when stated, their measurement goals have little to do with the prediction of nontest behavior. In contrast, the California Psychological Inventory (CPI) (Gough 1975) was developed with the explicit goal of assessing factors associated with competency and real world effectiveness. The theoretical basis of the CPI—"folk theory"—is underdeveloped, but no more so than inventories based on the Murray need system. Finally, the CPI rests on the empirical theory of item responses. The conceptual clarity underlying it has translated into empirical productivity and indisputable evidence regarding the utility of personality measures in applied contexts (see Cobb 1962; Goodstein & Schrader 1963; Mahoney, Jerdee, & Nash 1960; Rawls & Rawls 1968). One of the more impressive demonstrations of the CPI's practical utility has been the study of police performance. Hogan (1971) examined the relationship of CPI scores, rated performance, and class standing at a police academy. He reports that highly rated officers are capable, confident, reasonable, rational, independent, and energetic. These results have been replicated in different samples and at different times by Hogan and Kurtines (1975), Spielberger et al. (1979), Mills and Bohannon (1980), and Johnson and Hogan (1981). This success is especially striking when contrasted with the performance of other measures used on this population.

NEW DEVELOPMENTS

As noted above, we believe that many of the problems associated with using personality measures in industry are a function of conceptual confusions. We intimated earlier that socioanalytic theory (Hogan 1982; Hogan, Jones, & Cheek 1983) provides a sensible answer to questions regarding the meaning of test scores and what dimensions to assess when doing personality measurement. We also pointed out that trait words are the language of personality and that they mark the categories that observers use to evaluate the actions of others; in particular, observers are concerned with evaluating others with regard to their potential contribution to the goals and welfare of mutual or shared groups. Because all groups must do much the same things to survive, the structure of trait vocabularies should be cross-culturally similar if not actually universal, and this may be the case (see White 1980). If there is a universal structure underlying trait vocabularies, describable in terms of a finite set of dimensions, then every personality inventory should assess these dimensions more or less efficiently.

Two sources support this conclusion. On the one hand, work by Browne and Howarth (1977) shows that the item pools of several personality inventories can be reduced to 15 dimensions, which themselves can be collapsed into the dimensions of Adjustment (social shyness, mood swings, emotionality, hypochondriasis, and inferiority), Prudence (impulsiveness, superego), Ambition (persistence, submission, dominance, general activity), Sociability (sociability, social conversation), and Likability (suspicion/trust, cooperative/considerate). Curiously, Intellectance (quick-witted versus slow-witted) is missing from Browne and Howarth's final list. On the other hand, Hogan and Johnson (reported in Johnson 1981) sorted the CPI item pool into the six categories Intellectance, Adjustment, Ambition, Prudence, Sociability, and Likability. They found that the content scales thus formed had good internal consistency and predicted job performance in samples of police officers and consulting engineers as well as the original CPI scales. The point here is not to criticize the structure or construction of the CPI. Rather, the point is to suggest that existing personality inventories assess, in a more or less efficient manner, the same small number of dimensions, *and* that these dimensions are related to everyday performance in the world of work.

In conjunction with the fundamental work of Norman (1963), the foregoing suggests that there is now a systematic basis for doing personality inventory construction. Specifically, the inventory of the future should sample from each of the primary dimensions that observers use to evaluate actors (such as Intelligence, Adjustment, Ambition). As an exercise in scale construction, a group of us at Johns Hopkins set about doing this four years ago. Taking each of the major trait dimensions one at a time, and bearing in mind the earlier comments about item response theory, we asked what kinds of things an actor would do to persuade others that he or she is bright, well-adjusted, leaderlike, conscientious, sociable, and likable. In the case of Intellectance, for example, we concluded that people who are evaluated as intelligent usually have good memories, perform well in school, and make good decisions.

We devised six primary scales of varying length, each with an alpha reliability of about .90. Each scale is composed of a set of homogeneous item composites (HICs) (Zonderman 1980). These HICs are like miniature scales; each has an alpha reliability of .50 or better, and each correlates more highly with its parent scale than with any other (for details see Hogan 1982). But, most important, we found we could represent the domain of traitlike behaviors in six scales composed of 45 HICs.

In conducting analyses with this test, it is possible to run them at either the scale or the HIC level. Analyses at the HIC level allow a very discrete patterning of predictors on criterion data in a way that faithfully reproduces the complexity of meaningful, real world criterion data. At the same time the results are interpretable in psychological terms because the HICs are distinct psychometric units.

On theoretical grounds we expected that a personality inventory constructed in the manner just described would be a valid predictor of job performance in the everyday world. There were two reasons for this expectation. On the one hand, the dimensions scaled are the primary dimensions of interpersonal evaluation within the context of viable, ongoing groups—and the dimensions reflect competence rather than psychopathology. On the other hand, with this inventory actors are forced to describe themselves in terms of the dimensions that observers naturally use to make evaluations. In the six validity studies we have completed to date, these expectations have been met.

For example, in a study of volunteers at Navy research bases in the Antarctic, Busch, Schroeder, and Biersner (1982) found that performance was a function of being bright, introverted, and not easily bored. Persons who were sociable and craved excitement in their lives received low peer ratings for their performance over the six-month winter. Although the overall correlation with performance was only about .40, this represents a substantial improvement over merely selecting personnel on the basis of technical competence—a practice that has led to some near tragedies at the remote antarctic research stations during the long winter.

In a study of explosive ordnance disposal technicians at the combined services training school at Indian Head, Maryland, we defined performance in training three ways: in terms of the number of courses a student had to repeat; in terms of academic standing; and in terms of the pass/fail criterion. The HPI provided a reasonable prediction of each of these criteria; more interesting, however, was the finding that a separate pattern of scores was associated with each criterion. Persons who didn't repeat courses were dogged and conforming; persons with high academic standing were bright and academically motivated; persons who simply survived the training program were self-confident and devil-may-care. The point about this set of analyses is not that the HPI outperformed the other predictors in the study (including the ASVAB) but that the HPI was very sensitive to the kinds of criterion data used.

A third study (Hogan, Hogan, & Busch 1983) used the HPI to predict one aspect of job performance—service orientation—among hospital workers. Once again the HPI worked well, but the important finding from this set of analyses is that, in several comparisons, there were no reliable differences between black and white workers, who, in terms of educational level, were approximately equivalent to Army recruits.

In a fourth study the HPI was used to predict delinquency in two kinds of analyses. In the first, delinquents were compared with nondelinquents. In the second, HPI scores were regressed against self-reported delinquency in college students. The results were similar across the analyses and quite strong—zero-order correlations between single HICs and the criterion as high as .70. The portrait of the "typical delinquent" emerging from these analyses is a person who is tough, alienated, thrill-seeking, and exhibitionistic.

In a fifth study we correlated HPI scores with rated performance in a group of 110 secretarial/clerical employees (all women, 80 white, 25 black, 5 hispanics) from a large insurance corporation. The resulting regression equation ($r = .47$), which emphasized adjustment, conformity, and likability, outperformed typical clerical aptitude measures. The news: we found no black/white differences.

In a sixth study we correlated HPI scores with rated performance for a group of 50 (27 men, 23 women) professional/technical employees in the same insurance company. Collapsing across sex, we found a multiple r of .32. There were no sex differences, and the 30-item regression equation emphasized self-confidence, sociability, and an anti-intellectual style (a preference for baseball over opera).

The foregoing studies show that the HPI is a robust predictor of a range of everyday job performance outcomes. The point, however, is not to tout the HPI but to illustrate the value of a particular way of thinking about personality and interpersonal behavior, and a method of inventory construction that follows from this way of thinking. In a simplified way, the key elements in this perspective are the following:

1. Trait words are used by observers to evaluate actors in terms of their potential as resources for the observers' group.
2. The structure of trait vocabularies is much the same across groups.

3. Actors behave so as to create specific impressions in observers. They do this both in public and in responding to psychological tests.
4. The foregoing information can be used as a theoretical and systematic basis for constructing personality inventories.
5. The case of the HPI shows that, when inventories are constructed this self-conscious way, they are quite useful predictors of everyday performance.

The bottom line on all this is that when due regard is given to the relevant conceptual issues, personality measures work about as well as aptitude measures in the prediction of job performance. Because they are largely independent of aptitude measures, they can add substantial incremental validity. Even better, however, is the news that they don't discriminate as badly as aptitude measures. And best of all, personality measures allow us to capitalize on what real people have always known—that attitude is generally more important than aptitude in everyday performance.

FUTURE TRENDS

We would like to suggest a broad issue and three narrower but more researchable problems that seem amenable to the kinds of measurement efforts we have been discussing.

Integrating Personality Psychology and Organizational Theory

The broader issue involves the need for a more formal integration of personality psychology and organizational theory wherein personnel selection could be made more responsive to organizational dynamics—that is, to the organization as an evolving system over time, an organization that is dependent on and responsive to changing external conditions such as business cycles, and to changing role requirements for an individual as he or she moves up or across an organization.

Katz and Kahn (1978), for example, conceptualize organizational development in terms of three stages. Stage 1 involves the initial definition of task demands and development of "appropriate production or technical structures." Stage 2 concerns the development of stable managerial structure and social organization, with roles, norms, and goals designed to ensure the reliability of performance. Authority structures, traditions, policies, and procedures evolve to facilitate routinization, predictability, and production systems maintenance. Stage 3 concerns developing systems by which the now mature organization can adapt to, and interact with, a dynamic environment.

The typical large defense or airframe company is a useful example. Such a firm often has a divisional structure with somewhat parallel and mature divisions, each having a product line (X37, X47, X57) or family of products (missiles A, B, C). Yet the firm is constantly planning new generations of products and proposing new projects to the government. To facilitate the proposal or prototype stage of a new project, a new division may be formed and core personnel recruited from existing divisions. A special kind of person is necessary at the beginning, when production structures—indeed, the product itself—have yet to be defined. Authority structures, lines of communication, and informal alliances have yet to be negotiated; there are few traditions or rules for how to proceed; tolerance for change and ambiguity, and vast amounts of energy and career risk are demanded. If the project is given the go-ahead, all structures are subsequently stabilized, reliability of performance becomes the focus, and production costs start down the learning curve.

The large firm may be able to draw upon a sizable pool of individuals with similar levels of experience, aptitude, and training in order to staff its divisions, each of which may be at a different stage of development. The interesting assessment question, however, concerns how to identify those employees who might best serve the organization's needs and goals during each phase of the developmental cycle. We believe that personality assessment strategies could productively be adapted to identify personnel able to operate under varying conditions of risk, structure, predictability, and organizational climate. It may be possible, for example, to use current career-choice typologies (see Holland 1966) to improve personnel assignments (regardless of one's specialty or status in the organization) by considering the needs of an organization at a particular stage of its developmental cycle.

Responses to EEOC: Fast-Tracking Women and Minorities

Personality assessment strategies also seem appropriate to the solution of a recent problem resulting from pressure for affirmative-action planning. Corporate affirmative-action plans involve setting target employment levels for women and minorities throughout the organizational hierarchy. However, many organizations have faced a shortage of appropriately experienced female and minority candidates for upper-level positions, and thus have had to develop fast-track, enriched management development programs to provide a broad and varied experience base (Thornton & Byham 1982).

To succeed in such a program, however, a person must be intellectually and dispositionally prepared to rise to the challenge. In addition to undergoing an intensified learning experience, such candidates must buck long-established social systems in the organization. Candidates must be able to assert their rights, persevere under stress, display competence, build their own support relationships and alliances, and quickly adopt a managerial perspective. Former relationships and group identifications will likely wither as a managerial perspective is adopted. The characteristics required to meet these challenges again would seem amenable to straightforward personality measurement, and a wealth of available theory and data suggest selection strategies.

For example, recent research has established that those women who score high on "masculinity" scales (reflecting an instrumental orientation and characteristics such as independence, decisiveness, and assertiveness) are better-adjusted, more open to experience, more persevering problem solvers, more willing to trust their skill rather than their fate or luck, less fearful of success, more extraverted, higher in self-esteem, more easily able to take personal crisis (such as divorce) in stride, and more politically sophisticated (see Taylor & Hall 1982). Perhaps more important, women high in instrumental characteristics were found in a study of 50 business organizations to be more acceptable to incumbent managers and personnel directors as candidates for management trainee positions (Hansson, O'Connor, Jones, & Mihelich 1980).

Assessing Older Workers

Currently available personality tests have not proven reliable with older adults. Test items are likely to have been written for and normed on younger and better-educated persons. Older persons also may fatigue more easily, may not like being asked the sorts of questions often included in personality tests, and may be more inhibited and subject to response sets. The clinical and counseling literature is beginning to deal with these issues (see George & Bearon 1980; Mangen & Peterson 1982). However, these questions have generally been ignored in the area of industrial assessment, for a number of reasons. Much formal assessment is at the entry level, and thus by definition focuses on younger adults. Also, assessment center participation has historically been by nomination of one's supervisor, a process that may be subject to age stereotypes. In addition, until recently the mandatory retirement age of 65 kept industry from having to deal with issues involving the aging.

Several factors, however, have recently made the question of assessing older workers more interesting. Changes in the Age Discrimination in Employment Act have extended the range of protected status to age 70, prohibiting personnel policy or procedure that results in disparate treatment or impact because of age, and the EEOC has been progressing with precedent-setting cases. Another factor is the suggestion of an age bias in assessment center technology (which typically does not use personality measures). Performance on the widely used in-basket test has sometimes been found, for example, to correlate negatively with age (Meyer 1970), as have overall assessment ratings (Burroughs, Rollins, & Hopkins 1973; Thornton & Byham 1982). In addition, there has been little research focusing on age-related selection criteria for retention in stressful or demanding jobs, or on retrainability.

Available evidence suggests that, at least in jobs not involving physical or time stress, older workers of all kinds remain productive and dependable into their late sixties (see Fleisher & Kaplan 1980; Coates & Kirby 1982). Similarly, there are few normative cognitive changes in that period (see Schaie 1981), nor is there evidence of much normative personality change with age (McCrae & Costa 1982; Neugarten 1977). It would thus seem useful to adapt for use with older adults those personality scales that might be useful in employee selection elsewhere, and to use such instruments in making decisions regarding retraining, reassignment, retention, and retirement planning.

Organizational/Job Stress

In summarizing the literature, McGrath (1976) suggested several general sources of stress in organizations: task-based stress, such as difficulty, ambiguity, load; role-based stress, such as role conflict, ambiguity, change; stress intrinsic to the behavior setting, such as crowding, undermanning; stress intrinsic to the physical environment, such as physical danger; stress of the social environment, such as isolation, disagreement. In addition, he emphasized the importance of what the individual brings to the setting in terms of dispositional vulnerabilities, perceptual style, and so on.

Views regarding how to manage organizational/job stress generally focus on "human factors-human performance" interventions (see Alluisi & Fleishman 1982) or on management's role in providing predictability, a supportive organizational climate, role clarity, stress management programming, a better person-environment fit, and social support (see the ISR Model: French, Caplan, & Harrison 1982; Katz & Kahn 1978, p. 384). These approaches, however, assume management's ability to stabilize and control the production and social systems of an organization.

The economic recession of the early 1980s demonstrated clearly that stability and predictability are seldom obtainable for any period of time. This recession forced much of the business community into retrenchment, thereby reducing predictability regarding the status of employment itself, much less how particular jobs are to be carried out. Market and production strategies were revised to permit corporate survival, and organizational structures changed accordingly (in some cases experiencing 40-50 percent reductions in the work force).

Under such circumstances, those people who best serve an organization are likely to be dispositionally prepared to cope with stressful environments; this would include tolerance for risk and ambiguity, self-confidence, drive, ambition, lack of anxiety, inner locus of control, and the stamina and emotional reserves to withstand stress in the absence of structure and a supportive, predictable climate for long periods of time. Such personality characteristics are readily assessed, and could be used to select key personnel who can function effectively in such environments.

Susan Kobasa's related notion of the hardy personality seems useful in this context. The hardy personality is conceptualized to involve a combination of three dispositional characteristics: personal commitment, feeling in control, and responding to change as an interesting and challenging experience. In this research, elements of the hardiness construct appear to be associated with resistance to stressful life events, for example, among lawyers (Kobasa 1982) and among corporate managerial personnel (Kobasa, Maddi, & Kahn 1982).

Finally, considerable evidence has begun to accumulate regarding the health-protective effects of social support (see Gottlieb 1983). Supportive social relationships in the family, community, or work place are believed to provide the emotional and logistical resources that help to buffer against the negative consequences of stressful life events. Little attention has focused, however, on those variables that might be associated with being able to develop support networks in times of need. We believe that a number of personality characteristics are important in defining such relational competence and in defining the likelihood of organization members effectively developing support networks in time of stress. These variables are central to recent theory in the field of personal relationships generally (Duck &

Gilmour 1981), and include loneliness (Jones 1982), perspective-taking ability (Davis 1983), and social reticence (Jones & Russell 1982).

REFERENCES

Alluisi, E.A., & Fleishman, E.A., eds. *Human performance and productivity,* vol. 3, *Stress and performance effectiveness.* Hillsdale, N.J.: Erlbaum, 1982.

Baehr, M.E., Furcon, J.E., & Froemel, E.C. *Psychological assessment of patrolman qualifications in relation to field performance* (Law Enforcement Assistance Administration project # 046). Washington, D.C.: U.S. Government Printing Office, 1968.

Bartol, C.R. Psychological characteristics of small-town police officers. *Journal of Police Science and Administration,* 1982, *10,* 58–63.

Bernardin, H.J. The relationship of personality variables to organizational withdrawal. *Personnel Psychology,* 1977, *30,* 17–27.

Bernstein, I.H. Security guards' MMPI profiles: Some normative data. *Journal of Personality Assessment,* 1980, *44,* 377–380.

Bernstein, I.H., Schoenfeld, L.S., & Costello, R.M. Truncated component regression, multicollinearity and the MMPI's use in a police officer selection setting. *Multivariate Behavioral Research,* 1982, *17,* 99–116.

Bingham, W.V. Psychology applied. *Scientific Monthly,* 1923, 16.

Browne, J.A., & Howarth, E.A. A comprehensive factor analysis of personality questionnaire forms. *Multivariate Behavioral Research,* 1977, *12,* 399–427.

Buchwald, A.M. Verbal utterances as data. In H. Feigl & G. Maxwell, (eds.), *Current issues in the philosophy of science.* New York: Holt, 1961, 461–468.

Burroughs, W.A., Rollins, J.B., & Hopkins, J.J. The effect of age, departmental experience and prior rater experience on performance in assessment center exercises. *Academy of Management Journal,* 1973, *16,* 335–339.

Busch, C.M., Schroeder, D.H., & Biersner, R.J. Personality attributes associated with personal and social adjustment in small, isolated groups. Paper presented at the 53rd annual convention of the Eastern Psychological Association, Baltimore, 1982.

Buss, A.H. *Self-consciousness and social anxiety.* San Francisco: Freeman, 1980.

Butterfield, H.C., & Warren, S.A. The use of the MMPI in the selection of hospital aides. *Journal of Applied Psychology,* 1962, *46,* 34–40.

_____. Prediction of attendant tenure. *Journal of Applied Psychology,* 1963, *47,* 101–103.

Campbell, J.P., Dunnette, M.D., Lawler, E.E. III, & Weick, K.E., Jr. *Managerial behavior, performance, and effectiveness.* New York: McGraw-Hill, 1970.

Cattell, R.B., Eber, H.W., & Tatsuoka, M.M. *Handbook for the sixteen personality factor questionnaire (16PF)*. Champaign, Ill.: Institute for Personality and Ability Testing, 1970.

Cheek, J.M. Aggregation, moderator variables, and the validity of personality tests: A peer-rating study. *Journal of Personality and Social Psychology,* 1982, *43,* 1254–1269.

Coates, G.D., & Kirby, R.H. Organismic factors and individual differences in human performance and productivity. In E.A. Alluisi and E.A. Fleishman (eds.), *Human performance and productivity,* vol. 3, *Stress and performance effectiveness.* Hillsdale, N.J.: Erlbaum, 1982.

Cobb, B.B. Problems in air traffic management: A prediction of success in air traffic controller school. *Aerospace Medicine,* 1962, *33,* 702–713.

Comrey, A.L. *EITS Manual for the Comrey Personality Scales.* San Diego, Calif.: Educational and Industrial Testing Service, 1970.

Costello, R.M., Schoenfeld, L.S., & Kobos, J. Police applicant screening: An analogue study. *Journal of Clinical Psychology,* 1982, *38,* 216–221.

Davis, M.H. Measuring individual differences in empathy: Evidence for a multidimensional approach. *Journal of Personality and Social Psychology,* 1983, *44,* 113–126.

Duck, S., & Gilmour, R. *Personal relationships,* vol. 1, *Studying personal relationships.* London: Academic Press, 1981.

Eiduson, B.T. 10-year longitudinal Rorschachs on research scientists. *Journal of Personality Assessment,* 1974, *38,* 405–410.

Eysenck, H.J. *The biological basis of personality.* Springfield, Ill.: Thomas, 1967.

_____. *Readings in extraversion-introversion,* vol. 2, *Fields of application.* London: Staples, 1971.

_____. General features of the model. In H.J. Eysenck (ed.), *A model for personality.* New York: Springer-Verlag, 1981, 1–37.

Eysenck, H.J., & Eysenck, S.B.G. *The description and measurement of personality.* London: Routledge & Kegan Paul, 1969.

Fagerstrom, K.O., & Lister, H.O. Effects of listening to car radio, experience, and personality of the driver on subsidiary reaction time and heart rate in a long-term driving task. In R.R. Mackie (ed.), *Vigilance.* New York: Plenum, 1977, 73–86.

Fleisher, D., & Kaplan, B.H. Characteristics of older workers: Implications for restructuring work. In P.K. Ragan (ed.), *Work and retirement: Policy issues.* Los Angeles: Ethel Percy Andrus Gerontology Center, University of Southern California Press, 1980.

French, J.R.P., Jr., Caplan, R.D., & Harrison, R.V. *The mechanisms of job stress and strain.* New York: John Wiley, 1982.

George, L.K., & Bearon, L.B. *Quality of life in older persons: Meaning and measurement.* New York: Human Sciences Press, 1980.

Ghiselli, E.E. The validity of aptitude tests in personnel selection. *Personnel Psychology*, 1973, *26*, 461–477.

Goodstein, L.P., & Schrader, W.J. An empirically derived managerial key for the California Psychological Inventory. *Journal of Applied Psychology*, 1963, *47*, 42–45.

Gottlieb, B.H. Social support as a focus for integrative research in psychology. *American Psychologist*, 1983, *38*, 278–287.

Gough, H.G. The conceptual analysis of psychological test scores and other diagnostic variables. *Journal of Abnormal Psychology*, 1965, *70*, 294–302.

_____. *Manual for the California Psychological Inventory*. Palo Alto, Calif.: Consulting Psychologists Press, 1975.

Guilford, J.P., & Zimmerman, W.S. *The Guilford-Zimmerman Temperament Survey: Manual*. Beverly Hills, Calif.: Sheridan Supply, 1949.

Guilford, J.S., Zimmerman, W.S., & Guilford, J.P. *The Guilford-Zimmerman Temperament Survey Handbook*. San Diego, Calif.: Educational and Industrial Testing Service, 1976.

Guion, R.M., & Gottier, R.F. Validity of personality measures in personnel selection. *Personnel Psychology*, 1965, *18*, 135–164.

Gyorgy, B. Felsoszintu vezetok vizsgalata Rorschach-teszttel [Examination of top-level managers by Rorschach test]. *Magyar pszichologiai szemle*, 1979, *36*, 361–374.

Hale, M. History of employment testing. In A.K. Wigdor & W.R. Garner (eds.), *Ability testing: Uses, consequences, and controversies*, pt. 2, *Documentation Section*. Washington, D.C.: National Academy Press, 1982.

Hansson, R.O., O'Connor, M.E., Jones, W.H., & Mihelich, M.H. Role relevant sex typing and opportunity in agentic and communal domains. *Journal of Personality*, 1980, *48*, 419–434.

Harrell, T.W., & Harrell, M.S. The personality of MBA's who reach general management early. *Personnel Psychology*, 1973, *26*, 127–134.

Hase, H.D., & Goldberg, L.R. The comparative validity of different strategies of deriving personality scales. *Psychological Bulletin*, 1967, *67*, 231–248.

Hobert, R., & Dunnette, M.D. Development of moderator variables to enhance the prediction of managerial effectiveness. *Journal of Applied Psychology*, 1967, *51*, 50–64.

Hockey, G.R.J. Effects of noise on human efficiency and some individual differences. *Journal of Sound Vibrations*, 1972, *20*, 299–304.

Hogan, J., Hogan, R., & Busch, C. How to measure service orientation. Unpublished manuscript, University of Tulsa, 1983.

Hogan, R. Personality characteristics of highly rated policemen. *Personnel Psychology*, 1971, *24*, 679–686.

_____. The gifted adolescent. In J. Adelson (ed.), *Handbook of adolescent psychology*. New York: Wiley, 1980.

_____. A socioanalytic theory of personality. In M. Page & R. Dienstbier (eds.), *Nebraska symposium on motivation*. Lincoln: University of Nebraska Press, 1982, 55–89.

Hogan, R., Jones, W.H., & Cheek, J.M. Socioanalytic theory: An alternative to armadillo psychology. In B. Schlenker (ed.), *Self and identity: Presentations of self in social life*. New York: McGraw-Hill, 1983.

Hogan, R., & Kurtines, W. Personological correlates of police effectiveness. *Journal of Psychology*, 1975, *91*, 289–295.

Hoiberg, A., & Pugh, W.M. Predicting navy effectiveness: Expectations, motivation, personality, aptitude, and background variables. *Personnel Psychology*, 1978, *31*, 841–852.

Holland, J.L. *The psychology of vocational choice*. Waltham, Mass.: Ginn & Company, 1966. Rev. ed. Waltham, Mass.: Blaisdell, 1973.

Hooke, J.F., & Krauss, H.H. Personality characteristics of successful police sergeant candidates. *Journal of Criminal Law, Criminology and Police Science*, 1971, *62*, 104–106.

Jessup, G., & Jessup, H. Validity of the Eysenck personality inventory in pilot selection. *Occupational Psychology*, 1971, *45*, 121–123.

Johnson, J.A. The "self-disclosure" and "self-presentation" views of item response dynamics and personality scale validity. *Journal of Personality and Social Psychology*, 1981, *40*, 761–769.

Johnson, J.A., & Hogan, R. Vocational interests, personality and effective police performance. *Personnel Psychology*, 1981, *34*, 49–53.

Jones, W.H. Loneliness and social behavior. In L.A. Peplau & D. Perlman (eds.). *Loneliness: A sourcebook of current theory, research and therapy*. New York: Wiley-Interscience, 1982.

Jones, W.H., & Russell, D. The social reticence scale: An objective instrument to measure shyness. *Journal of Personality Assessment*, 1982, *46*, 629–631.

Katz, D., & Kahn, R.L. *The social psychology of organizations*. New York: John Wiley & Sons, 1978.

Kihlstrom, J.F. On personality and memory. In N. Cantor & J.F. Kihlstrom (eds.), *Personality, cognition, and social interaction*. Hillsdale, N.J.: Erlbaum, 1981.

Kobasa, S.C. Commitment and coping in stress resistance among lawyers. *Journal of Personality and Social Psychology*, 1982, *42*, 707–717.

Kobasa, S.C., Maddi, S.R., & Kahn, S. Hardiness and health: A prospective study. *Journal of Personality and Social Psychology*, 1982, *42*, 168–177.

Loevinger, J. Objective tests as instruments of psychological theory. *Psychological Reports*, 1957, *3*, 635–694 (monograph # 9).

Mahoney, T.A., Jerdee, T.H., & Nash, A.N. Predicting managerial effectiveness. *Personnel Psychology*, 1960, *13*, 147–163.

Mangen, D.J., & Peterson, W.A. *Research instruments in social gerontology*, vol. 1. *Clinical and social psychology*. Minneapolis: University of Minnesota Press, 1982.

Matarazzo, J.D., Allen, D.V., Saslow, G., & Wiens, A.N. Characteristics of successful policemen and firemen applicants. *Journal of Applied Psychology*, 1964, *48*, 123–133.

McClelland, D.C. *The achieving society*. Princeton: Van Nostrand, 1961.

_____. *Power: The inner experience*. New York: Invington-Halsted-Wiley, 1975.

_____. Entrepreneurship and management in the years ahead. In C.A. Bramlette, Jr. (ed.), *The individual and the future of organizations*. Atlanta: College of Business Administration, Georgia State University, 1977, 46–67.

_____. Is personality consistent? In A.I. Rabin, J. Aronoff, A.M. Barclay, & R.A. Zucker (eds.), *Further explorations in personality*. New York: John Wiley & Sons, 1981, 87–113.

McClelland, D.C., & Burnham, D.H. Power is the great motivator. *Harvard Business Review*, 1976, *54*, 100–110.

McCrae, R.R., & Costa, P.T. Self-concept and the stability of personality: Cross-sectional comparisons of self-reports and ratings. *Journal of Personality and Social Psychology*, 1982, *43*, 1282–1292.

McGrath, J.E. Stress and behavior in organizations. In M.D. Dunnette, (ed.), *Handbook of industrial and organizational psychology*. Chicago: Rand McNally, 1976.

Meehl, P.E. The dynamics of "structured" personality tests. *Journal of Clinical Psychology*, 1945, *1*, 296–303.

Merian, E.M., Stefan, D., Schoenfeld, L.S., & Kobos, J.C. Screening of police applicants: A 5-item MMPI research index. *Psychological Reports*, 1980, *47*, 155–158.

Meyer, H.H. The validity of the in-basket-test as a measure of managerial performance. *Personnel Psychology*, 1970, *23*, 297–307.

Michaelis, W., & Eysenck, H.J. The determination of personality inventory factor patterns and intercorrelations by changes in real-life motivation. *Journal of Genetic Psychology*, 1971, *118*, 223–234.

Mills, C.J., & Bohannon, W.E. Personality characteristics of effective state police officers. *Journal of Applied Psychology*, 1980, *65*, 680–684.

Mills, C.J., & Hogan, R. A role-theoretical interpretation of personality scale item responses. *Journal of Personality*, 1978, *46*, 778–785.

Mills, M.C., & Stratton, J.G. The MMPI and the prediction of police job performance. *FBI/Law Enforcement Bulletin*, 1982.

Moser, U. Eine methode zur bestimmung der widerstandsfahigkeit gegenuber der konflikts reaktivierung unter verwendung des Rorschachtests, dargestellt am problem der pilotenselektion [Rorschach test procedure for assessing competence of coping with conflict reactivation, as applied to aircraft pilot selection]. *Schweizerische Zeitschrift für Psychologie*, 1981, *40*, 279–313.

Murdy, L.B., Sells, S.B., Gavin, J.F., & Toole, D.L. Validity of personality and interest inventories for stewardesses. *Personnel Psychology*, 1973, *26*, 273–278.

Murphy, J.J. Current practices in the use of psychological testing by police agencies. *Journal of Criminal Law, Criminology and Police Science*, 1972, *63*, 570–576.

Neugarten, B.L. Personality and aging. In J.E. Birren and K.W. Schale (eds.), *Handbook of the psychology of aging.* New York: Van Nostrand Reinhold, 1977.

Norman, W.T. Toward an adequate taxonomy of personality attributes. *Journal of Abnormal and Social Psychology*, 1963, *66*, 574–583.

Olson, H.A. Personality characteristics of law students: A Rorschach study with emphasis on selection for law school. *Dissertation Abstracts International*, 1973, *33*, 3957B (University Microfilms no. 73–2480).

Parisher, D., Rios, B., & Reilley, R.R. Psychologists and psychological services in urban police departments: A national survey. *Professional Psychology*, 1979, *10*, 6–7.

Porter, L.W., & Steers, R.M. Organizational, work and personal factors in employee turnover and absenteeism. *Psychological Bulletin*, 1973, *80*, 151–176.

Rawls, D.J., & Rawls, J.R. Personality characteristics and personnel history data of successful and less successful executives. *Psychological Reports*, 1968, *23*, 1032–1034.

Saunders, B.T., & Pappanikou, A.J. Minnesota Multiphasic Personality Inventory sub-scale indices of effective child-care personnel. *Devereux Schools Forum*, 1970, *6*, 19–25.

Saxe, S.J., & Reiser, M. A comparison of three police applicant groups using the MMPI. *Journal of Police Science and Administration*, 1976, *4*, 419–425.

Schaie, K.W. Psychological changes from midlife to early old age: Implications for the maintenance of mental health. *American Journal of Orthopsychiatry*, 1981, *51*, 199–218.

Scheier, M.F., Buss, A.H., & Buss, D.M. Self-consciousness, self-report of aggressiveness, and aggression. *Journal of Research in Personality*, 1978, *12*, 133–40.

Shaw, L., & Sichel, H. *Accident proneness.* Oxford: Pergamon, 1970.

Sparks, C.P. Paper-and-pencil measures of potential. In G.F. Dreher & P.R. Sackett (eds.), *Perspectives on employee staffing and selection.* Homewood, Ill.: Irwin, 1983.

Spielberger, C.D., Spaulding, H.C., Jolley, M.T., & Ward, J.C. Selection of effective law enforcement officers: The Florida police standards research project. In C.D. Spielberger (ed.), *Police selection and evaluation: Issues and techniques.* New York: Praeger/Holt, Rinehart & Winston, 1979, 231–251.

Taylor, M.C., & Hall, J.A. Psychological androgyny: Theories, methods, and conclusions. *Psychological Bulletin*, 1982, *92*, 347–366.

Thornton, G.C., III & Byham, W.C. *Assessment centers and managerial performance.* New York: Academic Press, 1982.

Toole, D.L., Gavin, J.F., Murdy, L.B., & Sells, S.B. The differential validity of personality, personal history, and aptitude data for minority and nonminority employees. *Personnel Psychology,* 1972, *25,* 661–672.

Underwood, B., & Moore, B.S. Sources of behavioral consistency. *Journal of Personality and Social Psychology,* 1981, *40,* 780–785.

Webster, E.G., Booth, R.F., Graham, W.K., & Alf, E.F. A sex comparison of factors related to success in naval hospital corps school. *Personnel Psychology,* 1978, *31,* 95–106.

White, G.M. Conceptual universals in interpersonal language. *American Anthropologist,* 1980, *82,* 75–81.

Wiggins, J.S. *Personality and prediction: Principles of personality assessment.* Reading, Mass.: Addison-Wesley, 1973.

Worthy, J.C. *Planned executive development: The experience of Sears, Roebuck and Co* (Personnel Series #137). New York: American Management Association, 1951.

Zdep, S.M., & Weaver, H.B. The graphoanalytic approach to selecting life insurance salesmen. *Journal of Applied Psychology,* 1967, *51,* 295–299.

Zonderman, A.B. Inventory construction by the method of homogeneous item composites. Unpublished manuscript, Johns Hopkins University, 1980.

3

The Role of Person-Environment Fit in Job Performance and Satisfaction

Michael R. Patsfall and Nickolaus R. Feimer

INTRODUCTION

In recent years a number of researchers have noted the importance of creating and sustaining congruity between the needs of the individual and those of the organization (Downey, Hellriegel, & Slocum 1975; Friedlander and Margulies 1969; Pritchard and Karasick 1973; Morse 1975). The concept of person-environment (P-E) fit addresses this issue. The idea behind P-E fit is simply that there are qualities of environments that have the potential to match the qualities of individuals, with behavior being a consequence of the degree of achieved congruence (Murray 1938; Pervin 1968; Stern, Stein, & Bloom 1956; Stern 1970). From an organizational perspective, the greater the match between the individual's needs and the environmental attributes, the greater will be the potential for the individual's satisfaction and achieved performance (Pervin 1968; Downey, Hellriegel, & Slocum 1975).

Concurrently with the evolution of conceptualizations of P-E fit, the concept of organizational climate was generating a considerable amount of interest. Intended initially to represent an objective referent for variation in organizational environments (Forehand & Gilmer 1964), organizational climate has come to represent individuals' perceptions of the organizational environment (Schneider 1983). As the latter, the concept of organizational climate provides a conceptual link between analysis at the organizational and individual levels (Field and Abelson 1982). That is, it constitutes a link in the nomological net between constructs of process and structure, for example, and organizational outcomes such as satisfaction and effectiveness. Furthermore, although there are a number of ways to define and measure the organizational environment, the use of perceptual measures of organizational climate is the most common. (See Payne & Pugh 1976 for a discussion of objective and structural aspects in relation to climate.)

The purpose of this chapter is to provide an integration of the concepts of P-E fit and organizational climate. First the theoretical and empirical basis of both organizational climate and P-E fit will be presented. Next the empirical work on the effect of climate on performance and satisfaction will be presented, highlighting studies that have investigated the effects of interactions between the environment and personality on performance and satisfaction.

THE NATURE OF CLIMATE

Forehand and Gilmer (1964) initially defined organizational climate as a set of characteristics that distinguish among organizations, are relatively enduring, and influence the behavior of members of the organization. In recent years there has been an increasing interest in subsystem or work group, as well as individual or psychological, climate. "Organizational climate" refers to an aggregated measure of individuals' perceptions of the climate, presumably after some consensus is demonstrated (Guion 1973). "Psychological climate" refers to the individual's perceptions of the environment, which may be idiosyncratic and unique. This increasing specificity of the climate construct has been precipitated by recognition of climate at the suborganizational level (Drexler 1977) and heterogeneity of climate perceptions (Jones & James 1979).

Later definitions of climate (Hellriegel & Slocum 1974; Gavin & Howe 1975) were similar to earlier versions, but acknowledged the possibilities of subgroup and psychological climate. Schneider (1983), for example, has described climate, whether organizational or psychological, as an assessed molar perception or an inference made by researchers on the basis of assessments that are perceptions of organizational practices. In his view, climate is ". . . a psychological variable which is an attribution about the setting; a way for people to make sense out of all the stimuli around them" (Schneider 1983, p. 109). According to Siegel and Kaemmerer (1978), Campbell, Dunnette, Lawler, and Weick's (1970) definition of climate is the most widely accepted. In their opinion, climate refers to a

". . . set of characteristics specific to an organization that can be ascertained from the way in which the organization relates to its members and to its environment. For the members of the organization, climate is reflected in the attitudes and expectancies held toward the organization" (Siegel & Kaemmerer 1978, p. 553).

Figure 1
Conceptual Model of Climate

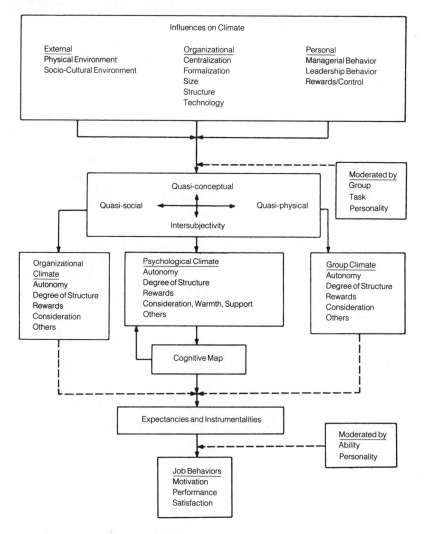

Source: From R.H.G. Field and M.A. Abelson, Climate: A reconceptualization and proposed model, *Human Relations,* 1982, *35,* pp. 181–201. Reprinted with permission.

Field and Abelson (1982) have presented the most recent and comprehensive model of climate (see Figure 1). In their model the psychological climate takes a central role while organizational and group climates are seen to take on decreased importance with regard to job-related behaviors. The model enumerates several sources of influence on climate, which may be external to the organization, organizational, or person-oriented. The psychological interpretation of social and physical facts, and the representation of problems to be solved and goals to be attained, constitute the quasi-physical, quasi-social, and quasi-conceptual facts that comprise the life space (in Lewin's [1936] terms) of the individual. Intersubjectivity is the subjective difference between persons of which the individual is aware. The individual's cognitive representation of these quasi-facts, which constitute the psychological climate, are exemplified by the four most common dimensions of climate as enumerated by Campbell et al. (1970), although other, more situation-specific dimensions may occur.

According to the Field and Abelson (1982) model, a schema is created from the individual's psychological climate, which filters future incoming information and has a feedback effect on the psychological climate (Guion 1973; Schneider 1973). The schema permits the individual to construct expectancies and instrumentalities that, moderated by ability and/or personality, result in the job behaviors of interest. The model implies that organizational and group climate may or may not influence the outcome behaviors, but psychological climate always does. Personality and ability factors are posited as potential moderators between these expectancies and instrumentalities and job behaviors, as Friedlander and Margulies (1969) and Downey, Hellriegel, and Slocum (1975) have shown.

CURRENT ISSUES IN CLIMATE RESEARCH

The use of climate as a measure of perceived environmental qualities requires a brief discussion of several important issues that have emerged from the climate literature: the dimensionality of climate, the unit of analysis and subsystem climates, the relationship between climate and satisfaction, and the measurement of climate.

Dimensionality of Climate

The specification of general dimensions that characterize organizational climate has been a central issue in climate research. Campbell et al.

(1970) reviewed a series of studies and concluded that at least four dimensions of climate seemed to emerge consistently: Individual Autonomy; Degree of Structure; Reward Orientation; and Consideration, Warmth, and Support. In a later review Hellriegel and Slocum (1974) concluded that while the core of climate dimensions specified by Campbell et al. may predominate, there also is considerable diversity in emergent climate dimensions.

Schneider (1983) has presented an alternative conceptualization of climate dimensions. He has suggested that any organization has a multitude of climates, largely because the employees are exposed to thousands of events and practices, and form these into clusters of related sets based on their perceived meaning. Conceptually it is still not clear whether this results in multiple climates (in the sense of perceiving multiple environments) or a single climate with multiple dimensions. Theoretically and empirically there is reason to believe that what we perceive is a single, organized molar environment (Ittelson 1973). However, this does not mean that the molar environment is unidimensional. On the contrary, it is suggested that what Schneider refers to as multiple climates are taken here to be simply the multiplicity of climate dimensions.

A related issue is the stability of climate dimensions across samples. To date, there is evidence of both stability and inconsistency in climate dimensions in similar but distinct organizational contexts. Stern's (1970) factor analyses of the Organizational Climate Index revealed similar climate dimensions across three disparate samples. Likewise, Jones and James (1979) found that the dimensions of climate in one sample generalized to two other, very different samples. On the other hand, Johannesson's (1973) cluster analyses of climate items revealed different clusters for the different samples.

In general, the evidence suggests that there is a small number of stable climate dimensions that tend to represent differences among organizational settings. However, sample- and organization-specific dimensions are likely to be manifest, suggesting that a single, omnibus multitrait measure is unlikely to be entirely representative of an organizational setting.

Unit of Analysis and Subsystem Climates

Another problematic issue in climate research is the determination of the appropriate level of analysis. That is, individual scores on climate measures are often aggregated in some way to result in a climate score that purportedly reflects the climate at an organizational level. Guion (1973) has criticized this approach, questioning the validity of organizational-level scores if there was no assessment of degree of consensus among individuals. Howe (1977) has defined two criteria that would indicate the presence of organizational climate. One, as suggested by Guion, is the demonstration of consensus within a group or organization on one or more perceptual climate dimensions. The other is the demonstration of significant differences between two or more organizations or groups on the climate dimensions. Empirically, Jones and James (1979) demonstrated that aggregated measures were appropriate only for homogeneous units (for ranks of Navy shipboard personnel, not for departments or ships), and could only predict performance at that level.

The distinction between psychological and work group climates is predicated on the assumption that a number of subclimates (that is, a number of different groups or clusters, each demonstrating within-group consensus) may coexist within the organization. At its simplest, according to Gavin and Howe (1975), psychological climate becomes organizational climate when there is a significant consensus on climate perceptions among organizational members. When individuals tend to agree on climate perception at levels below the total organization, group climates may be said to exist (Powell and Butterfield 1978).

Gavin and Howe (1975) have reported empirical evidence for subsystem or group climates. They discovered significant differences by echelon on four of six climate dimensions: Lack of Hindrance, Rewards, Esprit, and Trust/Consideration. Overall, however, echelon accounted for only about 10 percent of the climate variance, while differences between organizations accounted for 43 percent. Johnston (1976) also has demonstrated that different subgroup climates may coexist within an organization. When employees were divided into "generations" (those employees who had been with the company since its inception and those who had been with the company for two years or less), Johnston found that the first generation of employees perceived a significantly different (and generally more positive) climate than did the second-generation employees.

Other evidence also suggests that the presence of subgroup climates within a single organization is not uncommon. For example, Pritchard and Karasick (1973) found that both the local office and the larger organization contributed to climate perceptions. Payne and Mansfield (1973) showed that the higher in the hierarchy an employee was, the more the climate was perceived as friendly, less authoritarian, and innovative. Finally, Schneider and Bartlett (1970) found that while insurance agency managers and assistant managers agreed on what the relevant dimensions of climate were in the organization, there was a lack of congruence between their perceptions of the existing climate.

The recognition of subgroup climate has clear implications for the prediction of performance and satisfaction. Johnston (1976), for example, has suggested that the failure of climate studies to show a strong relation between perceived climate and performance may be due to the failure to acknowledge the importance of situational factors on individual behavior. Such things as level in hierarchy, personality factors, longevity, and environmental demands in different geographic locations could result in different subsystem climates. If subsystem climates exist within an organization, the use of perceptual measures based on the assumption that one pervasive climate characterizes the organization would clearly result in suboptimal prediction of performance and satisfaction.

Climate and Satisfaction

It has been suggested that climate is redundant with attitudinal constructs, primarily satisfaction (Johannesson 1973). This is based on the assumption that feelings influence the descriptions of perceptions or influence the perceptions themselves. In a series of cluster analyses of organizational climate items and two satisfaction measures, Johannesson (1973) found that clusters tended to include scales from each of the measures. He interpreted these findings as suggesting that the climate scales were redundant with the satisfaction measures, and measured no unique construct of climate. Payne, Fineman, and Wall (1976) disagreed with Johannesson's (1973) conclusions, however, pointing out that the median correlations among the 22 first-order clusters were moderate at best (for instance, r = .25 to .33) and not high enough to suggest that the measures of climate and satisfaction were the same.

Downey, Hellriegel, Phelps, and Slocum (1974) also found relationships among climate factors and satisfaction scales, but since they found other factors that mediated the relationship between climate and satisfaction, they concluded that the two concepts were not redundant. From the patterns of correlations among climate dimensions, organizational practices, and performance that La Follette and Sims (1975) explored, they concluded that satisfaction and climate relate differently to performance measures. And while both climate and satisfaction correlated with organizational practices in the La Follette and Sims study, the correlations between climate and practices were generally much higher than those between satisfaction and practices.

The confusion over the distinction between measures of climate and satisfaction has been aggravated by measurement strategies that have "built-in" redundancy between the two constructs. A number of climate measures have been derived largely from items in existing satisfaction measures, resulting in inherently substantial correlations between climate and satisfaction. However, as Schneider (1983) has summarized, the evidence suggests that when belief facets (climate) and affective facets (satisfaction) are operationalized separately, climate and satisfaction measures do not correlate highly. Thus, it appears that climate, on both theoretical and empirical grounds, can be validly distinguished from satisfaction. However, the research does suggest that there are some meaningful relationships between climate and satisfaction, an issue to be discussed subsequently.

The Measurement of Climate

With some exceptions (Schneider & Bartlett 1968, 1970; Halpin & Croft 1963; Stern 1970), most existing perceptual measures of climate are constructed for use in any type of business organization (Hellriegel & Slocum 1974). Stern (1970) and his colleagues developed a family of environment indices, three of which are for measuring high school, college, and evening college environments. The fourth version, the Organizational Climate Index (OCI), was developed to be a general instrument capable of use in any "formal administrative structure" (Stern 1970, p. 15). The OCI measures press (perceived capacity of the environment to fulfill personality needs) with regard to 30 dimensions, constructs initially developed by Murray (1938). The instrument is a more generalized version of the College Climate Index, which has been shown to have good internal consistency, test-retest reliability, and the ability to discriminate among colleges and universities (Stern 1970). The OCI has the advantage of already having a matching personality measure, the Activities Index, with which to assess 30 needs parallel to the dimensions of press in the OCI. Stern (1970) reported the OCI was successful in discriminating among the organizational climates found in different subgroups. It discriminated among 63 Peace Corps training programs, administrative climates in 43 schools, and 3 geographically disparate industrial sites.

Payne and Pheysey (1971) were concerned specifically with business organizations when they reconceptualized and altered the OCI to reflect concepts more directly related to the structure and functioning of work organizations and less with the structure and functioning of individual personalities. The refurbished scale, the Business Organization Climate Index (BOCI), has 24 dimensions that cluster into 6 broad categories: Authority, Restraint, Work Interest, Personal Relations, Routine or Control, and Wider Community. In general, they concluded that the scales of the BOCI appear to measure different constructs than did the original OCI. Because Payne and Pheysey were not interested in parallel items to measure personality needs, these were not developed, which makes use of the BOCI to measure P-E fit more difficult.

The Group Dimensions Descriptive Questionnaire (GDDQ) (Hemphill & Westie 1950) was an early attempt at measuring the impact of a group on its members. It contains items for 14 dimensions that are, like most climate measures, oriented toward the social aspects of the immediate group environment. Thus the GDDQ may be a good measure for work group-level analyses, especially for assessing social functioning in the environment.

Halpin and Croft's (1963) Organizational Climate Description Questionnaire (OCDQ) has been adapted for business organization use by Friedlander and Margulies (1969). The OCDQ shows low correlations between its subscales and other educational climate instruments, probably because of its narrow focus. In addition, it seems to be a general measure of organizational interpersonal behavior rather than an instrument measuring only educational environments.

Moos and his colleagues (Moos 1974a, 1974b, 1974c, 1974d; Moos, Insel, & Humphrey 1974; Moos and Trickett 1974; Moos and Gerst 1974) have also developed a family of climate scales applicable to small-scale organizational and group settings. These inventories each consist of nine to ten climate scales, originally developed to assess the social climate of psychiatric wards (Moos & Houts 1968; Moos 1974d), and subsequently modified to be appropriate to educational settings (Moos & Trickett 1974; Moos & Gerst 1974), community programs (Moos 1974a), correctional institutions (Moos 1974b), and family, work, and group environments (Moos, Insel, & Humphrey 1974). Subscales of each measure show some discriminant validity, and are generally able to discriminate among individuals in different roles within settings (for instance, staff versus patients in psychiatric wards). In addition, a number of the subscales for each of the inventories are similar to the four general dimensions of organizational climate reported by Campbell et al. (1970).

With respect to assessing P-E fit, the difficulty with most measures of climate is that there are no parallel measures of personality. The Stern scales are an exception, but they are primarily for educational institutions.

Without parallel, or isomorphic, dimensions of climate and personality, *a priori* hypotheses must be made relating particular expected interactions between a given personality dimension and a related climate dimension. In the next section the relationship between measures of personality and climate will be explored more fully.

PERSONALITY AND CLIMATE

One emphasis in climate research has been the use of climate scales for the characterization of and discrimination among environments. That is, from both a theoretical and a practical perspective, it is desirable to show that variance in environmental perception scales is smaller within environments than between environments. While this is generally the case, (Gerst & Moos 1972; Moos 1974e, 1975; Pace & Stern 1958; Stern 1970), there is often substantial within-group variance as well (Ellsworth & Maroney 1972; Golding 1977; James & Jones 1974; Payne & Pugh 1976; Guion 1973; Schneider & Bartlett 1970). Golding (1977), for example, has asserted that, on average, only about 25 percent of the variance in environmental perception scales is accounted for by differences between environments, leaving the major portion of the variance due to individual differences and error.

An interesting question that arises in considering such individual differences in climate perceptions, is their relation to personality variables. McFee (1961) assessed the relationship between one of Stern's climate measures, the College Characteristics Index (CCI), and his personality measure, the Activity Index (AI). These instruments measure 30 parallel dimensions of need and press (that is, environment/climate) based on Murray's (1938) manifest need system. McFee found that correlations between corresponding climate and personality scales ranged from -.01 to +.06, with none being significantly different from zero.

Later studies by Stern (1962, 1970) confirmed McFee's findings. He found an average correlation between corresponding AI-CCI scales of ‖.08‖, with a maximum correlation of .34. Stern (1970) also factor-analyzed the AI and CCI both separately and together. He found that the 23 orthogonal factors of the joint factor analysis were the same as the 11 and 12 orthogonal factors that characterized the CCI and AI individually. On the basis of these studies, Stern concluded that the perception of the college environment was independent of personality.

Other studies (Mitchell 1968; Marks 1968; Kish, Solberg, & Uecker 1971; Downey, Hellriegel, & Slocum 1975; Johnston 1974), however, have provided evidence that personality and perceived climate are more closely related. Mitchell (1968) found that 9 of the 30 High School Climate Index (HSCI) scales were significantly correlated with 50 percent or more of the personality scales he employed (from the California Psychological Inventory, the SRA Youth Inventory, and the Brown-Holtzman Survey of Study Habits). All 30 of the HSCI scales were associated with at least one personality scale; in particular, the California Psychological Inventory Achievement via Conformance, Socialization, and Sociability scales correlated significantly with more than 40 percent of the HSCI scales.

Marks (1968) demonstrated that items from the College and University Environment Scale (CUES) (Pace 1969) varied systematically as a function of their relationship to scales of the Personality Research Form (PRF) (Jackson 1968). Marks cross-classified CUES items with regard to their scale content (dimensions of Practicality, Awareness, Community, Scholarship, and Propriety) and their certitude (certainty of response accuracy). The proportion of PRF scales significantly correlating with CUES items was from 8 percent to 38 percent for high-certitude items and from 40 percent to 100 percent for low-certitude items. This suggests not only that personality is related to perceived climate but also that the degree of the relationship is affected by the ambiguity of the environmental attribute being perceived. The PRF dimensions accounting for most of the relationships were Affiliation, Succorance, Achievement, and Understanding.

Downey, Hellriegel, and Slocum (1975) found that cognitive complexity was related to perceptions of a corporate setting. They administered two measures of the perceived uncertainty of a corporation's environment and structure and an abridged version of Bieri's (1955) measure of cognitive complexity. They found that cognitive complexity significantly differentiated between high- and low-median-split groups for both perceived uncertainty variables.

A pair of studies in small-scale organizational settings likewise supports a link between personality and perceived climate. In a psychiatric ward Kish, Solberg, and Uecker (1971) found significant differences between extreme high and low locus of control groups on 7 of 14 scales on the Ward Atmosphere Scale (Moos & Houts 1968). In a small consulting firm Johnston (1974) measured climate by content analysis of in-depth interviews, describing the quality of the individual-organizational relationship along 25 categories. Personality dimensions of Activity, Task Orientation, and Interpersonal Orientation were measured using the Thematic Apperception Test. T-tests based on median splits of the personality dimensions were computed for all climate dimensions. There were seven significant differences in climate for the task orientation dichotomy, and eight significant differences for the activity dichotomy.

Finally, other individual-difference measures, related but somewhat distinct from personality indices, have been found to relate to perceived climate. Gavin (1975), for example, cluster-analyzed employees on the basis of their responses to requests for biographical and historical data, along dimensions such as Stability, School Adjustment, Social and Physical Well-being, and Vocational Choice. A threefold classification of subjects (atonic, work-oriented, and socially oriented) produced significant differences in climate dimensions of Perceived Hindrance, Rewards, and Esprit. The atonic employees were higher in Perceived Hindrance than the socially oriented or work-oriented groups, who were comparable with each other. The socially oriented group was highest (most favorable) on Rewards, while the work-oriented group had the least favorable perceptions of Rewards. Finally, on the Esprit factor, the socially oriented cluster had the most favorable perceptions, while the work-oriented cluster had the least favorable.

Hackman and Lawler (1971) also used a personality-like individual-differences measure to differentiate between job attitudes and perceived climate. They found that employees in the upper third of Degree of Desire for Higher-order Need Satisfaction had higher correlations between job attitudes (Satisfaction, Motivation, and Involvement) and the climate dimensions of Variety and Autonomy.

In general, the evidence from a number of studies tends to support at least a moderate relationship between personality and perceived climate. Only the Stern (1962, 1970) and McFee (1961) studies fail to support such a relationship. Owing to the diversity of both climate and personality measures employed in the studies reviewed, a clear and unencumbered specification of the relationship between these variable sets is not yet possible, but groundwork has clearly been laid for further, fruitful exploration.

ORGANIZATIONAL CLIMATE AND ORGANIZATIONAL OUTCOMES

The preceding section presented evidence indicating that personality exercises some influence upon perceived climate. However, the utility of such relationships ultimately hinges on the consequent link between perceived climate and organizational outcomes, such as performance and satisfaction. In this section evidence is presented (Litwin & Stringer 1968;

Schneider, Parkington, & Buxton 1980; Friedlander & Greenberg 1971; McCarrey & Edwards 1973; Gavin & Howe 1975; Schneider & Hall 1972; Friedlander & Margulies 1969; Lawler, Hall, & Oldham 1974) that supports a link between these variables, and thus provides a basis for the use of models of P-E fit for purposes of organizational analysis.

Litwin and Stringer (1968) were among the first to demonstrate a relationship between climate and both performance and satisfaction. They manipulated leader behavior to emphasize group member motivations of achievement, affiliation, or power. They viewed the organizational climate as the degree to which the organization fosters expectancies and incentives for its members that are favorable to the expression of all three motives. It was assumed that different climates would emerge by the leader's emphasizing different group norms, such as cooperation, conflict avoidance, warmth, and nonpunishment in the affiliation condition. Generally, the three groups were distinguished by differences in perceived climate. The affiliation group was higher on scales of Reward and Warmth, the power emphasis group was higher on Conflict and Structure, and the achievement group was higher on perceptions of Risk and Responsibility. Most pertinent, however, was the finding that the achievement group showed greater productivity, and members of the power group were less satisfied and less innovative in their performance.

A pair of studies by Schneider and his colleagues (Schneider & Snyder 1975; Schneider, Parkington & Buxton 1980) provides mixed support for the link between climate and performance. Schneider and Snyder (1975) found relatively low correlations between climate dimensions such as Managerial Support, Structure, Conflict, Concern, and General Satisfaction, and measures of insurance agency productivity. The climate measures were, however, related to turnover. Schneider, Parkington, and Buxton (1980), however, reported significant correlations between customer perceptions of service quality in bank branches and climate dimensions of Enthusiasm, Managerial Functions, and Retaining Customers. Customer perception of service quality was also related to the support system dimensions of Personnel Support and Equipment Supply Support.

In an evaluation of an actual training program for the hard-core unemployed, Friendlander and Greenberg (1971) examined a number of potential contributors to job satisfaction and performance. They found that background, demographic variables, and attitudes toward work were not predictive of job performance. Climate measures, on the other hand, were predictive of one or more measures of effectiveness. In general, those employees who perceived the environment to be supportive were rated as more competent and congenial, and were attributed with the more positive qualities of being friendly, smart, and conscientious. It should also be noted that workers and supervisors were very different in their perceptions of support. On all three aspects of support, workers viewed the environment as being significantly less supportive than did supervisors.

For another series of studies (McCarrey & Edwards 1973; Gavin & Howe 1975; Schneider & Hall 1972; Friedlander & Margulies 1969; Lawler, Hall, & Oldham 1974; Downey, Hellriegel, & Slocum 1975; Pritchard & Karasick 1973), it appears that the effects of climate on performance and satisfaction are quite variable, depending upon the range of climate and criterion (performance and satisfaction) measures employed, as well as a variety of contextual factors. For example, McCarrey and Edwards (1973), in a study of scientific achievement, found that different climate dimensions were related to different performance factors. No set of orthogonal climate components was associated with high scientific performance along all three performance factors used (Creative Productivity, Quality of Publications, and Impact of Publications). Of six climate dimensions for three organizations, Gavin and Howe (1975) found only dimensions of lack of Hindrance (for two organizations) and Trust/Consideration (for one organization) to be correlated with supervisors' ratings of effectiveness. Schneider and Hall (1972) found that position level in the priesthood moderated the relationship between the number of activities performed and climate perceptions. The correlation between the climate dimension of Work Challenge and amount of the activity dimension of Community Involvement was $r = .42$ for assistant pastors and $r = .05$ for pastors.

Friedlander and Margulies (1969) also found that different dimensions of climate predict different aspects of satisfaction. Regression analysis demonstrated, for example, that the best prediction of interpersonal satisfaction was given by a combination of climate descriptions of Esprit and lack of Hindrance. On the other hand, satisfaction with opportunities for advancement was best predicted by Thrust (leader-oriented goal directiveness), Intimacy, and lack of Hindrance. Lawler, Hall, and Oldham (1974) found that each of six climate dimensions was significantly correlated with at least two of six aspects of satisfaction (such as Fulfillment, Security, Pay). Downey, Hellriegel, and Slocum (1975) found main effects on Supervisor, Pay, and Co-worker Satisfaction due to climate (Decision Making, Rewards, Structure, Promotion, and Openness) and personality (Sociability). Interactions between climate and personality were also found to affect different aspects of job satisfaction. Finally, Pritchard and Karasick (1973) found 10 of 11 dimensions of climate to be significantly correlated with satisfaction as measured by the Minnesota Satisfaction Questionnaire.

It has been suggested by Meglino (1976) that some of the conflicting results regarding climate and performance can be accounted for by the effects of social facilitation. Where dimensions of climate have been evaluative, the effects on performance have depended on whether the performance dimension was well learned (Hall & Lawler 1969) or was a new set of responses (Friedlander & Greenberg 1971). These findings suggest, in keeping with Zajonc's (1965) results, that when performance is either a set of well-learned responses or a relatively simple response, an evaluative climate facilitates performance. When performance is complex and a relatively new behavior, an evaluative climate tends to impede performance. Typically, measures that tap an evaluative climate are embedded in other constructs. For example, Meglino (1976) points out that in Friedlander and Greenberg (1971), the evaluative items are found in support dimensions, and support was the only climate dimension to relate significantly to effectiveness.

The evidence presented thus far suggests that perceptions of the environment (that is, climate) can have a significant impact on both satisfaction and performance. Such impacts, however, may be on quite specific aspects of satisfaction and performance dimensions. We turn now to the concept of P-E fit and its possible role in determining organizational outcomes.

THE NATURE OF P-E FIT

Although others have noted the importance of the environment in affecting behavior (Lewin 1951; Sells 1963; Hunt 1965), it was Murray (1938) who originally proposed a taxonomy and model for person-setting interaction. In his model the environment gratifies or obstructs, to varying degrees, the satisfaction of the individual's needs. Congruence occurs when the individual develops a positive sentiment toward the environment when, through interaction, the individual has a positive cathexis in the environment.

Murray (1938) conceptualized needs as a biophysiological force, but later viewed them more simply as dispositional constructs: "[A need] . . . is a state, in short, that is characterized by the tendency to actions of a certain kind" (Murray 1951, p. 435). Stern (1970), amplifying Murray's position, points out that psychological needs are functional in nature, "being identified with the goals or purposes that an interaction serves for the individual" (p. 6). In addition, it is assumed that needs are revealed in the characteristic, spontaneous modes of behavior used by the individual in life transactions.

On the environmental side, the construct of press is analogous to needs. The unique, private, and phenomenological view each person has of the events in which he/she is taking part constitutes one type of press, called beta press. When individuals tend to share interpretations of the surrounding world, a distinction is made between the private beta press and the consensual beta press. Finally, Murray provides for an objective referent to the environment, the alpha press, which may be assessed by the inferences that observers make about the events in which others participate; these inferences are likely to be different from those made by the participants. It is these inferences that may form the basis for a taxonomy of situational variables. Disparity in the alpha and beta presses arises out of need-driven selective attention and cognitive distortion of environmental stimulation, as well as through simple errors in judgment.

It is assumed that needs and press are complementary in affecting behavior outcomes. For example, a given individual with a need to affiliate with others will experience a positive result in an environment that offers maximal opportunities for such interactions. The relation between a given psychological need and the relevant environmental press is described by Stern (1970) as being isomorphic. Need-press congruence is, then, based on some form of psychological symmetry between the person's needs and the environmental press. An organism activated by a need may seek a press or act to avoid one—or, more frequently, the organism encounters a press and a need is activated by the encounter. The behavioral event is seen as the result of an interaction between internal and external forces.

Although compelling in many regards, Murray's model of P-E fit is not without its pitfalls. One problem is the difficulty in translating the constructs of need and press into measurable phenomena. Ultimately, all aspects of need and press are fundamentally phenomenological, leading to a substantial reliance on self-report. This is most problematic for the delineation of the alpha press, which most often will be indirectly measured through an aggregation of beta press measures or, at best, through the assessment of the consensual beta press.

Another difficulty in Murray's model is that the implications of incongruence between needs and press are not clear. It is implicit in Murray's model that maximal congruence would be reflected by parallel scores on corresponding measures of need and press, and that any degree of incongruence is suboptimal. However, in theory, a person with a low need should be satisfied with a press that is any level above that need.

ALTERNATIVE FORMULATIONS OF PERSON-ENVIRONMENT INTERACTIONS

One reason that Murray's theory regarding need-press interaction has not generated more programmatic research relates to the ambiguity surrounding the nature of interactions in general. Pervin and Lewis (1978) describe five different meanings of the term "interaction," described briefly below:

1. Descriptive interaction—mere description of two or more persons in social interaction, without any conceptual or theoretical understanding of it.
2. Statistical interaction—an interaction between variables described in analysis of variance terms. This supports viewing interactions as mechanistic and unidirectionally causal, and provides little information about the underlying relationships between variables. In addition, Schneider (1983) suggests that such interactions rarely occur in natural settings, since selection forces tend to restrict the range of settings or persons, and hence yield few significant interaction terms.
3. Additive interaction—independent variables contribute only in an additive, linear fashion, and any one independent variable can be assessed independently of the others.
4. Interdependent interaction—the effects of a set of variables (because of their inseparable nature in real settings) can be understood only in terms of their reciprocal effects. This view holds that persons and situations cannot be understood in isolation from each other, and the central issue is the manner in which the situational and person components influence each other.
5. Reciprocal action-transaction—similar to interdependent interaction in process emphasis but includes the idea that variables are continually influencing one another in a multidirectional way. That is, one variable may influence a second, which in turn influences the first.

Unfortunately, in most P-E studies the manner in which the concept of interaction is being used is not made explicit. In practice, it is conceptualized statistically (Pervin & Lewis 1978). This is understandable, in that it is the meaning typically associated with common research design and, as Pervin and Lewis note, there is a lack of methodology reflecting more complex formulations of interactions.

Despite the dearth of appropriate conceptualizations of the P-E interaction process, a few notable efforts have emerged that are pertinent to organizational contexts (Stern 1970; Schneider 1983; James, Hater, Gent, & Bruni 1978; Pervin 1968; Kaplan 1983). Stern (1970), for example, building upon Murray's need-press framework, describes the empirical assessment of congruence in terms of the actual combination of need and press that characterizes spontaneously occurring groups. In his view, congruent relationships provide a sense of satisfaction and fulfillment for the involved individuals, and it is assumed that the sense of fulfillment and satisfaction resulting from need-press congruence will be revealed in such variables as Achievement and Productivity. Conversely, need-press dissonance presents a state of imbalance that results in discomfort and stress, which is assumed to impair functioning in the work place through low morale, conflict, and decreased productivity and efficiency.

Alternatively, Schneider (1983) has provided a developmental-process model of interactionism in an organizational context. He suggests that particular types of people start particular types of organizations, with particular goals in mind, and select others who are compatible and similar in their focus and goals. Indeed, he suggests that considerable selection seems to occur early in the choice of career (Holland 1973) and organization (Wanous 1980). The effect is to narrow the range of "types" of people in any given setting, which contributes to the homogeneity of perceived climate within settings.

Given the selection pressures and restriction in range of people, Schneider suggests that rather uniformly high P-E fit would be expected within settings. However, there are other concurrent events in the development of an organization that may mitigate extreme range restriction in people and ideal P-E fit. For example, as an organization evolves, its goals and its subunit goals may slowly but dramatically change, and employees may shift to different departments. In addition, initial selection procedures are fallible in matching people to jobs. In many instances, people and jobs are matched on the basis of quite specific task-level characteristics rather than on other dimensions that may be important for determining P-E fit, such as social or interpersonal features. Thus, it may be that there are indeed selection pressures that seem to increase the homogeneity within settings, pressing toward increasing P-E fit, but there still seem to be factors that keep these selection factors from working absolutely. The degree of P-E fit remains an issue.

James et al. (1978), adopting a cognitive-social learning position, have emphasized individual differences in the perceptual component of the interaction process, which they feel has been neglected in organizational research. They suggest that individual-differences variables in climate perceptions have been neglected for at least two reasons. One is that there has been a tendency for researchers to be interested in organizational climate as a situational attribute, and to have treated differences between persons as error variance. The other reason is an ahistorical emphasis in climate research that presumes climate perceptions are functional and adaptive. These perceptions bend to the need to develop an adaptive P-E fit in each new situation (James et al. 1978). These authors suggest that research in cognitive-social learning theory and interactional psychology suggest a number of classes of variables that may help explain important individual differences in climate perceptions, including cognitive construction competencies, encoding strategies, behavior-outcome expectancies, self-regulatory systems, and subjective stimulus values.

Finally, Kaplan (1983) has offered a cognitive model of P-E fit based on the notion of informational compatibility. In this model P-E compatibility derives from the harmony of basic informational processes that all individuals must use to function in the world. Instead of focusing on individual differences in personality or needs, this approach emphasizes environmental requisites that people in general share. Thus, by examining the sources of mental activity (external or environmental versus personal or internal) and the type of mental activity (images, or the perception and knowledge one has about what one is dealing with versus one's plans or actions), one can distinguish among various modes of dealing with the environment. Incompatibility derives from interference with these mental activities. It should be noted, however, that Kaplan's focus is not on individual differences and the ability of specific individuals, given those differences, to meet the demands of the environment. Rather, it is on providing a characterization of those aspects of the environment that facilitate or hinder the carrying out of plans or activities in general.

P-E FIT AND ORGANIZATIONAL OUTCOMES

Although much work has been done on P-E fit in the context of educational institutions (Pace & Stern 1958; Stern 1970; Pervin 1968), and to a lesser extent of occupational stress and health (French 1973; French, Rogers & Cobb 1974), relatively few investigators have explored the relation between P-E fit and performance and satisfaction. However a few pertinent studies have emerged (Downey, Hellriegel, & Slocum 1975; Pritchard & Karasick 1973; Lawler, Hall, & Oldham 1974; Schneider & Olson 1972; Hackman & Lawler 1971; Morse 1975; Coburn 1975; Fredericksen, Jenson, Beaton, & Bloxom 1972; Andrews 1967), focusing largely on the congruence between dimensions of personality and dimensions of organizational climate. In general, the evidence suggests that the concurrent use of measures of persons and of environments does indeed lead to prediction of pertinent outcome measures. A more detailed discussion of these studies, and their implications for the prediction of performance and satisfaction, follows.

Downey, Hellriegel, and Slocum (1975) assessed the congruence between personality dimensions Self-Confidence and Sociability and six climate dimensions: Decision Making, Warmth, Risk, Openness, Rewards, and Structure. The effects of degree of congruence were assessed with regard to two performance indices and five dimensions of job satisfaction. Twelve of 48 possible main effects were significant, all for the job satisfaction variables. These involved primarily the climate dimensions of Decision Making, Rewards, and Structure. The only significant main effect due to personality was that of Sociability on the dimension of Supervisor Satisfaction. Eight of 72 potential interactions were significant, and two of these were for performance measures. These were due to high Sociability interacting with high Reward system in one case, and with high Structure in the other, both resulting in high performance. Unfortunately, the authors did not offer any theoretical explanation for the interactions on performance. For satisfaction, the interactions were primarily for the three Job Description Index scales that are people-oriented (Work, Supervisor, Coworker), and not for Pay and Promotion, which tend to be more policy- or structure-oriented.

Rather than examining all possible interactions between the personality and climate variables, as Downey et al. (1975) did, Pritchard and Karasick (1973) examined specific pairings of personality and climate variables. On the basis of the parallel meanings of the dimensions chosen, they hypothesized that performance and satisfaction would be higher when managers high in needs of achievement, order, and dominance perceived climates to be high in achievement motivation, structure, and status polarization, respectively. It was also hypothesized that the outcome variables would be higher when subjects high in need for autonomy perceive their environment to be both high in autonomy and low in decision centralization.

The needs were measured by the Edwards Personal Preference Schedule (Edwards 1959), which is based on Murray's (1938) manifest need system. Of 12 such interactions studied, 3 were significant. There was a significant interaction between the climate dimension of Status Polarization and need for dominance, with managers high in need for dominance showing greater satisfaction and performance in a climate of low status polarization. This was contrary to what was predicted, and was interpreted to suggest that the number of managers who perceived their opportunity for relative power and dominance would be greater in a climate where there was less differentiation between managerial levels. There was also a significant interaction between the managers' need for autonomy and the climate dimension of Decision Centralization, but again the effect was not in the predicted direction. For subjects low in need of autonomy, performance was higher when decision centralization was low. It is interesting that there were no main effects due to personality (needs) on performance or satisfaction. There was a main effect for the climate dimension of Status Polarization on performance, and the climate dimensions of Achievement, Social Relations, Status Polarization, and Decision Centralization were significantly related to job satisfaction.

Lawler, Hall, and Oldham (1974) found relationships between 5 of 6 organizational process variables and climate variables in 21 research and development laboratories. Climate was used as an intervening variable between structural and process variables, and outcome variables of performance and satisfaction. Five empirically derived climate factors (Competence Potency, Responsibility, Practicality, Risk, and Impulsivity) were found not to relate to any of the structural variables (such as Size or Span of Control), but all process variables except one correlated with at least one climate variable. The more closely performance reviews were tied to compensation, the more climate was perceived as competent, responsible, practical, risk-oriented, and impulsive: the more autonomy there was regarding projects, the more general assignments that were given, and the more informal research budgets were available. In addition, there was an inverse relationship between the frequency of performance reviews and the perception of risk orientation.

Of greater interest in the context of the present discussion, however, is the finding that climate was related to administrative and overall performance, but not to technical performance. Overall performance was measured by a composite of six objective indices concerning contracts, budgets, and the like. Technical and administrative performance was research directors' ratings on a percentage estimate scale. The Responsibility factor was related to both the administrative and the overall performance. Competence and Risk orientation were significantly related to administrative performance, while Practicality and Impulsivity were related to overall objective performance.

Also of interest are the findings of Lawler, Hall, and Oldham (1974) with regard to satisfaction. Each climate measure was significantly related to at least two of six satisfaction dimensions. As with performance, satisfaction increased as the climate was more competent, practical, risk-oriented, and impulsive. Comparisons of correlations among variables of structure, process, performance, and satisfaction show that climate tends to be more strongly related to all of these variables than structure and process are related to performance and satisfaction. This suggests that structure and process have their impact on performance and satisfaction through climate. In addition, the relation between process and climate is much stronger than between structure and climate. In contrast with some past research (Porter & Lawler 1965), structural variables were not found to be highly related to satisfaction.

Using a path-goal framework, Schneider and Olson (1972) postulated that effort was an interaction between individual differences (the degree to which rewards are valued) and a climate of reward (the degree to which effort is rewarded with valued rewards). They found a positive relationship between valued intrinsic rewards (security, social, autonomy, and self-realization) and effort in a hospital that rewarded effort, but not in a hospital in which rewards were based on tenure. Apparently pay for effort serves as a cue to employees valuing particular intrinsic rewards that the organization sanctions and encourages.

Andrews (1967) found that the "dominant firm values" (an aggressive, entrepreneurial achievement orientation versus a conservative, lack-of-growth orientation) interacted with individual differences in need for achievement and need for power to determine corporate effectiveness. For the achievement-oriented company, the correlation between need achievement and progress in the company was positive, while it was negative for power. The opposite was true for the conservative company, where progress was positively correlated with need for power and negatively with need for achievement, suggesting that climate can affect predictor-criterion relationships. Similarly, Litwin and Stringer (1968), in a field study conducted in a utility company, found that for workers with a high need for achievement, a climate low on dimensions of Responsibility, Identity, Risk, and Warmth resulted in high turnover and dissatisfaction.

Hackman and Lawler (1971) examined climate dimensions with referents at the task level: Autonomy, Variety, Task Identity, and Feedback. Performance ratings were found to correlate with Variety and Autonomy, while absenteeism correlated negatively with Task Identity. Employees were split into groups based on their degree of self-reported desire for higher-order need satisfaction. Employees in the top third were found to have higher correlations between job attitudes and Variety and Autonomy, but there were no significant relationships to performance and absenteeism.

In a field experiment, Morse (1975) examined the effects of congruence between five personality dimensions and the degree of certainty (routineness and predictability) of clerical and hourly jobs on self-estimates of competence. He measured the personality dimensions: Tolerance for Ambiguity, Attitude toward Authority, Attitude toward Individualism, Cognitive Complexity, and Arousal-seeking Tendency. New applicants who clustered on the high end of all or most of these dimensions were assigned to low-certainty jobs, while those falling on the lower end were assigned to high-certainty jobs. The rest of the applicants were placed in jobs through the company's regular selection procedure. On the basis of ratings taken shortly after placement and eight months later, both congruence groups had significantly higher self-ratings of competence than the employees placed in the conventional manner. Furthermore, there were no differences in self-estimates of competence between the two job-congruent groups, even after eight months. It should be noted, however, that no measure of actual performance was taken, and it is not clear what construct, or set of constructs, self-estimated competence actually refers to.

Coburn (1975) used a congruence model to assess the effects of personal and job-related attributes on outcome measures. Incongruence was operationalized as either perceived excessive job complexity or excessive job simplicity. Job demands perceived to be beyond one's capabilities presumably would lead to negative job experiences and feelings of self-deficiency. Job demands perceived as far below one's capabilities ostensibly would lead to frustration. Both conditions were expected to lead to decreased psychological and physical well-being. Work perceived to be overly complex was not disliked more than congruent work, but was associated with more reported psychological distress and poorer physical health. Work perceived to be overly simple, however, was disliked more than congruent work, and also was related to increased psychological distress. Problems with physical health were less evident than for those with overly complex jobs.

Another aspect of congruity is concerned with the compatibility of the organizational variables themselves. In a laboratory study Fredriksen et al. (1972) manipulated two climate dimensions: Innovation (manifested by the presence or absence of rules for accomplishing tasks) and Closeness of Supervision. Although productivity was generally higher in the innovative climate, it was more predictable when the two climate conditions were logically consistent (that is, when the environment had no rules and loose supervision or had rules and close supervision). Production was lower in inconsistent climates, when rules were paired with loose supervision or no rules were paired with close supervision. Not surprisingly, the different climates led to different methods of work. The loose condition led to more direct peer contact than did the restrictive condition.

In general, the foregoing set of studies suggests that both measures of P-E congruence and statistically defined interactions can predict performance and satisfaction. However, the evidence is still fragmentary, and a great deal more empirical evidence is required before an acceptable level of knowledge concerning the implications of P-E fit for performance and satisfaction is achieved.

SUMMARY AND CONCLUSIONS

The foregoing discussion illustrates the utility of the concept of P-E fit for the prediction and understanding of organizational behavior. The conceptual models of P-E fit reviewed suggest that congruence between the needs of individuals and the characteristics of an organizational setting will determine the individuals' behavior. The extant empirical evidence generally supports this view, and in particular suggests that personality characteristics influence perceptions of organizational characteristics (that is, climate), and that personality and organizational characteristics independently and jointly influence organizational outcomes, such as performance and satisfaction.

Despite the clear indications of the utility of P-E fit for organizational analysis, there is little reason to be sanguine. The empirical evidence is still fragmentary, and there is still a great deal of ambiguity surrounding the manner in which P-E fit, or P-E interaction, is best operationalized and measured. In the future, programmatic theoretical and empirical efforts must be directed at both the refinement of models representing the P-E interaction process, and the measurement of organizational characteristics in a manner that allows a clear link to the personality domain. An implication of the latter point is that measures of organizational characteristics (or climate) that discriminate only among organizational settings and do not reflect individual differences in the perception of those settings, lack an important component of variance that, in part, determines performance and satisfaction. In the final analysis this suggests nothing more than what we have always known: that persons and organizations are inextricably linked.

REFERENCES

Andrews, J.D.W. The achievement motive and advancement in two types of organizations. *Journal of Personality and Social Psychology*, 1967, *6*, 163–168.

Bieri, J. Cognitive complexity-simplicity and predictive behavior. *Journal of Abnormal and Social Psychology*, 1955, *51*, 263–268.

Campbell, J.P., Dunnette, M.D., Lawler, E.E., III, & Weick, K.E., Jr. *Managerial behavior, performance, and effectiveness.* New York: McGraw-Hill, 1970.

Coburn, D. Job-worker congruence: Consequences for health. *Journal of Health and Social Behavior*, 1975, *16*, 198–212.

Downey, H., Hellriegel, D., Phelps, M., & Slocum, J. Organizational climate and job satisfaction: A comparative analysis. *Journal of Business Research*, 1974, *2*, 233–248.

Downey, H., Hellriegel, D., & Slocum, J. Congruence between individual needs, organizational climate, job satisfaction and performance. *Academy of Management Journal*, 1975, *18*, 149–155.

Drexler, J.A., Jr. Organizational climate: Its homogeneity within organizations. *Journal of Applied Psychology*, 1977, *62*, 38–42.

Edwards, A. *Edwards Personal Preference Schedule.* New York: Psychological Corporation, 1959.

Ellsworth, R., & Maroney, R. Characteristics of psychiatric programs and their effects on patients' adjustment. *Journal of Consulting and Clinical Psychology*, 1972, *39*, 436–447.

Field, R.G., & Abelson, M. Organizational climate: A reconceptualization and proposed model. *Human Relations*, 1982, *35*, 181–201.

Forehand, G.A., & Gilmer, B.V.H. Environmental variation in studies of organizational behavior. *Psychological Bulletin*, 1964, *62*, 361–382.

Fredriksen, W., Jenson, O., Beaton, A., & Bloxom, B. *Prediction of organizational behavior.* New York: Pergamon Press, 1972.

French, J.R.P., Jr. Person-role fit. *Occupational Mental Health*, 1973, *3*, 15–20.

French, J.R.P., Jr., Rogers, W., & Cobb, S. Adjustment as person-environment fit. In G.V. Coelho, D.A. Hamburg, & J.E. Adams (eds.), *Coping and adaptation.* New York: Basic Books, 1974.

Friedlander, F., & Greenberg, M. Effect of job attitude, training, and organization climate on performance of the hard-core unemployed. *Journal of Applied Psychology*, 1971, *55*, 287–295.

Friedlander, F., & Margulies, N. Multiple impacts of organizational climate and individual value system upon job satisfaction. *Personnel Psychology*, 1969, *22*, 171–182.

Gavin, J.F. Organizational climate as a function of personal and organizational variables. *Journal of Applied Psychology*, 1975, *60*, 135–139.

Gavin, J.F., & Howe, J.G. Psychological climate: Some theoretical and empirical considerations. *Behavioral Science*, 1975, *20*, 228–240.

Gerst, M.S., & Moos, R.H. The social ecology of university student residences. *Journal of Educational Psychology*, 1972, *63*, 513–525.

Golding, S.L. The problem of construal styles in the analysis of person-situation interactions. In D. Magnusson and N.S. Endler (eds.), *Personality at the crossroads*. Hillsdale, N.J.: Erlbaum, 1977, 401–408.

Guion, R.M. A note on organizational climate. *Organizational Behavior and Human Performance*, 1973, *9*, 120–125.

Hackman, J., & Lawler, E.E., III. Employee reactions to job characteristics. *Journal of Applied Psychology Monograph*, 1971, *55*, 259–286.

Hall, D., & Lawler, E.E., III. Unused potential in research and development organizations. *Research Management*, 1969, *12*, 339–354.

Halpin, A., & Croft, D. *The organizational climate of schools*. Chicago: University of Chicago Press, 1963.

Hellriegel, D., & Slocum, J.W. Organizational climate: Measures, research and contingencies. *Academy of Management Journal*, 1974, *17*, 255–280.

Hemphill, J.K., & Westie, C.M. The measurement of group dimensions. *Journal of Psychology*, 1950, *29*, 325–342.

Holland, J.L. *The psychology of vocational choice* (rev. ed.). Waltham, Mass.: Blaisdell, 1973.

Howe, J.G. Group climate: An exploratory analysis of construct validity. *Organizational Behavior and Human Performance*, 1977, *19*, 106–125.

Hunt, J. McV. Traditional personality theory in the light of recent evidence. *American Scientist*, 1965, *53*, 80–96.

Ittelson, W.H. Environment perception and contemporary perceptual theory. In W.H. Ittelson (ed.), *Environment and cognition*. New York: Seminar Press, 1973.

Jackson, D.N. *Personality research form*. Goshen, N.Y.: Research Press, 1968.

James, L.R., Hater, J.J., Gent, M.J., & Bruni, J.R. Psychological climate; Implications from cognitive social learning theory and interactional psychology. *Personnel Psychology*, 1978, *31*, 781–813.

James, L.R., & Jones, A.P. Organizational climate: A review of theory and research. *Psychological Bulletin*, 1974, *81*, 1096–1112.

Johannesson, R.E. Some problems in the measurement of organizational climate. *Organizational Behavior and Human Performance*, 1973, *10*, 118–144.

Johnston, H.R., Jr. Some personality correlates of the relationships between individuals and organizations. *Journal of Applied Psychology*, 1974, *59*, 623–632.

_____. A new conceptualization of source of organizational climate. *Administrative Science Quarterly,* 1976, *21,* 95–103.

Jones, A.P., & James, L.R. Psychological climate: Dimensions and relationships of individual and aggregated work environment perceptions. *Organizational Behavior and Human Performance,* 1979, *23,* 201–250.

Kaplan, S. A model of person-environment compatibility. *Environment and Behavior,* 1983, *15,* 311–332.

Kish, G., Solberg, K., & Uecker, A. Locus of control as a factor influencing patients' perceptions of ward atmosphere. *Journal of Clinical Psychology,* 1971, *27,* 287–289.

La Follette, W.K., & Sims, H.P., Jr. Is satisfaction redundant with organizational climate? *Organizational Behavior and Human Performance,* 1975, *13,* 257–278.

Lawler, E.E., Hall, D.T., & Oldham, G.R. Organizational climate: Relationship to organizational structure, process, and performance. *Organizational Behavior and Human Performance,* 1974, *11,* 139–155.

Lewin, K. *Principles of topological psychology.* New York: McGraw-Hill, 1936.

_____. *Field theory in social science.* New York: Harper & Row, 1951.

Litwin, G.H., and Stringer, R.A., Jr. *Motivation and organizational climate.* Boston: Division of Research, Harvard Business School, 1968.

Marks, E. Personality and motivational factors in response to an environmental description scale. *Journal of Educational Psychology,* 1968, *59,* 267–274.

McCarrey, M.W., & Edwards, S.A. Organizational climate conditions for effective research scientist role performance. *Organizational Behavior and Human Performance,* 1973, *9,* 439–459.

McFee, A. The relation of student needs to their perceptions of a college environment. *Journal of Educational Psychology,* 1961, *52,* 25–29.

Meglino, B.M. A theoretical synthesis of job performance and the evaluative dimension of organizational climate: A social psychological perspective. *Academy of Management Review,* 1976, *1,* 58–65.

Mitchell, J.V. The identification of student personality characteristics related to perceptions of the school environment. *School Review,* 1968, *76,* 50–59.

Moos, R.H. *Community Oriented Programs Environment Scale manual.* Palo Alto, Calif.: Consulting Psychologists Press, 1974. (a)

_____. *Correctional Institutions Environment Scale manual.* Palo Alto, Calif.: Consulting Psychologists Press, 1974. (b)

_____. *The social climate scales: An overview.* Palo Alto, Calif.: Consulting Psychologists Press, 1974. (c)

_____. *Ward Atmosphere Scale manual.* Palo Alto, Calif.: Consulting Psychologists Press, 1974. (d)

_____. *Evaluating treatment environments: A social ecological approach.* New York: John Wiley & Sons, 1974. (e)

_____. *Evaluating correctional and community settings.* New York: John Wiley & Sons, 1975.

Moos, R.H., & Gerst, M.S. *University Residence Environment Scale manual.* Palo Alto, Calif.: Consulting Psychologists Press, 1974.

Moos, R.H., & Houts, P. The assessment of the social atmosphere of psychiatric wards. *Journal of Abnormal Psychology,* 1968, *73,* 595–604.

Moos, R.H., Insel, P.M., & Humphrey, B. *Family, Work & Group Environment Scales manual.* Palo Alto, Calif.: Consulting Psychologists Press, 1974.

Moos, R.H., & Trickett, E.J. *Classroom Environment Scale manual.* Palo Alto, Calif.: Consulting Psychologists Press, 1974.

Morse, J. Person-job congruence and individual adjustment and development. *Human Relations,* 1975, *28,* 841–861.

Murray, H.A. *Exploration in personality.* New York: Oxford University Press, 1938.

———. Toward a classification of interaction. In T. Parsons and E.A. Shils (eds.), *Toward a general theory of action.* Cambridge, Mass.: Harvard University Press, 1951, 434–464.

Pace, C.R. *College and University Environmental Scales (CUES)* (2nd ed.) Princeton, N.J.: Educational Testing Service, 1969.

Pace, C.R., & Stern, G. An approach to the measurement of psychological characteristics of college environments. *Journal of Educational Psychology,* 1958, *49,* 269–277.

Payne, R.L., Fineman, S., & Wall, T.D. Organizational climate and job satisfaction; A conceptual synthesis. *Organizational Behavior and Human Performance,* 1976, *16,* 45–62.

Payne, R.L. & Mansfield, R.M. Relationships of organizational climate to organizational structure, context, and hierarchical position. *Administrative Science Quarterly,* 1973, *18,* 515–526.

Payne, R.L., & Pheysey, D.C. G.G. Stern's Organizational Climate Index: A reconceptualization and application to business organizations. *Organizational Behavior and Human Performance,* 1971, *6,* 77–98.

Payne, R.L., & Pugh, D.S. Organizational climate and structure. In M. Dunnette (ed.), *Handbook of industrial and organizational psychology.* New York: Rand McNally, 1976.

Pervin, L.A. Performance and satisfaction as a function of individual-environment fit. *Psychological Bulletin,* 1968, *69,* 56–68.

Pervin, L.A., & Lewis, M. Overview of the internal-external issue. In L.A. Pervin & M. Lewis (eds.), *Perspectives in interactional psychology.* New York: Plenum Press, 1978.

Porter, L.W., & Lawler, E.E., III. Properties of organization structure in relation to job attitudes and job behavior. *Psychological Bulletin,* 1965, *64,* 23–51.

Powell, G.N., & Butterfield, D.A. The case for subsystem climates in organizations. *Academy of Management Review,* 1978, *3,* 151–157.

Pritchard, R.D., & Karasick, B.W. The effects of organizational climate on managerial job performance and job satisfaction. *Organizational Behavior and Human Performance,* 1973, *9,* 126–146.

Schneider, B. The perception of organizational climate: The customers' view. *Journal of Applied Psychology*, 1973, *57*, 248–256.

_____. Organizational climates; An essay. *Personnel Psychology*, 1975, *28*, 447–479.

_____. Work climates: An interactionist perspective. In N.R. Feimer and E.S. Geller (eds.), *Environmental psychology: Directions and perspectives.* New York: Praeger, 1983.

Schneider, B., & Bartlett, C.J. Individual differences and organizational climate. I: The research plan and questionnaire development. *Personnel Psychology*, 1968, *21*, 323–334.

_____. Individual differences and organizational climate. II: Measurement of organizational climate by the Multi-trait, Multirater matrix. *Personnel Psychology*, 1970, *23*, 493–512.

Schneider, B., & Hall, D.T. Toward specifying the concept of work climate: A study of Roman Catholic diocesan priests. *Journal of Applied Psychology*, 1972, *56*, 447–455.

Schneider, B., & Olson, L.K. Effort as a correlate of organizational reward system and individual values. *Personnel Psychology*, 1972, *23*, 313–326.

Schneider, B., Parkington, J.J., & Buxton, V.M. Employee and customer perceptions of service in banks. *Administrative Science Quarterly*, 1980, *20*, 252–267.

Schneider, B., & Snyder, R.A. Some relationships between job satisfaction and organizational climate. *Journal of Applied Psychology*, 1975, *60*, 318–328.

Sells, S.B. An interactionist looks at the environment. *American Psychologist*, 1963, *18*, 696–702.

Siegel, S.M., & Kaemmerer, W.F. Measuring the perceived support for innovation in organizations. *Journal of Applied Psychology*, 1978, *63*, 553–562.

Stern, G.G. The measurement of psychological characteristics of students and learning environments. In S.J. Messick and J. Ross (eds.), *Measurement in personality and cognition.* New York: John Wiley, 1962.

_____. *People in context.* New York: John Wiley & Sons, 1970.

Stern, G.G., Stein, M.I., & Bloom, B.S. *Methods in personality assessment.* Glencoe, Ill.: Free Press, 1956.

Wanous, J.P. *Organizational entry: Recruitment, selection and socialization of newcomers.* Reading, Mass.: Addison-Wesley, 1980.

Zajonc, R.B. Social facilitation. *Science*, 1965, *149*, 269–273.

4

Research Findings from Personality Assessment of Executives

V. Jon Bentz

INTRODUCTION

Sears's involvement with measurement of executive behavior began in the early 1940s when the company asked the late Dr. L.L. Thurstone to develop a procedure for selecting and assessing executive talent. The original and continuing purpose of that effort was to measure general executive competence—the ability to move effectively and flexibly through a range of tasks and assignments within a relatively non-technical company.

The tests selected by Thurstone, listed in Table 4.1, are still in use. They are not now the last word in instrument design; however, using one set of tests for nearly 40 years has obvious benefits. For instance, the distribution of attributes within the Sears executive population has remained remarkably stable over time (as indicated in Table 4.2, where mean scores from a 1953 random sample are compared with those of the 1978 population). This consistency, plus the fact that these tests were standardized on the population at large, makes possible a definitive statement about the nature of the Sears executive population.

In Figure 4.1 the vertical line down the middle represents the average score provided by the test authors; the horizontal bars extending to the right and left represent the divergence of the executive group from the authors' normative sample. This graphically portrays that executive research begins with a restriction-of-range problem on the predictor side of the equation. Monumental problems exist on the criterion side of the equation. One of the

TABLE 4.1
Variables Contained in the Sears Executive
Battery of Psychological Tests

American Council on Education Psychological Test

  L—Comprehension of words, language, and verbal ideas: verbal reasoning
  Q—Quantitative, numerical problem solving: logical reasoning
  T—Quickness of learning

Guilford-Martin Personality Inventories

  S—Outgoing friendliness: social ease
  T—Reflective awareness of what's happening to self and surrounding
  D—Freedom from depression: optimism, cheerful outlook
  C—Emotional control, predictability of temperament
  R—Spontaneity, flexibility, impulsiveness

  G—Energy: general activity, quickness of movements
  A—Social ascendency, assume leading role when part of a group
  M—Masculinity (not used in interpretation), nonsqueamishness
  I—Self-confidence, assurance to act without need for support
  N—Lack of nervous anxiety: composure under pressure

  O—Objectivity in judging, without emotional involvement
  Ag—Agreeableness, avoidance of conflict
  Co—Cooperative tolerance, fair-mindedness, noncritical

Allport-Vernon Scale of Values

Theoretical	—Concern for why things are as they are
Economic	—Concern for money, profit, and general values of marketplace
Aesthetic	—Concern for the interrelated harmony of form, line, color, and structure
Social	—Concern for general social welfare
Political	—Concern for personal status and prestige
Religion	—Concern for orthodox religious values (variable not used in interpretation)

Kuder Preference Inventory—Preference for activities and tasks related to:

Mechanical	—Involvement with mechanical ideas, things, and principles
Scientific	—Involvement with physical sciences
Computational	—Involvement with numerical and computational tasks
Persuasive	—Involvement with selling, promoting, and persuading
Artistic	—Involvement with art and artistic production
Literary	—Involvement with literary expression, writing, and authorship
Music	—Involvement with music and musical production
Social service	—Involvement with serving, helping, and assisting others
Clerical	—Involvement with routine, repetitive, detailed clerical tasks

Source: Prepared by author.

TABLE 4.2
Comparison over Time of Sears Executive Battery
Means and Standard Deviation

Executive Battery	1953 Sample			1978 Population		
	Mean		N	Mean		N
Linguistic	75.10	18.51	2,458	71.36	16.34	16,005
Quantitative	43.50	11.89		45.82	10.26	
Total	118.50	27.76		117.17	23.46	
Sociable	9.80	7.39	2,923	7.78	6.62	17,384
Reflective	33.60	10.02		32.22	7.48	
Optimism	8.90	7.28		7.19	5.65	
Emot. control	14.40	8.08		13.43	6.67	
Serious vs. carefree	42.06	9.65		45.44	9.04	
General activity	13.46	4.42		15.28	4.37	
Social leadership	26.86	5.77		29.02	5.37	
Dominance	22.85	5.16		24.56	5.08	
Self-confidence	41.58	5.49		43.56	4.41	
Composure	32.70	6.69		33.59	5.76	
Objective	59.62	10.08		61.88	8.99	
Agreeable	38.30	9.28		38.63	8.93	
Tolerance	78.18	14.35		79.98	13.69	
Theoretic	28.97	6.14	2,548	29.31	5.97	15,826
Economic	35.80	7.05		35.83	6.93	
Aesthetic	19.35	7.58		19.10	7.71	
Social	29.45	5.88		27.88	5.92	
Political	33.40	6.90		35.20	6.65	
Religious						
Mechanical	64.60	20.88	2,888			
Computational	35.51	11.70				
Scientific	57.02	10.89		Comparable data		
Persuasive	95.40	20.09		not available		
Artistic	42.86	14.27				
Literary	53.38	15.04				
Musical	14.70	9.54				
Social service	75.60	17.73				
Clerical	52.48	13.69				

Source: Prepared by author.

FIGURE 4.1

Graphic Presentation of Sears Executive Population

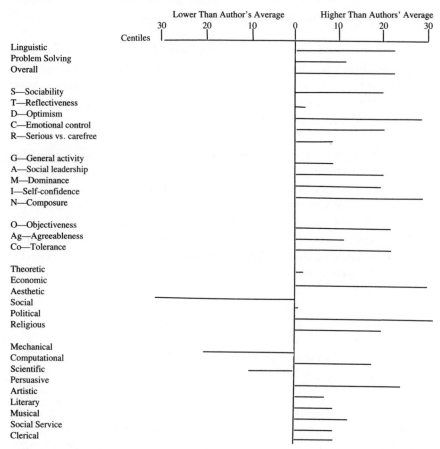

Source: Prepared by author.

greatest is that in most executive research there is but one criterion source for each subject in a sample. Accepting the presence of some error in every criterion measure, the one-for-one subject/criterion source represents both problem and challenge for executive research. It is possible to be swamped by criterion error variance even in very carefully designed executive research studies. The added facts that most executives perform well and that the substantive nature of executive performance tends to be elusive, create real criterion problems. These are but some of the matters contributing to the incredibly complicated milieu in which research on executive behavior occurs.

In this chapter I will discuss a number of research studies using the Sears Executive Battery (where personality assessment is a central concern). I shall avoid complex intragroup comparisons and mainly stay away from specific interpretation within a study. I would like to present a broad array of data and attend to overall results for various executive populations, treating general trends within and across studies. In doing so, I also shall refer to some personality measurements not included in the Sears Executive Battery, and I hope to discuss predictors within the context of a wide range of performance criteria.

INITIAL SELECTION OF MANAGEMENT PERSONNEL: THE SECOND LOOK PROGRAM

In the initial selection of managerial talent, we interview potential candidates on college campuses. Those who would have been hired on the basis of an on-campus contact are invited to a central location where both they and Sears can take a "second look" and come to a more informed mutual decision.

Our Second Look Program is a mini assessment center. Candidates are assessed in two highly structured interviews, one concerning personal history and the other dealing with life goals. The Sears Executive Battery of Psychological Tests is administered and candidates participate in a mixed-motive-design leaderless group problem-solving situation. Interviewers and observers of performance in the group problem situation (who have been carefully trained) evaluate candidates on the variables listed in Figure 4.2. They then make a selection recommendation of Yes, No, or Undecided. A psychologist evaluates the psychological test results and, on the basis of clinical judgment, makes similar recommendations. Five independent recommendations are made (one from a psychologist's judgment of the overall adequacy of test data, one each from two independent interviewers, and one each from two observers of the group problem situation) and entered into an empirically developed decision-making model. Yes or No decisions are made in about 68 percent of all cases, and the staff discusses the relative merits of the Undecided cases. Ultimately, all candidates are assigned to one of three categories: Offer, Discuss, No Offer. Some who fell in No Offer or Discuss categories were hired.

Those hired are assigned to a year's on-the-job training program in one of several training stores. At the end of the year, their performance is carefully evaluated by a training coordinator. The entire process is illustrated in Figure 4.2, which lists the predictor variables at the top and the criterion variables at the bottom.

Each dimension of the Management Trainee Final Rating consists of a descriptive paragraph defining various levels of behavior within the dimension (an example of a criterion definition appears in Figure 4.3). The behaviors are evaluated on a nine-point scale, each point representing a portion of the normal curve.

The Reactions to Problems criterion consists of 24 items. Item format is shown in Figure 4.4. The instrument has been factor-analyzed; the three factorially defined dimensions result in the criteria described under Reactions to Problems.

The Personal Effectiveness/Semantic Differential Criterion Questionnaire was developed to obtain a measurement of personal impact. It is a 53-item personality evaluation form that, when factor-analyzed, yields the seven dimensions listed in Figure 4.2.

The Management Trainee Evaluation Form (containing 31 performance elements, each rated on a 1 to 99 scale) has been factor-analyzed and provides the three criterion dimensions listed in Figure 4.2.

Let us discuss some of the validity results from this study.

Validity of the Decision Model Recommendation: Second Look Program

An empirically derived decision model systematically combines ballots from the two interviews, the group problem-solving situation, and the Executive Battery clinical judgment evaluation to arrive at one of three hiring recommendations. The data in Table 4.3 clearly demonstrate the validity of the decision model recommendation. Comparison of the performance of the two extreme groups (No Offer versus Offer) indicates a number of significant differences. In addition, the performance level of the Offer

FIGURE 4.2
Flow Chart of Second Look Assessment Process and Performance Measures Used in Study

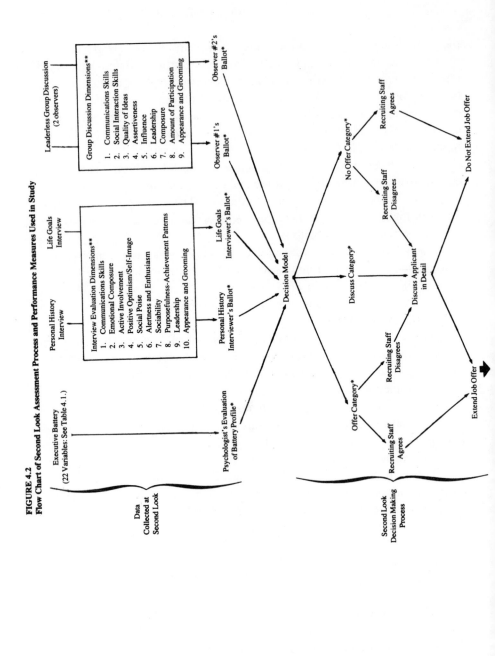

ONE   YEAR   TRAINING   PROGRAM

Performance Evaluation Measures (26 Variables)†

Performance Data Collected After One-Year Training Program

Store Rank

Dimension scores for each of the nine dimensions measured by the Management Trainee Final Rating Questionnaire. These performance dimensions are:

1. Flexibility in Handling Work Assignments
2. Ability to Comprehend the Technical Details and Procedures Comprising the Various Departments Within the Store
3. Emotional Involvement
4. Oral Communications
5. Open-mindedness
6. Attitude
7. Personal Judgment
8. Personal Organization
9. Aggressiveness

Dimension scores for each of the three dimensions measured by the Reaction to Problems Questionnaire, and the total score across all items. These performance dimensions are:

1. Product of Creative and Original Ideas
2. Personal Enthusiasm and Improving upon the Ideas of Others
3. Independence in Problem Solving
4. Total Score

Dimension scores for each of the seven dimensions measured by the Personal Effectiveness Semantic Differential Questionnaire and the total score across all items. These performance dimensions are:

1. Open-mindedness and Interpersonal Effectiveness
2. The Highly Motivated, Energetic Leader
3. Sophisticated Intellectually Alert Leader
4. Sociable and Warm Team Worker
5. Sensitive, Kind Person
6. Personal Impact
7. Health
8. Total Score

Dimension scores for each of the three dimensions measured by the Management Trainee Evaluation Form and the total score across all items. These performance dimensions are:

1. Interpersonal Effectiveness
2. Functional Utility of Executive Abilities
3. Productivity and Task Performance
4. Total Score

---

*Variables used as predictors in the raw score form.

**Variables used as predictors in standardized form.

†Variables used as criteria in standardized form.

Note: Group discussion evaluations from the two observers were added, resulting in one set of nine predictor variables. Interview dimension evaluations from each interview were used separately as predictors.

Source: Prepared by author.

FIGURE 4.3
Definition of Criterion Variables Used for Final Store Rating and Nine-Point Scale

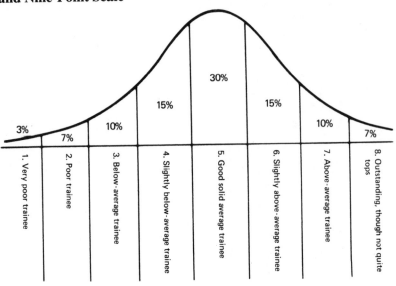

Source: Prepared by author.

group is higher than that of the No Offer group for all performance criteria, though not all differences are significant. This indicates the validity of the procedure.

Validity of the Executive Battery for the Total Group

Table 4.4 presents the significant (p < .05) correlations of Executive Battery variables with the one-year follow-up criteria for the total group of management trainees. Many significant relationships were obtained, and all but one of the 26 performance criteria were successfully predicted by Executive Battery scales. Several comments on these findings are in order:

1. Mental ability measures predicted 16 of the performance criteria, and these relationships make quite good psychological sense.
2. Overall mental ability is related to store rank (essentially a measure of overall performance); mental ability measures are related to grasping the technical knowledge necessary for performing in an executive capacity; linguistic reasoning is related to oral communications skills.

FIGURE 4.4
Supervisory Creativity Rating Form

The following statements are concerned with describing the way checklist people work with, or, handle problems, ideas and/or assignments that are a part of their Sears responsibilities.

Please read each statement carefully and place a checkmark beside the alternative that best describes the person.

1. Contributes more of his/her own ideas to assignments (s)he works on than does the average Sears executive.

    _____ Yes, (s)he's like this.
    _____ No, but contributes as many of his/her own ideas as does the average Sears executive.
    _____ No, contributes somewhat fewer of his/her own ideas than does the average Sears executive.

2. Given an unfamiliar problem, his/her first reaction is to consult a book, manual, or another person.

    _____ Yes, (s)he's like this.
    _____ No, (s)he's likely to try and think it through on his/her own before consulting another source.

3. By comparison with other executives in Sears, (s)he is outstandingly creative.

    _____ Yes, by comparison (s)he is.
    _____ No, though (s)he tends to be creative, (s)he is not outstandingly so.
    _____ (S)He is no more or no less creative than the average Sears executive.
    _____ (S)He is somewhat less creative than the average Sears executive.

Source: Prepared by author.

3. Persons with higher mental ability are more productive and demonstrate greater creativity and independence in problem solving.

    Executive Battery personality variables also provided excellent prediction of later performance, as did other Executive Battery scales. In gen-

TABLE 4.3
Job Performance Levels of Decision Model Categories

Performance Criteria	Decision Model Categories									t_{I-III}	t_{I-II}	t_{II-III}
	I No Offer			II Discuss			III Offer					
	Mean	SD	N	Mean	SD	N	Mean	SD	N			
Store Ratings												
Store rank	4.200	2.000	25	4.883	1.875	86	5.035	1.937	216	-2.027*	-1.556	-0.632
Flexibility	-.331	.959	25	-.082	.959	86	.068	1.012	217	-1.871†	-1.333	-1.179
Technical knowledge	-.478	1.082	25	-.120	.993	86	.093	.969	217	-2.771**	-1.541	-1.751†
Emotional involvement	-.24	.894	25	-.032	.945	86	.028	1.030	216	-0.947	-0.673	-0.467
Oral communications	-.24	1.147	25	-.023	.890	86	.079	1.003	216	-3.034**	-2.530*	-0.823
Open mindedness	-.124	.803	25	.063	.932	86	-.017	1.042	215	-0.491	-0.898	0.620
Attitude	-.024	.935	25	-.048	.960	86	.026	1.022	216	-0.568	-0.219	-0.577
Personal judgment	-.238	.865	25	.014	.890	86	.024	1.053	216	-1.195	-1.244	-0.078
Personal organization	-.139	1.201	25	-.131	1.014	86	.067	.964	217	-0.981	-0.033	-1.587
Aggressiveness	-.555	.930	25	-.054	1.022	84	.084	.977	217	-3.102**	-2.176*	-1.082
Semantic Differential												
Interpersonal effectiveness	-.187	1.006	24	.147	.944	86	-.037	1.017	209	-0.684	-1.499	1.443
Motivated leadership	-.579	1.220		.003	.970	86	.062	.964	209	-2.988**	-2.429*	-0.477
Alert leadership	-.448	1.059		.042	.904	86	.041	1.016	209	-2.228*	-2.241*	-0.008
Sociable team worker	-.312	1.028		.233	.863	86	-.055	1.030	209	-1.156	-2.599*	2.286*
Sensitivity	-.218	1.042		.195	.953	86	-.047	.997	209	-0.791	-1.824†	1.921†

Trainee Evaluation	Personal impact	-.210	1.123	24	.084	.938	86	.000	.998	209	-0.961	-1.288	0.669
	Health	-.105	.963	24	.109	1.015	86	-.023	.987	209	-0.386	-0.916	1.036
	Total	-.351	1.049	24	.121	.964	86	-.006	.999	209	-1.591	-2.064*	1.003
	Interpersonal effectiveness	-.311	1.014	24	.024	.949	86	.023	1.014	209	-1.525	-1.494	0.008
	Functional use of abilities	-.295	1.053	24	-.095	.962	86	.069	1.000	209	-1.676†	-0.875	-1.295
	Productivity	-.248	1.109	24	-.067	.986	86	.051	.986	209	-1.386	-0.767	-0.935
	Total	-.308	1.068	24	-.045	.975	86	.049	.996	209	-1.647	-1.135	-0.742
Reaction to Problems	Creativity	-.539	1.161	24	-.125	.953	86	.107	.972	209	-3.012**	-1.776†	-1.876†
	Enthusiasm & improving on ideas	-.345	1.034	24	.036	.997	86	.023	.991	209	-1.712†	-1.630	0.102
	Independent problem solving	-.406	1.201	24	-.037	.952	86	.056	.983	209	-2.123*	-1.568	-0.746
	Total	-.498	1.190	24	-.088	.973	86	.087	.967	209	-2.730**	-1.721†	-1.411

*p < .05 **p < .01 †p < .10

Note: Data are presented in standardized form.

Source: Prepared by author.

TABLE 4.4
Significant Predictor-Criterion Relationships for Executive Battery Variables: Total Group (N = 329)

Criteria → Predictors ↓	Store Ratings										Semantic Differential								Trainee Evaluation				Reaction to Problems			
	Store Rank	Flexibility	Technical Knowledge	Emotional Involvement	Oral Communications	Open-Mindedness	Attitude	Personal Judgment	Personal Organization	Aggressiveness	Interpersonal Effectiveness	Motivated Leadership	Alert Leadership	Sociable Team Worker	Sensitivity	Personal Impact	Health	Total	Interpersonal Effectiveness	Functional Use of Abilities	Productivity	Total	Creativity	Enthusiasm & Improving on Ideas	Independent Problem Solving	Total
Quantitative reasoning	121	187	253				124	154	128	124		120			-116					182	133	128	142		149	144
Linguistic reasoning			188		208				111											146	113		194		170	180
Overall	114	140	258		202				142	126										194	147	133	210		196	201
Sociability	-109																									
Reflectiveness	-143	-113				-112	-121	-122			-141	-123		-218	-113			-147	-147					-147		
Optimism	-120	-112				-143		-110					-116	-126												
Emotional control																										
Serious vs. carefree																										
General activity			115							174																
Social leadership										123																
Dominance						109	147																			
Self-confidence	153	130	118		137	133						159														
Composure																										

Objectivity
Agreeable-
ness

Tolerance	134	182	173		155	143	143	127	134		113	192		119		137		149	132

								122	194	176	168

Theoretical

Economic	184	137	122		127		155	115		194		114		
Aesthetic	-152	-130			-182			-125		-183	-110	-113	-127	-115
Social	-112		-116	-131				-148					-140	
Political	215	174	161	127	114	149	120	180		151	124	147	114	
Religious														

(continued columns)

Economic		113	120	120			
Aesthetic	-110		-144	-112			
Social	-111	-131	-141	-135			
Political	135	192	162	172	128	135	141

E.B. evalu-
ation

E.B. evaluation	173	183	162	137	112	160	108	118	152	113	161	138	140	157	129 154

Decision
model

category	116	130	127	146	154	128	111	188	166

Note: Decimal points have been omitted for all correlations. Underlined correlations are significant at p < .01; other correlations are significant at p < .05.

Source: Prepared by author.

eral, there is strong evidence for the validity of the Executive Battery in predicting the performance of management trainees.

The Executive Battery evaluation made by the psychologists (EB evaluation at the bottom of Table 4.4) predicted 16 performance measures. This allows a clinical versus statistical comparison of predictive validity.

Validity of the Structured Interviews

The results of the structured interviews (presented in Table 4.5) are of particular interest. They demonstrate that the life goals interview is a better predictor of performance than is the personal history interview, even though the same dimensions are evaluated during both interviews. The different results cannot be attributed to systematic differences between interviewers, since the same people generally conduct both types of interviews (but with different applicants). Neither can divergent results be attributed to a difference in understanding the meaning of the evaluation dimensions within the two types of interviews. Moreover, it seems unreasonable to hypothesize that evaluation dimensions are inappropriate for the personal history interview. The structure of both interviews is such that information and behaviors relevant for an evaluation on each of the dimensions should be elicited.

An examination of the formats indicates that the life goals interview requires more thought-provoking problem-solving responses than does the personal history interview. Consequently, both structured interviews were reworked with emphasis on making the personal history interview a more probing and thought-evoking process.

Validity of the Reworked Personal History Interview

Follow-up validity data for the reworked personal history interview are in Table 4.6. While criteria remained the same, refinements occurred in the definition of interviewer predictor evaluations. The smaller number of cases in this study reflects a reduction in hiring under adverse economic conditions.

Comparison of data from Tables 4.5 and 4.6 shows a marked improvement in prediction. Note the excellent prediction of the interview variables Social Poise, Positive Optimism, and Emotional Control. There is considerable strength in the prediction of the three trainee evaluation factorial dimensions and for the Reactions to Problems criterion Production of Creative Ideas.

I would like to draw special attention to the predictor variable Appearance in Tables 4.5 and 4.6. We try to prevent a biasing influence within the interview by requiring a separate evaluation for personal appearance. We ask the interviewer to judge candidates on how they present themselves with whatever physical equipment they possess. The Appearance variable obviously has a pervasive effect upon judgments of interviewers and superiors alike.

Relationship Between Interview and Executive Battery Scales

Before leaving interview data, let us look at the relationship between interview and psychological test data. Since the two data sets are independent, correlations between them represent a kind of validity—or at least an attempt to extend our understanding of dynamics within the interview situation. Table 4.7 presents correlations between the interview data and Executive Battery variables. These data tend to replicate earlier observations.

VALIDITY RESEARCH WITH THREE EXECUTIVE GROUPS

I shall now turn from initial selection to research with three very different executive groups: women executives engaged in buying, executives in manufacturing, and people in mainstream retail store staff positions.

Study of Women Executives Engaged in Buying

Two groups of women executives engaged in buying were studied separately. The two positions (buyer and assistant buyer) share common job elements. Many job activities are identical, with the major difference being extent of responsibility. In addition, buyers are a select group and the promotion an assistant buyer might typically expect would be to buyer. For these reasons it makes good sense to combine data into one group.

I wish there were time to give more details concerning the nature and treatment of criterion data. Briefly, the Promotion Potential criterion appearing in Figure 4.5 was adapted to this research; the Reactions to Problems criterion was also used. Since the research was conducted in one location, it was possible to gather criteria from multiple sources. As a result, criteria were analyzed by the Campbell/Fiske multitrait/multimethod matrix method for determining convergent and discriminant criterion validity.

TABLE 4.5
Significant Predictor-Criterion Relationships for Interview Predictor Variables: Total Group (N = 329)

Criteria → Predictors ↓	Store Ratings										Semantic Differential								Trainee Evaluation				Reaction to Problems			
	Store Rank	Flexibility	Technical Knowledge	Emotional Involvement	Oral Communications	Open-Mindedness	Attitude	Personal Judgment	Organization	Aggressiveness	Interpersonal Effectiveness	Motivated Leadership	Alert Leadership	Sociable Team Worker	Sensitivity	Personal Impact	Health	Total	Interpersonal Effectiveness	Functional Use of Abilities	Productivity	Total	Creativity	Enthusiasm & Improving on Ideas	Independent Problem Solving	Total
Personal History Interview																										
Communication skills			113		120								110										131			
Emotional composure					130								133													
Active involvement																										
Positive optimism/self-image																										
Social poise																										
Alertness and enthusiasm																										
Sociability																										
Purposefulness-achievement patterns																148							142			111
Leadership																										
Appearance and grooming																										
Ballot																										

	Store Rank	Flexibility	Technical Knowledge	Emotional Involvement	Oral Communications	Open-Mindedness Attitude	Personal Judgment	Personal Organization	Aggressiveness	Interpersonal Effectiveness	Motivated Leadership	Alert Leadership	Sociable Team Worker	Sensitivity	Personal Impact	Health	Total	Interpersonal Effectiveness	Functional Use of Abilities	Productivity	Total	Creativity	Enthusiasm & Improving on Ideas	Independent Problem Solving	Total
life goals Interview																									
Communication skills	114	147			174			111	142													148	149	129	169
Emotional composure				127																					111
Active involvement									112													113			
Positive optimism/self-image	138	121							146																
Social poise																		114				135	114	137	144
Alertness and enthusiasm	113		117		158				111																
Sociability											119												137		122
Purposefulness-achievement patterns	131	116	129		112	114	115		172																
Leadership	127	155							178			117					121	126	128			141	138		142
Appearance and grooming	163	204	148	118	160	187	178	162	159				129	146			142	128	121	142		114	151	132	140
Ballot	113			119				123	143		119	114	133	164			159	118	118	146		127	151	154	159
								116	123								119						123	119	

Note: *Decimal points have been omitted for all correlations. Underlined correlations are significant at p < .01; other correlations are significant at p < .05.

Source: Prepared by author.

TABLE 4.6
Reworked Personal History Interview: Validity Data for Second Look Follow-up, 1980

Personal History	Store Ratings (N = 68)										Reaction to Problems			Trainee Evaluation			Semantic Differential (N = 58)					
	Store Rank	Flexibility	Technical Knowledge	Emotional Involvement	Oral Communication	Open Mindedness	Attitude	Personal Judgment	Personal Organization	Aggressiveness	Production of Creative Ideas	Personal Enthusiasm	Independent Problem Solver	Inter-Personal Effectiveness	Functional Utility of Executive Ability	Productive and Task Performance	Open-minded & Interpersonal Effectiveness	Motivated, Energ. Leader	Sophisticated, Energ. Leader	Sociable, Warm Team Worker	Sensitive, Kind	Personal Impact
Communication	-068	-028	-116	149	125	-030	180	107	086	-088	229	197	038	084	201	110	159	147	134	109	153	175
Alertness	109	170	059	227	326*	248	176	210	108	087	290*	257	148	343**	318*	239	281**	207	175	300*	124	094
Social poise	129	223	099	400**	385**	227	280*	268*	250	162	280*	298*	198	289*	395*	316*	239	295*	335*	149	147	225
Self-confidence	128	131	185	167	233	157	212	116	218	159	278*	197	122	098	284*	171	087	258	262*	081	041	-000
Sociability	121	253	122	183	200	254	365*	212	164		187	311*	179	309*	275*	319**	335*	213	162	284*	265*	215
Positive optimism	238	313*	197	209	279*	320*	363**	266*	192		320*	426**	319*	441**	417**	436**	392**	332*	170	372**	216	083
Purposeful	027	110	001	241	152	100	262*	046	209	-057	328*	236	187	220	315*	254	299	199	208	187	218	112
Active involvement	-057	199	-003	154	226	253	240	312*	240	046	171	164	038	140	150	145	224	126	142	114	176	093
Leadership	168	261*	247	226	214	266*	276*	139	240	148	335*	320*	152	232	339**	259**	324*	323*	286*	229	331*	126
Emotional control	112	156	097	262*	266*	077	139	224	086		371**	323*	222	222	388**	289**	191	292*	289*	133	122	194
Appearance	214	195	054	459**	216	275*	423**	299*	322*	036	285*	455**	434**	391**	473**	480**	311*	288*	181	234	183	328*
Ballot	181	191	160	-084	267*	032	108	257	-007	276*	114	134	-001	185	105	-012	261	244	210	281*	178	087

*p < .05
**p < .01

Source: Prepared by author.

TABLE 4.7
Executive Battery Scores Related to Interview Data: Second Look Follow-up Study, 1980 (N = 496)

Executive Battery	Life Goals Interview												Personal History Interview											
	Communication	Alertness	Social Poise	Self-Confidence	Sociability	Positive Optimism	Purposeful	Active Involvement	Leadership	Emotional Control	Appearance	Ballot	Communication	Alertness	Social Poise	Self Confidence	Sociability	Positive Optimism	Purposeful	Active Involvement	Leadership	Emotional Control	Appearance	Ballot
Mental Ability																								
Linguistic	073	-030	-015	-025	-007	-069	-024	-003	-003	-044	-110*	-013	137**	009	000	018	-058	-033	-009	002	-022	058	-063	006
Problem solving	076	039	018	-022	044	-042	-021	039	016	-036	-053	-009	141**	035	031	038	-042	022	-025	057	047	074	-004	043
Total	083	-001	002	-027	019	-065	-026	014	002	-045	-092*	-011	157**	022	015	028	-055	-011	-019	026	009	073	-039	025
Personality Traits																								
Sociability	-190**	-217**	-188**	-229**	-223**	-201**	-164**	-201**	-215**	-137**	-115*	132*	-105*	-184**	-155**	-131**	-167**	-124**	-165**	-161**	-148**	-125**	-051	-163**
Reflectiveness	-051	-099*	-040	-051	-053	-073	002	-053	019	-093*	-089*	003	-021	-062	-067	-072	-132**	-053	-016	-046	-048	-081	-123**	-024
Optimism	-115*	-058	-056	-081	-069	-108*	-089*	-094*	-087	-057	-080	-071	-052	-063	-057	-055	-039	-034	-092*	-074	-078	-049	-076	-089*
Emotional control	-087	-010	-025	-059	008	-072	-059	-055	-030	-049	-078	-059	-027	-050	-052	-055	-017	-078	-057	-051	-028	-063	-039	
Serious vs. carefree	-005	107*	054	070	122**	029	005	041	043	037	-013	005	-039	023	-026	-011	007	032	-014	-001	008	006	-014	023
General activity	098*	165**	165**	129**	150**	116*	079	084	134**	079	066	077	094*	130**	069	126**	085	100*	114*	138**	118**	113*	-000	089*
Social leadership	079	118**	096*	126**	105*	114*	126**	112*	126**	048	048	104*	036	050	048	117**	055	089*	171*	127**	127**	075	014	091*
Dominance	-157**	-118**	-200**	-045	-139**	-123**	-100*	-097	-095*	-112**	-095*	-124*	-153**	-122**	-158**	-073	-190**	-131**	-072	-128**	-082	-117**	-053	-063
Self confidence	039	007	009	040	012	048	083	088	092*	014	020	082	033	069	045	095*	011	088	143**	107*	137**	057	001	114*
Composure	-022	-034	-059	-002	-067	-010	001	006	018	-033	-006	013	-052	-051	-020	-006	-032	-006	051	001	-006	-023	-009	014
Objectiveness	057	030	045	093*	-017	035	061	059	039	045	026	037	027	066	028	055	-002	029	079	051	069	-012	025	082
Agreeableness	-024	-038	-021	-059	-056	-008	-041	-042	-069	-013	-065	-022	-027	050	-013	-009	-030	010	004	011	011	-014	-018	062
Tolerance	058	008	039	014	-010	010	035	005	001	004	039	034	018	036	-045	-008	-000	010	004	011	011	-014	-023	-035
Motivations																								
Analytical	-092*	-121**	-101*	-074	-162**	-107*	-063	-100*	-059	-087	-048	-123*	-101*	-082	-093*	-090*	-078	-085	-090*	-094**	-101*	-071	-054	-101*
Economic	016	004	-069	034	-001	-003	051	023	043	-037	045	-024	-045	002	-032	047	-011	027	074	043	049	-056	-004	-018
Aesthetic	093*	061	099*	-027	031	014	014	059	026	-034	-034	064	068	053	041	-016	-006	-033	-026	045	-008	048	047	008
Social	064	071	087	-006	063	052	014	023	025	042	031	036	011	-009	021	034	034	032	-055	-035	-051	005	033	013
Political	004	008	-048	034	017	026	030	-001	031	-052	-058	023	076	038	042	107*	-009	025	092*	011	064	076	-017	046
Religious	-067	-036	009	017	034	037	-038	-007	-066	053	037	009	-004	-007	013	-002	047	029	-001	011	023	008	-003	039
EB Ratings																								
Mental alertness	038	001	-011	-040	014	-049	-037	-028	-006	-054	-099*	029	118**	025	016	032	-026	009	-007	036	017	072	-042	055
Personality	019	-001	-011	048	019	-006	091*	027	037	-043	-032	073	049	055	007	026	023	056	079	074	065	026	-020	083
Overall	085	046	047	028	046	033	065	040	056	-019	-038	057	155**	081	083	087	041	075	072	098**	077	093**	-030	088

*p < .05
**p < .01

Source: Prepared by author.

FIGURE 4.5
Potentiality Rating Scale

In considering the general executive ability of this person, how does s(he) compare with other Sears executives? (Read all alternatives before rating future potential of this person.)

_____ Compares with the upper 2% or 3% of Sears executives: could well become president or chairman of the board.

_____ Compares with the upper 2% or 3% but is not presidential caliber. Could, however, well become a territorial or staff vice-president.

_____ Compares favorably with the top 5% of Sears executives and could well become a *top* group or zone manager, general manager of a catalog distribution center, or fill some other very top job just below the vice-presidential level.

_____ Compares favorably with the top 5% of Sears executives, may not become a top group or zone manager, but certainly has the potential of becoming a national merchandising or operating department manager in Headquarters, a topflight store manager of a larger A store, catalog distribution center key staff, or fill some other important job of equally high responsibility in the company.

_____ Compares with the upper 15% (but not top 5%) of Sears executives and has the potentiality of being a good solid A store manager, an executive staff assistant or senior buyer in Headquarters, or of handling comparable high level responsibilities in a staff, group/zone, territorial, or Headquarters assignment.

_____ Compares with the upper 20% (but not top 15%) of Sears executives and has the potentiality of becoming an outstanding B store manager, a senior staff assistant, or of handling comparable major responsibilities in a catalog distribution center, zone/group, territorial, or Headquarters assignment (such as an outstanding buyer or retail sales manager).

_____ Certainly compares with the upper 30% (but not top 20%) of Sears executives and has the potentiality of becoming a solid B store manager, a solid Headquarters buyer, or is capable of turning in well above average performance in an executive capacity.

_____	Compares with the upper half (but not top 30%) of Sears executives and is capable of turning in above-average performance in an executive capacity.
_____	May not quite compare with the upper half but has good average executive potential.
_____	Definitely does not compare with the upper half, and is most likely in a position very near the upper limits of his/her ability.
_____	Is in the lower half, and is working above his/her level of competency.

Source: Prepared by author.

Two psychologists made independent evaluations of the overall quality of the Executive Battery profile. After making separate judgments* they met to resolve differences. This resulted in an overall Executive Battery quality evaluation.

Results from this research are presented in Tables 4.8-4.10. Table 4.8 contains predictor/criterion relationships for the total group, Table 4.9 presents these data in terms of multiple correlations, and Table 4.10 compares validities computed through multiple correlations and those obtained with the psychologists' clinical evaluation. While the psychologists' clinical evaluation demonstrates validity, it does not predict as effectively as do the multiple correlations.

From the data in these tables, particularly Table 4.8, we can draw the following conclusions:

1. Strong predictive validity exists for the total group.
2. Validity patterns replicate across rating sources. This is particularly true for the Promotability criterion.
3. Mental Alertness is the best single predictor of all criteria.
4. The Masculine/Dominance scale is the most powerful predictor (of all criteria) among the personality measures.

---

*The intercorrelations among psychologist sorts of profiles for the total group appear below. This indicates a high degree of consistency.

	I	II	Consensus
Psychologist I	—	823	960
Psychologist II		—	921
Consensus			—

TABLE 4.8
Correlations Between Sears Executive Battery Test Scores and Performance for Total Group of Buyers and Assistant Buyers

Test Variables / Criteria	Potentiality Personnel Consensus	Job Performance Personnel Consensus	Job Performance Immediate Superior	Potentiality Immediate Superior	Creative Problem Solving—A	Creative Problem Solving—B	Creative Problem Solving—Total	Job Performance Buying Staff	Potentiality Buying Staff
Mental ability									
Problem solving	.576**	.259**	.214*	.379**	.214*	.295**	.263**	.155	.289**
Linguistic	.520**	.227*	.167	.267**	.255*	.335**	.287**	.237*	.283**
Overall	.592**	.262**	.203*	.339**	.243*	.352**	.306**	.229*	.315**
Personality traits									
S—sociability	-.239*	-.070	-.117	-.206*	-.090	-.153	-.123	-.056	-.130
T—reflectiveness	-.198	-.074	-.170	-.125	-.037	-.169	-.096	-.022	-.049
D—optimism	-.278*	-.089	-.218*	-.185	-.194	-.230*	-.223*	-.045	-.193
C—emotional control	-.326**	-.106	-.272**	-.231*	-.249*	-.223*	-.254*	-.056	-.197*
R—serious vs. carefree	.160	.079	-.014	.072	-.112	.091	-.032	.051	.105
G—general activity	.068	-.011	.072	.055	.093	.179	.136	-.100	-.005
A—social leadership	.295*	.125	.171	.361**	.259*	.307**	.297*	.057	.170
M—dominance	.510**	.226*	.269**	.384**	.249*	.336**	.303**	.158	.226*
I—self-confidence	.346**	.084	.298**	.304**	.166	.261**	.218*	.115	.250*
N—composure	.338**	.144	.199*	.206*	.153	.116	.148	.089	.330**
O—objectiveness	.377**	.113	.239*	.311**	.160	.268**	.217*	.032	.213*
Ag—agreeableness	.068	-.093	-.013	-.141	-.031	.025	-.009	-.075	.004
Co—tolerance	.359**	.106	.079	.114	.080	.201*	.137	-.061	.132

Motivations

Analytical	.168	.158	.028	.099	.021	-.034	-.001	.151	.069
Economic	.052	.053	.181	.250*	.140	.080	.124	-.009	.131
Aesthetic	.213	.194*	-.009	-.035	-.004	.030	.011	.267**	.158
Social	-.388**	-.179	-.083	-.197	-.037	-.030	-.037	-.250*	-.350**
Political	.227	.061	.146	.211*	.088	.096	.097	.092	.190
Religious	-.263*	-.256**	-.217*	-.287**	.162	-.130	-.162	-.240*	-.202*

Vocational interests

Mechanical	.334**	.198*	.014	.055	.038	-.007	.022	.196*	.294**
Computational	-.012	.104	.249*	.117	.083	.110	.100	.041	.009
Scientific	.174	.061	.053	.007	-.041	-.111	-.073	.135	.162
Persuasive	.137	.057	-.056	.159	.045	.091	.068	-.126	.080
Artistic	.069	.074	-.160	-.165	-.137	-.195	-.171	.045	.044
Literary	.093	.072	.020	-.030	.039	.040	.042	.013	.117
Musical	.182	-.033	-.086	.036	-.029	.047	.002	-.086	-.004
Social service	-.289*	-.185	-.150	-.132	-.112	-.095	-.112	-.239*	-.173
Clerical	-.440**	-.179	-.066	-.145	-.189	-.187	-.200*	-.189	-.199*

Overall Executive Battery Profile quality score	.574**	.261**	.297**	.388**	.294**	.398**	.358**	.192	.354**

N =	72	104	100	99	99	99	99	101	101

* = .05 level of confidence
** = .01 level of confidence
Source: Prepared by author.

TABLE 4.9

Multiple Correlations Between Criteria and Executive Battery Scores for Total Buying Group

Criteria	Test Variables	Shrunken Multiple R	B Weights
Personnel department rating of performance (N = 100)	Religious	.272**	-.252
	Dominance	.298*	.303
	Mechanical	.320*	.107
			constant = 48.266
Immediate supervision rating of performance (N = 98)	Self-confidence	.299**	.057
	Computational	.352**	.037
	Clerical	.381**	-.018
	Religious	.404**	-.024
			constant = 3.210
Immediate supervision rating of potential (N = 98)	Quantitative	.384**	.040
	Social leadership	.490**	.090
	Religious	.513**	-.030
	Dominance	.531**	.061
	Agreeableness	.542**	-.046
	Serious vs. carefree	.544**	-.002
	Objectiveness	.550**	.034
	Optimism	.561**	.139
	Emotional control	.573**	-.101
			constant = .308
Immediate supervision creativity—A, production of ideas (N = 98)	Social leadership	.265**	.155
	Quantitative	.304**	.129
	Serious vs. carefree	.347**	-.201
	Activity	.374**	.337
	Emotional control	.400**	-.123
	Clerical	.403*	-.080
	Artistic	.422*	-.092
			constant = 24.078

Immediate supervision	Linguistic	.33**	.060
creativity—B,	Social leadership	.400**	.183
Application of Ideas	Artistic	.430**	-.051
(N = 98)	Clerical	.442*	-.085
	Computational	.456**	.098
	Scientific	.468**	-.066
	Reflective	.474**	-.039
	Activity	.485**	.167
	Social	.491**	.143
	Emotional control	.493**	-.149
	Composure	.503**	-.121
			constant = 20.180
Immediate supervision	Social leadership	.303**	.324
creativity	Quantitative	.366**	.219
total (A + B)	Artistic	.391**	-.194
(N = 98)	Clerical	.431**	-.180
	Serious vs. carefree	.435**	-.280
	Activity	.448**	.418
	Emotional control	.460**	-.352
	Composure	.472**	-.331
	Theoretical	.475**	-.242
	Religious	.483*	-.153
			constant = 72.390
Staff rating of	Aesthetic	.267**	.026
performance	Scientific	.294*	.013
(N = 100)	Dominance	.318*	.030
	Social service	.331*	-.012
	Musical	.349*	-.023
			constant = 4.037
Staff rating of	Social values	.350**	-.068
potential	Composure	.464**	.059
(N = 100)	Quantitative	.489**	.030
	Mechanical	.506**	.019
			constant = 2.967

*p < .05
**p < .01
 Source: Prepared by author.

TABLE 4.10
Comparison of Predictive Efficiency of Criteria by Psychologists' Quality Evaluation of Overall Executive Battery Profile and Multiple Regression

Predictor \ Criteria	Potentiality Personnel Consensus	Job Performance Personnel Consensus	Job Performance Immediate Superior	Potentiality Immediate Superior	Creative Problem Solving—A	Creative Problem Solving—B	Creative Problem Solving—Total	Job Performance Buying Staff	Potentiality Buying Staff
Overall Executive Battery Profile quality score	.528**	.410**	.329**	.301*	.301*	.486**	.409**	.255*	.232
Shrunken multiple correlation		.320**	.404**	.573**	.422*	.503**	.483*	.349*	.506**

* = .05 level of confidence.
** = .01 level of confidence.
Source: Prepared by author.

5. Strong Self-Confidence generalizes across several variables as a predictor of effectiveness.
6. A group of personality variables indicative of emotional strength (Optimism, Emotional Control, and Composure) relates to nearly all criteria. A kind of rugged emotional outlook is associated with effectiveness.
7. The more effective female buyer is strongly tied to objective reality, and her judgments are free from personal or emotional considerations.
8. A concern for the mechanics of how things run and an aversion to clerical pursuits reflect the interest patterns of the more effective buying executive.
9. Social competence and the aggressive assumption of responsibility and social leadership are associated with general effectiveness.
10. Current Job Performance, Potentiality, and Creative Problem Solving are all predicted at adequate levels of significance.
11. Effective Application of Ideas Produced is more strongly predicted than Production of Creative Ideas. "Ingenuity" rather than "pure creativity" makes good sense in terms of the nature of buying job requirements.
12. The psychological factors predicting effectiveness of female executives are not markedly different from those predicting effectiveness of other executives. It seems that "an executive is an executive is an executive" rather than there being differential concepts of executive behavior appropriate to gender identification.

A Study of Executives Engaged in Manufacturing

An interesting study was done with a large manufacturing organization affiliated with Sears. Extensive job analysis revealed a multitude of job elements that grouped logically into 23 criterion dimensions. A rating committee (composed of top management from the corporation) evaluated 179 manufacturing managers. Evaluations were supervised by a Sears Headquarters psychologist. Characteristics were rated on a 1 to 99 Scale.
The total group data in Table 4.11 demonstrate the following:

1. Mental ability is a strong predictor of performance.
2. Self-confidence predicts 18 of the 23 criteria. The ability to initiate and act without the need for external support is an extremely important predictor of executive performance in manufacturing.

TABLE 4.11
Significant Correlations (p < .05) of Test Battery Scales with Criteria for the Total Group of Manufacturing Managers

Group	Predictors	Forecasting	Scheduling	Structuring	Delegating	Relations	Direction	Decisions	Communicating	Persuading	Motivating	Developing	Selecting	Checking	Evaluating	Correcting	Initiative	Objectivity	Maturity	Dedication	Problem Solving	Community	Overall	Potential
TMA	Quantitative		17				19		17	18		16		21	21		16	16	25					-31
	Linguistics								19	19				16	18		16	16	26					-27
	Total score							15	19	20				19	21			16	27		31			-30
Guilford-Martin	Sociability				-24					-23	-16			-16										21
	Thinking																							
	Depression				-19			-19		-22	-17			-19					-18					23
	Cycloid							-18				-16							-17					
	Rathymia																							
	Activity		16				24	16	16		22			22		22	18							-24
	Ascendance				26		20	22		27	19			23			18		21					-30
	Masculinity											27	61					16						-22
	Inferiority	17	21	23	25	23	28	33	18	32	31	30		27		36	32	20	30				17	-30
	Nervousness										16	15							18					-19
	Objectiveness									18		16					16		21					
	Agreeableness																							
	Cooperativeness				19				19	17	17		43						30	37				-26

Correlation matrix of Allport-Vernon and Kuder scales.

	Theoretical	Economic	Aesthetic	Social	Political	Religious	Mechanical	Computational	Scientific	Persuasive	Artistic	Literary	Musical	Social service
Allport-Vernon														
Theoretical														
Economic	18													
Aesthetic	20	-17												
Social	21	-15	**25**											
Political	**25**	-19	15	**25ₛ**										
Religious	15	-24	**21**	18	-16									
Kuder														
Mechanical	19	19	20	-16	-20	-16								
Computational	19	19		-16	-23	16	18							
Scientific	16	16		23	-23	**29**		**21**						
Persuasive				23	-23	16	-18	16	19					
Artistic	19					-23	**-21**			**20**				
Literary						-32	**21**			**34**	22			
Musical	18									**24**	**21**	18		
Social service	-19			-21	19					**35**	**23**	**20**	**20**	
Clerical								17	-36	25	**21**	17	17	
N	179	179	179	110	179	112	179	179	179	167	22	179	179	106

N (continued): 179 179 179 42 42 16 179 179

Note: p < .01 for underlined correlations.
Source: Prepared by author.

3. A preference for selling and persuading others (Persuasive Interest) is associated with so many important criteria (15) that it must be requisite for executive effectiveness in manufacturing.
4. A strong concern for money, profit, and the economic value of the marketplace is a strong predictor (Economic Values).
5. Both importance of personal status and the natural assumption of the leading role when a member of a group are predictive of effective performance (Political Values and Social Ascendancy).
6. The criterion Promotion Potential is predicted by 14 psychological test variables.
7. Selling ideas to others in the face of resistance is a Persuasive Interest criterion predicted by a wide range (13) of mental ability, personality, and value variables.
8. Keeping track of efficiency, costs, and human performance is also predicted by 13 test variables (Checking Performance criterion).
9. Generating positive and productive attitudes in others (Motivating criterion) is also predicted by a large number of psychological variables.

In summarizing these results, a clinical interpretation of major predictor variables may be illuminating. In the Executive Battery a constellation of scores comprises the syndrome Competitive Leadership. This syndrome (and the variables associated with it) can be described as follows:

> Persuasive and socially assured, the person moves aggressively into a central role whenever part of a social or business group (Sociability, Social Ascendancy, Persuasive Interests). Confident to initiate and act without external support (Self-Confidence), the individual catches on rapidly (Mental Ability) and moves into action with energy and flexibility (General Activity and Serious versus Carefree). With heightened personal concern for status, power, and money (Political and Economic Values), the person will work hard to achieve positions that yield such rewards.

In our experience, behaviors pertinent to this combination of scores (amply reflected in the significant relationships presented in Table 4.11) are central to effective executive leadership. These variables are strongly represented in the validity findings for this group of manufacturing executives.

I would like to draw attention to yet another example of the validity of clinical judgments. Two psychologists did separate blind evaluations of each profile on the seven variables listed beside the captions Evaluator I and Evaluator II. They then resolved their differences and made a combined judgment concerning each test profile. This overall clinical judgment and those made by each evaluator were related to the criteria. The results in Table 4.12 are satisfying.

Research with Mainstream Positions in Retail Stores

There is a variety of executive positions within the retail setting. By and large these are held by executives who report to a store manager and contribute to the effectiveness of the individual unit. Research concerning success in these positions is important but complex. The positions are located in geographically dispersed units, each with its own market and economic and social characteristics. While task requirements are similar, they vary in complexity and specificity, depending on store size, location, and so on. To recognize all the variations through intricate sampling techniques leads to fragmentation and complicated research design. Even in a company the size of Sears, some cells end up with few cases in such designs. While the results I am about to describe are from a study whose design shares those complexities, I will deal only with the results for a total group composed of a sample of 862 retail executives.

Since all retail stores are assigned to one of about 40 administrative groups, it was possible to gather criterion data from the immediate supervising executives (such as store managers) and from the group staff as well. This made possible a multimethod/multitrait examination of criteria that consisted of the variables listed in Table 4.13.

In Table 4.14 (where results are presented for the total group), two things to notice are the large number of significant correlations and the low magnitude of these significant relationships. The highest correlation is .205, between Overall Mental Ability and the Promotability criterion. However, even low relationships have utility value when applied to very large populations. Keeping in mind the numbers and magnitude of the correlations, the following observations are made:

1. The patterning of significant results for the two independent evaluation sources is very similar.
2. Virtually all relationships make sense. The patterning of significantly predicted variables follows that of other studies.

TABLE 4.12
Significant Correlations (p < .05) of Profile Evaluation Scales with Criterion Scales for the Total Group of Manufacturing Managers

Evaluator	Predictor	Forecasting	Scheduling	Structuring	Delegating	Relations	Direction	Decisions	Communicating	Persuading	Motivating	Developing	Selecting	Checking	Evaluating	Correcting	Initiative	Objectivity	Maturity	Dedication	Problem Solving	Community	Overall	Potential
I	Total Profile	21	21	23	38	17	28	24	28	33	22	28		27	20	26	18	20	26				17	-44
I	Problem Solving	18	24					17	18	19		17		20	20				23				18	-34
I	Verbal Ability			18				19	21	24	16			17	19		17	18	27	31			19	-33
I	Overall						23	18	24	25		18		18	20		16	16	27				17	-37
I	Emotional				26			21		24	16	29		26		25	21	18	23					-17
I	Social		16	18	31	25		25	24	35	26	32		24		27	28	24	31	37	31			
I	Supervisory				31	16		25	19	30	24	18		17		20	27	22	35	35			17	-38
I	Motivation			15	21	16	21			20	21													-40
II	Problem Solving	18	22		21		22	17	17	20				20	20				23				18	-35
II	Verbal Ability							17	19	22							17	16	25				18	-32
II	Overall							19	22	24	17			20	18	22	17	15	27				17	-35
II	Emotional							22	22	25	27	21		16		28	16	16	23					-20
II	Social			19	31	21		24	20	34	23	25		22		26	21	16	26	34	32			-36
II	Supervisory		15	19	31	21	24	23	20	33	23	32	44	23		26	24	18	32	33				-36
II	Motivation					17	25			17	17			16			23	22						
	N	167	168	169	102	169	105	168	169	167	167	158	21	168	169	99	169	169	169	41	41	16	162	161

Note: p < .01 for underlined correlations.
Source: Prepared by author.

TABLE 4.13
Criteria Gathered, by Source of Evaluation, for Study of
Executives in Mainstream Retail Positions

Criterion Variable	Source of Evaluation	
	Store Managers	Group Staff
Ratings designed for study		
Technical knowledge	X	X
Work relationships	X	X
Merchandise/operating effectiveness	X	X
General overall evaluation	X	X
Overall average of all ratings	X	X
Promotion potential	X	X
Reaction to problems questionnaire *(factor scores derived from this sample)*		
Enthusiastic, aggressive pragmatist	X	
Confident, independent problem solver	X	
Inventive generator of creative ideas	X	
Constructive, inquisitive thinker	X	
Annual performance evaluation scores		
Technical knowledge	X	
Administrative effectiveness	X	
Work relations	X	
Response to superiors	X	
Directing subordinates	X	
Individual effectiveness	X	
Manager's general evaluation	X	
Overall score	X	

Note: All data gathering was supervised by a psychologist or (in the case of the annual performance evaluation) by a trained personnel representative.

Source: Prepared by author.

TABLE 4.14
Correlations Between Executive Battery Scores and Ratings for Total Group (N = 862)

Executive Battery	Store Ratings							Group Ratings							Checklist Performance Evaluation							
	Technical Knowledge	Work Relations	Administrative Effectiveness	Mdsing/Operating Effectiveness	General Evaluation	Overall	Promotability	Technical Knowledge	Work Relations	Administrative Effectiveness	Mdsing/Operating Effectiveness	General Evaluation	Overall	Promotability	Technical Knowledge	Administrative Effectiveness	Work Relations	Response to Superiors	Directing Subordinates	Individual Effectiveness	General Evaluation	Overall
Linguistic	089*	032	079*	059	062	170*	083*	152**	007	138**	141**	118**	121*	159**	110**	087*	015	033	038	058	083*	067
Problem solving	172**	069*	123**	135**	127**	137**	188**	176**	028	147**	192**	136**	149**	212**	148**	101**	037	070*	053	095*	125**	101**
Overall	141**	054	111**	101**	104**	111**	143**	184**	015	160**	181**	141**	149**	205**	145**	107**	028	056	052*	085*	116**	093
Sociability	-112**	-053	-060	-084*	-113**	-090*	-115*	-162**	-104**	-141**	-158**	-164**	-160**	-133**	-107**	-075*	-067*	-051	-090*	-102**	-103**	-092*
Reflectiveness	-095*	-069*	-079*	-113**	-096**	-098*	-024	-053	-008	-072*	-048	-055	-052	-023	-050	-055	-044	-060	-053	-048	-050	-055
Optimism	-065	-056	-050	-031	-068*	-058	-047	-124**	-058	-098**	-086**	-095**	-101**	-062	-037	-027	-026	-018	-008	-039	-032	-027
Emotional control	-016	000	-010	-009	-015	-010	-001	-082*	-035	-059	-065	-064	-067	-041	003	017	015	010	027	-007	006	013
Seriousness vs. carefree	137**	112**	103**	118**	150**	134**	091*	156**	133**	130**	131**	154**	155**	090*	162**	140**	129**	101**	165**	139**	145**	155**
General activity	129**	060	101**	136**	130**	120**	064	140**	067*	103**	140**	123**	126**	068*	164**	127**	080*	068	113**	144**	132**	131**
Social leadership	097**	055	075*	085*	093**	087*	090*	148**	088*	091*	148**	135**	134**	121**	100**	085*	061	054	104**	100**	084*	093*
Dominance	051	-014	001	047	020	022	094**	037	-023	018	077*	012	027	040	056	005	-009	024	002	034	036	022
Self-confidence	110	050	089**	087**	108**	097**	089**	173**	131**	142**	163**	167**	170**	084**	087*	054	027	015	039	072*	071*	057
Composure	-020	-022	-026	-042	-020	-029	030	045	057	038	017	022	040	025	-002	-018	-018	-001	-038	-012	-016	-020
Objectiveness	027	016	010	003	031	019	-046	129**	087*	093*	107**	107**	115**	009	036	018	-022	-013	-009	032	022	012
Agreeableness	-051	-021	-030	-053	-037	-042	-084*	-040	023	000	-062	-031	-024	-016	-048	-031	-031	-029	-052	-029	-034	-041

Tolerance	082*	027	070	049	072*	066*	-038	139**	039	122**	114**	113**	115**	053	098**	083*	033	016	044	070*	088**	068*
Analytical	-107**	-088**	-077	-086**	-095**	-098**	-075*	-104	-093**	-093**	-080*	-112**	-106**	-095*	-067*	-070*	-039	-027	-040	-059	-058	-057
Economic	083*	046	055	092**	076**	076*	140**	115**	008	069*	145**	098**	095**	087**	113**	084*	044	058	057	085**	112**	089*
Aesthetic	-075*	-069*	-061	-081*	-081*	-080*	-065*	-124**	-085**	-076*	-108**	-105**	-109**	-004	-092**	-058	-083*	-059	-089**	-086**	-097**	-087**
Social	-030	010	013	-017	009	-003	021	-024	008	-010	-052	-008	-019	031	-086**	-034	-019	-044	-025	-037	-049	-048
Political	097**	062	075*	096**	087**	091**	086**	155**	081*	129**	184**	162**	156**	098**	143**	128**	091**	095**	119**	114**	110**	126**
Religious	005	021	-020	-026	-021	-009	-092**	-012	075*	-005	-058	-015	-003	-096**	002	-022	019	-009	-002	-008	006	-004
Mechanical	059	050	059	077*	039	063	070*	053	029	010	080	050	049	037	031	-002	010	019	024	020	030	020
Computational	-012	-033	-013	002	-019	-016	042	024	-026	-007	024	-020	-001	-022	021	-021	-051	001	-073*	-012	-018	-027
Scientific	015	036	-000	040	029	026	030	029	008	023	042	015	026	024	-020	-043	018	004	-024	-016	-025	-017
Persuasive	080*	022	021	051	065*	051	115**	115	037	092**	133**	105**	106**	121**	096**	082*	034	050	057	078*	071	076*
Artistic	-108**	-051	-048	-097**	-084*	-084*	-120**	-069	-004	-026	-052	-049	-044	-043	-093**	-065	-060	-062	-067*	-100**	-082*	-083*
Literary	-054	-041	-015	-060	-052	-049	-022	-060	-076*	-044	-044	-053	-061	-028	-042	-055	-043	-025	-055	-053	-053	-052
Musical	-057	-070*	-062	-075*	-065*	-071	-066*	-072*	-050	-072*	-101**	-079*	-082*	-053	-019	-015	-035	-020	-026	-022	-014	-024
Social service	-030	029	-006	-008	-005	-005	-038	-052	-014	-043	-090*	-042	-053	-055	-026	-002	042	037	043	023	-010	-019
Clerical	021	-019	-002	-027	-003	-007	-062	042	-000	-005	-003	004	008	-088*	040	034	010	007	-024	006	039	018

*p <.05

**p <.01

Source: Prepared by author.

3. Both Store Managers' General Evaluation and Promotability are significantly predicted by 17 variables.

4. Merchandising or Operating Effectiveness is strongly predicted by 20 variables when evaluated by group staff.

5. The consistency of significant relationships between criteria and Mental Ability is impressive.

6. The Overall criteria are heavily predicted in each of the three sets of evaluations.

7. There is heavy prediction of the Technical Knowledge criteria in all three sets of data.

Table 4.15 shows the large number of significant correlations (all of low magnitude) between Executive Battery test variables and the four factorially defined criteria from the Reaction to Problems Questionnaire. The patterning of significant predictor/criterion relationships replicates those found with other criteria in the study.

Correlations between psychologists' clinical judgment of test results and criteria appear in Table 4.16. Again, the number of significant correlations is impressive, though the magnitude of the relationships is low.

Multiple correlations for selected criteria were all significant beyond the .01 level. They are summarized in Table 4.17, where comparisons in predictive efficiency can be made by source of criterion.

A minority group (N = 208) was extracted from the total group; data for it are presented in Table 4.18. There is similarity to total group results in both the patterning and the low magnitude of the significant correlations. Some differences in results do appear, particularly in predicting the annual performance evaluation criterion scores. The variable Tolerance (cooperative interpersonal trust) is significantly related to every performance evaluation score. The ability to view things in the terms of the reality of their occurrence (Objectivity) is also a pervasive predictor of performance evaluations. So is the personality variable (Serious versus Carefree) that measures flexibility of behavior and the acceptance of task interruptions as the person moves from one task to another. There is also strong prediction of criteria by Political Values.

In summary, results from these studies begin to form a strong pattern: across studies, patterns of validity emerge. Let us now move to three other studies.

TABLE 4.15
Correlations Between Reactions to Problems Factors and
Executive Battery Scores N = 862

	Total Group			
Executive Battery	Enthusiastic, Aggressive Pragmatist	Independent Problem Solver	Inventive, Creative Idea Generator	Constructive, Inquisitive Thinker
Linguistic	012	093*	084*	109**
Problem solving	095*	223**	203**	172*
Overall	051	165**	150**	154**
Sociability	-136**	-097**	-145**	-091*
Reflectiveness	-059	-088*	-051	-052
Optimism	-077*	-075*	-071*	-094*
Emotional control	-018	-029	-030	-029
Serious vs. carefree	143**	116**	119**	100**
General activity	108**	109**	113**	075*
Social leadership	119**	070*	141**	081*
Dominance	030	116**	089*	127**
Self-confidence	072*	095**	107**	191*
Composure	008	026	013	029
Objectiveness	012	035	008	008
Agreeableness	-035	-042	-052	-069*
Tolerance	052	053	053	035
Analytical	-092**	-055	-056	043
Economic	053	086**	110**	073*
Aesthetic	-059	-057	-065*	-032
Social	012	-035	-031	-052
Political	090**	129**	114**	092**
Religious	-002	-059	-054	-084*
Mechanical	034	091**	040	098**
Computational	008	021	051	049
Scientific	005	032	047	078*
Persuasive	048	092**	104**	037
Artistic	094**	-058	-091**	-093**
Literary	-036	-026	-061	-043
Musical	-089**	-072*	-082*	-058
Social service	048	-025	-016	-014
Clerical	031	-070	-048	-071*

*p < .05
**p < .01
Source: Prepared by author.

TABLE 4.16

Correlations Between Criteria and Executive Battery Ratings

Criteria ▼	EB Ratings ▶ Mental Ability	Personality	Overall
Store Ratings	N = 858		
Technical knowledge	138**	064	151**
Work relations	040	042	081
Administrative effectiveness	093**	047	104**
Mdsing/operating effectiveness	082*	030	111**
General evaluation	093**	068*	123**
Overall	097**	054	124**
Promotability	135**	068*	169**
Group Ratings	N = 723		
Technical knowledge	167**	142**	225**
Work relations	-001	063	050
Administrative effectiveness	100**	113**	164**
Mdsing/operating effectiveness	155**	126**	225**
General evaluation	102**	130**	173**
Overall	114**	125**	183**
Promotability	165**	086**	213**
Checklist Performance Evaluation	N = 845		
Technical knowledge	147**	059	113**
Administrative effectiveness	104**	037	082*
Work relations	048	013	018
Response to superiors	056	-007	022
Directing subordinates	065*	040	040
Individual effectiveness	085**	043	073
General evaluation	102**	039	090**
Overall	094**	035	069*

Reaction to Problem Factors	N = 585		
1. Enthus. aggress. pragmatic	036	056	095**
2. Independent problem solver	140**	070*	182**
3. Inventive, creative	128**	102**	168**
4. Critical thinker	111**	099**	170**

*p < .05
**p < .01
Source: Prepared by author.

LONG-TERM PREDICTIVE VALIDITY OF THE EXECUTIVE BATTERY

Test-Retest Study Related to Age

To address the issue of reliability at this point may be unusual; however, I would like to talk about some systematic retesting we have done. A national sample of 465 male executives was retested on the Guilford-Martin Personality Inventories. The fourfold design and results appear in Table 4.19. About half the men were less than 35 years old when they were tested originally. Time between test and retest varied from 1 to 20 years. Though stability differs in terms of specific personality variables, the predictability of scores across time is consistently greater for those originally tested somewhat later in life, regardless of whether the elapsed time after original testing was short or long. The correlation of scores for the younger executives is lower, regardless of how recent the original testing.

There are two ways of interpreting these findings. One way is to think about them in terms of reliability across time. However, when elapsed time is substantial, the issue of random error is not a matter of great importance. Therefore, these data fit more comfortably into the concept of trait stability.

While bearing on the issue of reliability and trait stability, these findings illustrate the dynamics of adult growth and reflect the image of the young man whose personality strengthens, deepens, and matures following graduation from college. It is impressive that for the total sample, the average across all scales and all age groups is .52, indicating stability of a high order for measurement of the adult personality.

TABLE 4.17
Multiple Correlations for Total, Mainstream Executive Positions in Retail Stores (N = 862)

Comparisons of Multiple Correlation, by Criterion Rating Sources

Criterion	Rating Source	Multiple R	No. of Var in Regression
Technical knowledge	-store manager	.331**	8
Technical knowledge	-group staff	.363**	11
Working relations	-store manager	.214**	6
Working relations	-group staff	.212**	5
Administrative effectiveness	-store manager	.299**	11
Administrative effectiveness	-group staff	.303**	10
Merchandising or operating effectiveness	-store manager	.310**	8
Merchandising or operating effectiveness	-group staff	.359**	11
General evaluation	-store manager	.313**	10
General evaluation	-group staff	.334**	10
Promotion potential	-store manager	.308**	9
Promotion potential	-group staff	.295**	6
Total rating (average all ratings)	-store manager	.307**	8
Total rating (average all ratings)	-group staff	.328**	10

Multiple Correlations Between Executive Battery Variables and Reaction to Problems Criterion Scores (rating source: store manager)

Criterion Variable—Factorial Scores	Multiple R	No. of Var in Regression
Enthusiastic aggressive pragmatist	.226**	7
Confident, independent problem solver	.293**	9
Inventive, generator of creative ideas	.327**	10
Constructive, inquisitive thinker	.282**	8

*p < .05
**p < .01
Source: Prepared by author.

TABLE 4.18
Correlations Between Executive Battery Scores and Ratings for Total Minority Group (N = 208)

Executive Battery	Store Ratings							Group Ratings							Checklist Performance Evaluation							
	Technical Knowledge	Work Relations	Administrative Effectiveness	Mdsing/Operating Effectiveness	General Evaluation	Overall	Promotability	Technical Knowledge	Work Relations	Administrative Effectiveness	Mdsing/Operating Effectiveness	General Evaluation	Overall	Promotability	Technical Knowledge	Administrative Effectiveness	Work Relations	Response to Superiors	Directing Subordinates	Individual Effectiveness	General Evaluation	Overall
Sociability	-201*	-086	-087	-116	-179**	-143*	-093	-062	-092	-062	-058	-103	-080	-056	-201**	-094	-058	-054	-153*	-128	-124	-129
Reflectiveness	-174**	-198**	-167*	-220**	-197**	-143*	-070	-083	-050	-126	-091	-116	-099	-088	-132	-147*	-148*	-153**	-143*	-153*	-179**	-166*
Optimism	-197**	-205**	-145*	-108	-188**	-183**	-101	-110	-115	-146*	-105	-148*	-133	-107	-194**	-173**	-183**	-133	-153*	-172**	-150*	-182**
Emotional control	-107	-151*	-109	-099	-131	-130	-036	-128	-109	-164*	-163*	-154*	-153*	-112	-132	-086	-156*	-114	-112	-138	-118	-132
Serious vs. carefree	162*	058	106	134	146*	131	183	089	074	085	059	110	089	057	213**	186**	096	143**	207**	190**	191**	195**
General activity	089	-035	029	097	048	049	026	048	-003	011	037	038	028	010	134	073	010	048	101	115	080	090
Social leadership	172*	046	084	149*	134	125	078	091	085	064	060	075	080	087	216**	123	063	067	186**	138*	136*	149*
Dominance	098	086	044	132	110	103	150*	071	059	066	132	088	089	174*	189**	149*	118	081	141	183**	133	174*
Self confidence	169*	113	134	153*	165*	160*	121	160*	214**	187**	180**	213**	204**	139	173	105	081	053	141	152*	133	134
Composure	017	074	-009	005	044	030	050	037	122	035	049	076	069	051	091	033	107	069	108	089	049	084
Objectiveness	130	158*	070	094	151*	134	043	121	152*	135*	132	161*	149*	024	219**	138	186**	142*	203**	213**	148**	193**
Agreeableness	036	132	018	018	083	093	002	086	157*	144	093	138	132	111	093	073	154*	125	091	143*	083	115
Tolerance	171*	108	112	122	141*	-006	143*	104	076	076	106	111	100	052	254**	175**	146*	150*	184**	216**	196**	207**
Analytical	-014	-048	-047	-045	-020	-036	-074	049	018	-002	010	020	020	-044	-026	-067	048	-024	011	-017	-062	-022
Economic	137*	128	091	152*	132	140*	175**	161*	096	128	159*	130	144*	090	176	193*	158*	127	140	111	215**	175**
Aesthetic	-139*	-117	-149*	-167*	-125	-152*	-095	-171*	-118	-135*	-139	-126	-147*	-048	-097	-107	-095	-036	-091	-121	-121	-103
Social	-098	-050	-037	-089	-062	-072	-013	019	021	010	-041	007	003	047	-161*	-102	-053	-122	-129	-127	-104	-126
Political	134	045	099	163*	121	123	086	191**	073	159*	217**	175**	173*	044	248**	234**	100	187**	220**	216**	212**	221**
Religious	-044	018	019	-037	-071	-028	-043	-187**	-054	-119	-172*	-157*	-146*	-114	-126	-126	-080	-122	-135*	-093	-125	-124

*p < .05
**p < .01

Source: Prepared by author.

TABLE 4.19
Stability of Guilford-Martin Scales Under Test-Retest Conditions

Age of Executives When Originally Tested

	20-34 Years of Age		35-50 Years of Age	
	Scale	Stability r	Scale	Stability r
	S	.535	S	.748
	T	.504	T	.555
	D	.450	D	.495
	C	.490	C	.453
1-9 Years Between Testings	R	.598	R	.647
	G	.723	G	.567
	A	.363	A	.638
	M	.538	M	.674
	I	.623	I	.489
	N	.491	N	.624
	O	.469	O	.418
	Ag	.491	Ag	.557
	Co	.540	Co	.533
	AVERAGE .524 N = 86		AVERAGE .568 N = 132	
	Scale	Stability r	Scale	Stability r
	S	.336	S	.423
	T	.403	T	.544
	D	.371	D	.540
	C	.330	C	.603
10-20 Years Between Testings	R	.497	R	.372
	G	.511	G	.574
	A	.413	A	.564
	M	.482	M	.621
	I	.375	I	.629
	N	.509	N	.569
	O	.426	O	.493
	Ag	.473	Ag	.625
	Co	.357	Co	.592
	AVERAGE .421 N = 141		AVERAGE .549 N = 106	

Time Elapsed Since Testing

Source: Prepared by author.

With this quality of stability, one can ask whether psychological tests, taken earlier in the life of an individual, predict current executive behavior. Let us examine results from two studies, both involving higher-level executives.

Long-Term Predictive Validity of Store Manager Performance

A study was done with a sample of 76 store managers. The average time between testing and gathering performance criteria was 17 years. Consequently, this is a true, long-term predictive study. Criteria were merchandising, operating, and people-related skills, as well as a general overall evaluation. Descriptions of these criteria and their measurement scale appear in Figure 4.6. To focus attention on personality assessment, only Guilford-Martin validity results are shown in Table 4.20.

Considerable validity is demonstrated. Both Merchandising and People-Related Abilities are strongly predicted. Prediction of overall effectiveness as a store manager is somewhat less strong. Operating ability is predicted by a single (though logical) score.

Thus far, I have done little more than indicate the general trends of validity findings. It may, therefore, be well to break out of that mold and provide an interpretation of at least part of these data. Let us look at the prediction of the criterion Merchandising Ability (in Table 4.20).

Prediction of Store Manager Merchandising Ability

Merchandising ability is significantly predicted by nine test variables, six of them at the .01 level of confidence (see Table 4.20). Assuming that significant correlations cluster together to form a behavioral syndrome, we can describe the person who effectively handles store manager merchandising tasks as follows:

> The store manager who effectively handles merchandising tasks is friendly, socially outgoing, and at ease in most situations (S—Sociability = -.331). Naturally assertive, he readily takes over the leadership of any group of which he is a part (A—Social Leadership = .269) and functions with assured self-confidence (I—Self-Confidence = .318). He also has a kind of fast-moving, enthusiastic exuberance that allows him to express himself readily (G—General Activity = .330; R—Impulsive = .348) and carry others along with him. He likes excitement and

FIGURE 4.6
Evaluations of Skills and Abilities

Rate all managers listed on the attached sheet (by ascribing a number between 1 and 99) on each of the following characteristics.

1. General skill and ability in performing the *merchandising* duties of a store manager's job.

1	10	20	30	40	50	60	70	80	90	99

Not good at merchandising but not sufficiently poor to be removed from the assignment	Solid, acceptable performance in the merchandising area of store management	A great merchandiser: in merchandising ability compares with the best the company has ever produced

2. General skill and ability in dealing with, *handling, and relating to all the people* who work in the store.

1	10	20	30	40	50	60	70	80	90	99

Not good at working with people but not sufficiently poor to be removed from the assignment	Solid, acceptable managerial performance in dealing with, handling, and relating to all people in the store	Great ability to work with, handle, and relate to people. Compares with the best the company has ever had

3. General skill and ability in performing the *operating* duties of a store manager.

1	10	20	30	40	50	60	70	80	90	99

Not good at performing operating duties but not sufficiently poor to be removed from the assignment	Solid, acceptable performance in operating areas of store management	Great in operating. Operating skill and ability compare with best the company has ever produced

4.   General *overall effectiveness* as a store manager.

1	10	20	30	40	50	60	70	80	90	99

Poorer store manager, but not so poor as to be removed from the assignment	Solid, acceptable store management performance	Great. Compares with the best store managers the company has ever produced

Source: Prepared by author.

change, and may be somewhat impatient with those who do not function as quickly or as enthusiastically as he does. Sensitive to the subtleties and nuances of situations (T—Reflectiveness = -.272), his thinking is also closely tied to reality. His high objectivity is unlikely to let personal feelngs or emotions color his evaluation of situations or ideas (O—Objectivity = .308). Cheerful and optimistic (D—Optimism = -.269), he has the kind of emotionally robust outlook that allows him to encounter a wide range of situations without being personally bothered (M—Dominance = .443).

The overall Executive Battery profile clinical evaluation predicts the Merchandising Ability criterion and only that criterion. In summarizing the study findings, we can say that tests taken many years ago predict current store manager performance. Considering the variation in time between testing and criterion measurement, these findings are impressive.

Long-Term Prediction of Upper-Level Executive Performance

We come now to a project where subjects had to be highly effective before they could be eligible for inclusion in the study. In recent years we have been concerned with qualities associated with upper-level executive effectiveness. On the basis of extensive analysis, an evaluation form was constructed to assist in identifying candidates for higher-level positions. Called the Qualifications Questionnaire, the instrument was composed of 51 items. Each item reflects an area of executive function representing complex skills, abilities, or characteristics.

TABLE 4.20
Relationship Between Retail Store Manager Sears
Executive Battery of Psychological Test Scores
and Job Performance Criteria

Performance Variables ▶ Test Variables ▼	Merchandising Ability	People-Related Ability	Operating Ability	General Overall Effective.	Alternate Ranking of Overall Ability
Personality					
S—Sociability†	-.331**	-.220	-.034	-.153	-.333**
T—Reflectiveness†	-.272*	-.286*	.044	-.157	-.252*
D—Optimism†	-.269*	-.361**	-.024	-.148	-.167
C—Stability†	-.099	-.215	-.141	-.097	-.130
R—Impulsive	.348**	.201	.084	.164	.377**
G—General Activity	.330*	.170	.173	.228*	.334**
A—Social Leadership	.269*	.226	.110	.163	.290*
M—Dominance	.443**	.391**	.213	.301**	.383**
I—Self-Confidence	.318**	.324**	.077	.192	.211
N—Composure	.134	.395**	.019	.082	.092
O—Objectivity	.308**	.280*	.107	.217	.177
Ag—Agreeableness	.052	.170	-.002	.019	-.066
Co—Tolerance	.169	.249	-.035	.093	.144
N =	76	59	76	76	64

* $p < .05$
** $p < .01$
†Inverse scales: a negative correlation is indicative of positive and more socially adaptive behavior.
Source: Prepared by author.

Data from the questionnaire were factor-analyzed. An early assumption was that the complex structure of the items might cause them to fall into one big general factor. Such was not the case. A clear and meaningful factor structure emerged. Titles of the nine factors were the following:

Factor	Title
I	Flexible physical, emotional, and intellectual strength that supports and translates into administrative action
II	Assured independence and ingenuity of intellectual and administrative functioning
III	Effective (people) leadership
IV	Administrative sensitivity and strength in setting standards and appraising performance
V	Effectiveness as a public representative of the company
VI	Integration of complex and diverse functions to move the organization forward
VII	Informed, competitive drive to improve and develop the business
VIII	Organizing and planning activities
IX	Foresight

Factor scores were then used as criteria and related to psychological test variables.

Two issues are important in considering the relationship between the psychological test scores of these 136 executives and the evaluation criteria. First, the psychological test data are old. The average elapsed time between taking the Executive Battery and being rated is 21 years. Second, those evaluated occupy high-level positions. Since they represent a select executive sample, the range of their test scores might well be restricted. This possibility was examined and, as shown in Table 4.21, restriction of range was found for several variables. Consequently, correlations for those variables were treated with appropriate corrections.

Table 4.22 presents both uncorrected and corrected correlations between scores on the Sears Executive Battery and factorially defined criterion scores from the Qualifications Questionnaire (N = 136). Where a variable produces a significant uncorrected correlation, the magnitude of the relationship is improved by correcting for restriction of range. There are no uncorrected significant correlations between mental ability and the criteria.

TABLE 4.21
Executive Battery Mean Scores and Standard Deviation
Comparison of Top-Level Executive Group with Total Population

	Evaluated Group			Sears Population		
	Mean Score	SD	N	Mean Score	SD	N
Mental Ability						
Linguistic	75.97	12.61	134	71.36	16.34	16,005
Problem Solving	48.75	7.47		45.82	10.26	
Overall	124.69	16.97		117.17	23.46	
Personality Traits						
Sociability	4.84	4.15	134	7.78	6.62	17,389
Reflectiveness	32.11	8.09		32.22	7.48	
Optimism	5.89	3.93		7.19	5.65	
Emotional control	12.81	5.64		13.43	6.67	
Serious vs. carefree	47.32	8.58		45.44	9.04	
General activity	16.82	4.40		15.28	4.37	
Social leadership	31.19	4.12		29.02	5.37	
Dominance	25.96	4.57		24.56	5.08	
Self-confidence	44.93	3.63		43.56	4.41	
Composure	34.36	5.61		33.59	5.76	
Objectiveness	63.14	8.12		61.88	8.99	
Agreeableness	37.87	9.10		38.63	8.93	
Tolerance	83.53	11.85		79.98	13.69	
Motivations						
Analytical	28.74	6.11	134	29.31	5.97	15,826
Economic	37.15	6.99		35.83	6.93	
Aesthetic	17.71	7.45		19.10	7.71	
Social	26.97	6.06		27.88	5.92	
Political	36.77	7.24		35.20	6.65	
Religious	32.57	7.95		32.80	8.86	

Vocational Interests

				*
Mechanical	31.46	11.95	131	
Computational	30.94	10.43		
Scientific	31.09	8.97		
Persuasive	58.23	12.54		
Artistic	19.77	8.49		
Literary	22.01	8.40		
Musical	12.40	5.75		
Social service	44.19	11.11		
Clerical	42.91	11.46		

Source: Prepared by author.

*Comparable Data Not Available

However, three significant corrected correlations exist between the Quantitative Problem Solving score and factor dimensions II, V, and VI. These are logical, intellectual function being strongly implied in all three criteria.

Factor VII, Informed, Competitive Drive to Improve and Develop the Business, is significantly predicted by ten psychological test variables. It is the strongest prediction of any criterion and the factor most likely to be predicted by personality variables.

Sociability, Social Leadership, and Carefree* are significantly related to every criterion variable. This strong patterning of results is shown in Table 4.22. Other variables (Self-Confidence, Political Values, and Persuasive Interests) are significantly related to many criteria. If a variable produces a significant relationship with one criterion, that relationship then generalizes by producing significant relationships with other criteria. These significantly predictive variables form the psychological syndrome described earlier as Competitive Leadership. This strong patterning of data, which includes higher scores from the Serious versus Carefree variable may portray the psychological dynamics of long-term predictive validity. It should be remembered that, on the average, the test data are 21 years old.

---

*The term "carefree" may be somewhat misleading. Originally the variable was called Rathymia, but Sears has used the more descriptive term Serious versus Carefree. On this variable, higher-scoring people make decisions readily, are flexible, and like variety. They tend to be zestful, enthusiastic, and spontaneous.

TABLE 4.22
Correlations Between Sears Executive Battery of Psychological Tests and Factor Scores from the Qualifications Questionnaire (U = uncorrected, C = corrected for attenuation)

Executive Battery Variables	Factor I		Factor II		Factor III		Factor IV		Factor V		Factor VI		Factor VII		Factor VIII		Factor IX		Total Scale	
	U	C	U	C	U	C	U	C	U	C	U	C	U	C	U	C	U	C	U	C
Mental ability																				
Linguistic	-029	-038	068	088	-026	034	-064	-083	060	078	012	016	-103	-133	-074	-096	109	141	-006	007
Quantitative	117	161	132	181*	-029	-040	053	073	165	227**	133	183*	005	007	088	121	070	096	102	140
Overall	028	039	107	148	-034	-047	-025	-035	116	160	067	093	-075	-104	-018	-025	111	153	039	054
Personality traits																				
Sociability	-251**	-400**	235**	-375**	-172**	-274**	-223*	-356**	-201*	-321*	-227**	-362**	-258**	-459**	-117	-187**	-155	-247**	-269**	-413**
Reflectiveness	-030		068		062		058		131		038		-059		003		026		010	
Optimism	-020	-029	005	007	076	109	041	053	019	028	034	049	-057	-082	089	128	-111	-160	014	020
Emotional control	012	-014	030	035	094	111	105	124	132	156	073	086	025	030	028	033	-057	-067	056	066
Serious vs. carefree	200*	103	214*	145	178*	141	178*	146	214*	154	192*	156	274**	253**	092	133	183*	166	229**	166
General activity	253**	330**	310**	404**	232**	302**	289**	377**	313**	408**	284**	370**	393**	512**	215*	280**	336**	438**	332**	433**
Social leadership	145	161	115	128	114	127	101	112	044	049	065	072	149	166	025	028	192*	213**	123	137
Dominance	123	149	108	131	078	095	021	026	143	174*	083	101	152	185*	026	032	249**	303**	118	143
Self-confidence	030		-023		-145		-123		-040		-034		004		-040		103		-040	
Composure	030	033	039	043	-061	-068	029	032	-027	-030	004	004	007	008	-031	-034	090	100	015	017
Objectiveness.	-092		-041		-063		-092		-050		-072		-093		-125		-067		-018	
Agreeableness																				
Tolerance	051	059	054	062	106	122	022	025	098		039	045	060	069	-085	-098	062	072	065	075

Motivations

Analytical	-084	095	-053	-103	-028	-048	-195	-124	013	-092
Economic	-064	-026	017	016	-120	-020	074	108	038	-030
Aesthetic	-118	068	-151	-119	-060	-094	-166	-234**	-053	-126
Social	-005	012	019	032	002	-040	-085	087	-131	018
Political	195*	173*	166	176*	168	104	304**	160	106	201*
Religious	053	014	040	052	047	066	017	131	008	051

Vocational interests

Mechanical	053	105	-116	-135	-082	-037	-073	-066	046	-089
Computational	-178*	192*	-226**	-154	-156	-136	-263**	063	-066	-207*
Scientific	-112	055	-117	080	-127	-067	-226**	058	-119	-121
Persuasive	110	153	198*	224*	164	157	296**	243**	156	199*
Artistic	029	043	121	060	-022	087	-064	077	027	042
Literary	008	-047	111	089	006	-066	-101	-146	-179*	071
Musical	038	-015	086	-025	116	036	025	083	-064	016
Social service	-006	000	030	055	-052	-105	-061	070	-112	040
Clerical	030	068	-053	030	023	-040	-034	015	-103	042

*p $<$ .05
**p $<$ .01

Source: Prepared by author.

Multiple Correlations Between Executive Battery Test Variables and Each Criterion Dimension

I have computed multiple correlations between Executive Battery variables and each of the factorially defined criterion variables. These data appear in Tables 4.23 through 4.31. For convenience, the final multiples are summarized in Table 4.32. Since the number of cases exceeds 100, these are all unshrunken multiple correlations.

TABLE 4.23

Multiple Correlations Between Executive Battery Scores and Factor I, Flexible Physical, Emotional and Intellectual Strength That Supports and Translates into Administrative Action

Executive Battery Variables	Multiple R
Social leadership	.264**
Masculine dominance	.320**
Economic values	.357**
Aesthetic values	.377**
Theoretical values	.395**
Artistic interests	.408**
Mental ability—quantitative	.422**
Computational interests	.433**
Clerical interests	.449**

**p $< .01$

TABLE 4.24
Multiple Correlations Between Executive Battery and
Factor II, Assured Independence and Ingenuity of Intellectual
and Administrative Functioning

Executive Battery Variables	Multiple R
Social leadership	.347**
Masculine dominance	.376**
Computational	.392**
Mental Ability—quantitative	.411**
Scientific interests	.431**
Mechanical interests	.455**
Composure	.474**
Serious versus carefree	.492**
Cooperative	.507**
Activity	.517**
Theoretical values	.525**
Mental ability—linguistic	.536**
Aesthetic values	.544**

**p $<$ .01

TABLE 4.25
Multiple Correlations Between Executive Battery Scores
and Factor III, Effective (People) Leadership

Executive Battery Variables	Multiple R
Social leadership	.235**
Composure	.326**
Aesthetic values	.364**
Artistic interests	.417**
Economic values	.446**
Masculine dominance	.470**
Computational interests	.501**
Clerical interests	.519**
Scientific interests	.544**
Sociability	.560**
Mechanical interests	.571**
Literary interests	.581**
Cooperative	.588**
Serious versus carefree	.597**
Mental ability—quantitative	.608**

**p $<$ .01

TABLE 4.26
Multiple Correlations Between Executive Battery and Factor IV, Administrative Sensitivity and Strength in Setting Standards and Appraising Performance

Executive Battery Variables	Multiple R
Social leadership	.278**
Composure	.337**
Aesthetic values	.363**
Scientific interests	.381**
Reflective	.396**
Activity	.412**
Objectivity	.431**
Mental ability—quantitative	.447**
Theoretical values	.457**
Mechanical interests	.468**
Artistic interests	.484**
Literary interests	.496**

$**p < .01$

TABLE 4.27
Multiple Correlations Between Executive Battery Scores and Factor V, Effectiveness as a Public Representative of the Company

Executive Battery Variables	Multiple R
Social leadership	.305**
Reflective	.350**
Cooperative	.401**
Religious values	.418**
Economic values	.445**
Masculine dominance	.466**
Mental ability—quantitative	.483**
Sociability	.498**
Activity	.507**
Composure	.536**

$**p < .01$

TABLE 4.28
Multiple Correlations Between Executive Battery Scores
and Factor VI, Integration of Complex and Diverse Functions
to Move the Organization Forward

Executive Battery Variables	Multiple R
Social leadership	.324**
Optimism	.341**
Emotional control	.461**
Cooperative	.375**

**p < .01

TABLE 4.29
Multiple Correlations Between Executive Battery and
Factor VII, Informed, Competitive Drive to Improve
and Develop the Business

Executive Battery Variables	Multiple R
Social leadership	.427**
Literary interests	.454**
Masculine dominance	.471**
Computational interests	.482**
Clerical interests	.500**
Aesthetic values	.510**
Objectivity	.520**
Emotional control	.535**

**p < .01

TABLE 4.30
**Multiple Correlations Between Executive Battery Scores
and Factor VIII, Organizing and Planning Activities**

Executive Battery Variables	Multiple R
Persuasive interests	.269**
Literary interests	.317**
Social leadership	.356**
Optimism	.394**
Emotional control	.466**
Aesthetic values	.488**
Theoretical values	.482**

**p $<$ .01

TABLE 4.31
**Multiple Correlations Between Executive Battery
and Qualifications Questionnaire Total Score**

Executive Battery Variables	Multiple R
Social leadership	.352**
Dominance	.382**
Optimism	.404**
Emotional control	.420**
Computational interests	.438**
Religious values	.450**
Composure	.461**
Mental ability—linguistic	.476**
Political values	.484**
Activity	.494**
Scientific interests	.504**
Cooperative	.514**
Reflective	.524**
Mental Ability—quantitative	.539**

**p $<$ .01

TABLE 4.32
Multiple Correlations Between Sears Executive Battery of
Psychological Tests and Factorially Defined Criterion Dimensions

Factor	Title	Multiple R
I	Flexible physical, emotional, and intellectual strength that supports and translates into administrative action	.449**
II	Assured independence and ingenuity of intellectual and administrative functioning	.564**
III	Effective (people) leadership	.608**
IV	Administrative sensitivity and strength in setting standards and appraising performance	.496**
V	Effectiveness as a public representative of the company	.536**
VI	Integration of complex and diverse functions to move the organization forward	.375**
VII	Informed, competitive drive to improve and develop the business	.535**
VIII	Organizing and planning activities	.482**
	All items together—total score	.539**

**p $<$ .01

As shown in the summary Table 4.32, the multiple correlations range from .375 to .608. The multiple for all items combined is .539. These are conservative estimates, since all multiples were computed with correlations that were uncorrected for restriction of range.

For all but one criterion, the first variable to enter the multiple is Social Leadership. It contributes heavily to every multiple correlation. Therefore, the quality of social aggressiveness it measures (taking over the dominant leadership role within a group) is one of the most important characteristics associated with long-term executive success. Indeed, social ascendancy and natural assumption of leadership responsibilities may well be one of the enabling characteristics prerequisite to long-term executive effectiveness.

The other variables associated with the syndrome Competitive Leadership do not contribute markedly to the multiple correlations (due to the high intercorrelations among these variables). Therefore, examination of variables that contribute to the multiples provides further insight into qualities necessary for long-term executive effectiveness. The following observations are pertinent:

1. Masculine Dominance enters into six of the nine multiples, as does lack of Computational Interest.
2. Mental Ability variables (notably the Quantitative score) appear in six of the nine multiples.
3. Emotional Strength variables (Composure, Optimism, Stability, and Objectivity) make real a contribution to the findings.
4. Theoretical, Economic, and Aesthetic values enter a number of the multiples. The Aesthetic variable is present in six.

These findings indicate that a broader range of psychological test variables contributes to long-term executive effectiveness than was evident in the earlier data. In Table 4.22 we again see the strong emergence of the psychological variables composing the syndrome Competitive Leadership. Since the average age of predictor data was 21 years, these findings are little less than remarkable.

Seven/Nine Year Follow-up of Managerial Trainees

Three successive groups of managerial trainees were carefully studied. I want to zero in on the performance evaluation data collected at the conclusion of the first year of training.

At the time these performance data were collected, we made unusual efforts to see that this would be done very well. Training coordinator raters were brought into Headquarters for instruction concerning performance evaluation principles and techniques. Later, evaluations were produced under the supervision of Headquarters psychologists who had trained the raters. Nearly a decade later we asked, "Do these early ratings predict long-range career progress and current executive effectiveness?" To answer this question, we sought appropriate objective criteria. Since the subjects all began as management trainees, their starting positions and salary levels were nearly the same. Therefore, the following objective measures of career progress are appropriate criteria for use in a follow-up investigation.

1. Number of job evaluation points awarded to current position held
2. Present compensation per year
3. Midpoint of salary compensation range

Other follow-up criteria were nine scores from the most recent company performance evaluation. With them we restate the question, "Do performance ratings made nearly a decade earlier predict career progress and current effectiveness?"

The data in Table 4.33 say "Yes," early evaluations do predict long-term career progress—and do so resoundingly.

Evaluations made nearly a decade earlier concerning Production of Creative and Original Ideas, Active Problem Solving (through enthusiastic willingness to tackle tough problems and improve on the ideas of others) and Independence of Problem Solving *do* predict long-range career progress, as indicated by two factors:

1. Growth in compensation over time
2. Growth in job responsibility, as measured by job evaluation points assigned to the incumbent's present position and the compensation midpoint of the position achieved.

The early Overall Performance ranking also predicts objective criteria of career progress. Five of the nine current Executive Performance Evaluation dimensions are predicted by three Reactions to Problems ratings. This finding bears emphasis; observations of problem solving, made nearly ten years earlier, predict current executive performance.

Table 4.33 also shows the relationship between six store ratings and long-range career progress. The Final Training Evaluations predict all objective indices of long-range career progress. Both sets of long-term predictors (the three Reaction to Problems variables and Final Store Ratings) are laden with personality content and/or implication. These data indicate that carefully executed performance evaluation ratings predict long-range career progress and do so as well as (or better than) psychological tests. Such findings certainly raise questions as to where we should place our professional efforts.

CONCLUSIONS

I have presented validity studies for a variety of executive groups in which predictors have been significantly related to a wide range of performance criteria, both objective and subjective in nature. It has been demonstrated that personality measures are reliable over a considerable time

TABLE 4.33

Seven-to-Nine-Year Prediction of Career Progress by Earlier Performance Ratings

Long-Range Career Progress / Early Evaluations	No. Job Evaluation Points	Midpoint Compensation	Compensation	1977 Perf. Eval.	Technical Knowledge	Knowledge Application	Administrative Effectiveness	Work Relations	Response to Superiors	Directive Subordinates	Personal Commitment	Overall
Original and creative production of ideas	302**	299**	293**							261*	213*	199*
Active problem solving	292**	290**	325**				206*		205*	304**	235*	223*
Independence in problem resolution	211	197*	200*							236*		
Overall effectiveness ranking	381**	390**	399**							282*	269**	
Store Ratings												
Flexibility		207*								216*		
Technical details	259**	251*	234**									
Oral communications	200*	207*	243**							275*		
Emotional involvement			186*								227	
Aggressiveness												
Attitude	193*	193*	178*					222*	222*	220*	205*	
N =	123	123	124	100	100	100	100	100	100	86	100	100

*p < .05
**p < .01

Source: Prepared by author.

span; tests taken years ago predict both job progress and current performance. From the perspective of this research it is appropriate to conclude that the pervasive academic bias against paper-and-pencil personality assessment is unjustified.

Considerable attention has been given to comparisons of statistical versus clinical validity. While statistical validity is generally stronger, clinical judgments of test data have been shown to be reliable and valid. In study after study, executive performance is predicted by the personality variables Sociability, Social Ascendancy, and Self-Confidence. These appear to be enabling characteristics, prerequisite to effective executive performance. Social ease may be a liberating characteristic, a platform from which other executive skills and abilities are launched.

There are consistent findings, across groups and across various criteria, that point to a generality of validity for the Sears Executive Battery. We are currently pursuing a validity generalization study with Dr. John Hunter of Michigan State University.

We have done two item-factor analyses of the Guilford-Martin Inventories. Although results have not been entirely consistent, similarities exist between factor structures. In both analyses, items realign to form different, sometimes entirely new dimensions—yielding fresh insights into the executive personality. Such factor analyses, plus the use of original and factorial dimensions within various research strategies, are promising avenues for future investigation.

Although the focus of this chapter has been on personality measurement, much evidence points to the important role that mental abilities play in predicting executive behavior. We should know more about how mental ability and personality interact to facilitate effectiveness in various adult roles, including that of the business executive.

Variables related to emotional conditions, while predictive, do not validate as strongly as expected. It is my hunch that the problem may be in the elusive nature of such measurement rather than in the real contribution that emotional health makes to executive effectiveness.

Thus far we have not found sufficient meaning in the content of the Guilford-Martin M Scale to include it in our interpretive repertoire. Guilford labeled this variable Masculinity, and there are differential scoring tendencies for males and females. Yet the many validities of M, for both male and female executive groups, require that we reexamine our position. Several leads are suggested. In both of our item-factor analyses, items from the M scale were realigned. In one factor analysis Guilford's M separated into three scales: Tough-Minded versus Tender-Minded, Squeamishness, and Fearfulness. In both analyses the Tough-Minded versus Tender-Minded items from M realigned with Emotional Stability, changing to something that looks like Emotional Strength. It may be that behavior measured by Guilford's M Scale contains an element of robustness that allows one to take things in stride and to cope with the vicissitudes of a demanding executive career. Such speculative ideas may ultimately provide important insights into executive behavior and emotional strength. These leads should be followed.

Research with structured interviews brought impressive validity results that show this ancient technique to have real vitality. Careful development of format and rigorous training of interviewers hold promise for future personality research.

In an organization where executive growth takes place through job mobility, the Promotability criterion is essential. Such a criterion is also an excellent (though indirect) assessment of current performance; no person will long be considered promotable if he or she is not performing well. That Promotion Potential is strongly predicted in nearly all studies is a finding of major import.

The Reaction to Problems criterion, used successfully in many studies, contains elements related to creativity and ingenuity in problem solving. Several analyses have also produced dimensions that look like the ability to receive and improve on the ideas of others. While this instrument is imperfect and factorially unstable in its present state, a better and more stable version may be used to uncover further knowledge about the nature of the creative or ingenious problem solver.

Finally, research with executives does not exist in the lofty realm of .70 correlations. We live with relationships of much more modest magnitude. Even so, when dealing with an organization the size of Sears, these magnitudes have impact. Considering that all projects used concurrent validity strategies, and recognizing the unavoidable presence of error variance in criterion measurements, the findings reported in this chapter are likely to be underestimates of true validity.

5

Sentence Completion Measures in Personnel Research: The Development and Validation of the Miner Sentence Completion Scales

John B. Miner

At this writing there are three Miner Sentence Completion Scales (MSCSs)—forms H, P, and T—each structured to serve a particular theoretical objective. Research and development with each of these projective scales are at distinctly different stages. The original MSCS, Form H, had its origins in the late 1950s; the other two are of much more recent vintage. Thus, the present discussion will focus much more on Form H, because that is where personnel research, organizational behavior research, and practical experience in psychological assessment have concentrated to the greatest extent. What has been learned from studying Form H should generalize to the other instruments, however; all are very similar in their basic structural properties.

The discussion starts with a historical description of how the various MSCS measures came to be developed, and how items were selected and scoring procedures were devised. This is a previously untold story. Many of the obstacles encountered differ substantially from those traditionally faced by personnel researchers concerned with mental ability and self-report personality measurement. The goal here is to sensitize future researchers to these difficulties, as well as to certain advantages of the sentence completion approach in personnel research, in the hope that knowledge in this area can be expanded without having to "reinvent the wheel" with each new instrument.

A second objective is to update previous treatments of MSCS validity and other psychometric properties. The last comprehensive review of validity research was published in 1978 (Miner 1978a). A great deal has happened since. These findings are considered in the second section of this chapter, along with a review of data from the pre-1978 period. Considerable evidence relating to other psychometric factors has been developed since the last full-scale treatment of this subject (Miner 1978b); this evidence, too, is covered in the second section.

The chapter concludes with an overview of the pluses and minuses of sentence completion measurement as used in industrial and organizational psychology. Many of the considerations in this field differ sizably from those that hold within clinical and other areas of psychology. For that reason, only very limited attention is given to the substantial body of research and experience that has evolved outside the industrial/organizational arena. Furthermore, the conclusions derive, with few exceptions, from a single, long-term research program; in large part they represent the views of one person. This, too, is an important caveat.

HISTORICAL DEVELOPMENT OF THE MSCS INSTRUMENTS

Projective techniques have not always enjoyed a very good press within industrial psychology, although at present a major reconsideration of earlier viewpoints appears to be under way (see Cornelius 1983). Given the traditional stance, it is not surprising that very few psychologists originally educated in the industrial/organizational field have contributed to the development of knowledge regarding the use of projective techniques in personnel research. In contrast, psychologists who originally were educated in the clinical area and personality theory, and later moved into the industrial/organizational field, did not face a similar constraint on their thinking. Thus it was much easier for them to work with projective techniques; they understood them better and valued them more. In the author's opinion, this type of cross-fertilization within psychology is important to its development. Increasing standardization of careers, it is hoped, will not serve to prevent it in the future.

Prior Experience with Projective Techniques

The writer was one of those educated in clinical psychology and personality theory who learned industrial/organizational psychology in large part "on the job," while doing personnel research within a corporate industrial relations setting. In fact, at Clark and Princeton universities, where he did his graduate work in the early 1950s, there was no course work in the industrial area at all.

Early Training and Research

Exposure to projective techniques on any meaningful scale first came in connection with an undergraduate thesis, while working with Silvan Tomkins on a study of alcoholics using the Thematic Apperception Test (TAT) (Miner 1950). Subsequent research with Thelma Alper, culminating in a master's thesis, utilized the Rorschach, TAT, and Tomkins-Horn Picture Arrangement Test (PAT) to study factors associated with the illusory (or empathic) motion phenomenon as produced through tachistoscopic presentations (Miner 1952, 1956).

The writer's experience with projectives beyond the master's level concentrated heavily on the PAT—first in collaborating on the basic standardization research for that instrument (Tomkins & Miner 1957, 1959) and then in a series of studies of various occupational groups. Among the latter were top-level executives and college professors (Miner & Culver 1955; Miner 1962a), tabulating machine operators (Miner 1960a, 1961), dealer-salesmen in the oil business (Miner 1962b), and, considerably later, management consultants (Miner 1971, 1973).

Impressions from Studies of Projectives

These experiences left certain impressions that accumulated to yield a strong preference for sentence completion measures in the personnel context. The Rorschach produces varying numbers of responses (items) from different people. Where the response rate is low, many of the test's measures tend to become unreliable for those individuals. Toward the top of the management hierarchy, protocols usually become very rich—as Piotrowski and Rock (1963) demonstrated at an early point—but in other contexts they can be equally barren, and reliable measurement is hard to obtain. Furthermore, it is difficult, if not impossible, to structure the highly abstract inkblots to focus on specific topics of theoretical and practical concern. Individual administration is time-consuming and cumbersome, thus making the Rorschach less attractive for personnel purposes. Although group procedures are available, they tend to thwart the use of an inquiry, thus reducing both the number of responses and the reliability of scoring.

The TAT can be structured to focus on particular topics, as McClelland, Atkinson, Clark, and Lowell (1976) have done in studying achievement motivation, and it can be group-administered, although the advantages of prompting are thereby lost. The major problem, however, is instrument unreliability, presumably caused, at least in part, by a limited number of cards (items) and, thus, stories (Miner 1980a). This difficulty can be overcome by reverting to the original 20-card test, but then the TAT becomes excessively cumbersome for most personnel purposes.

The Tomkins-Horn PAT was created specifically to cope with many of these problems. It is structured to focus primarily on the work setting, contains 25 items, and is capable of group administration. In addition, the arrangements can be scored in a standardized manner so as to eliminate problems of scorer reliability. In actual use, however, many of the measures contain few items, and instrument reliability therefore remains a problem. Accordingly, higher validities have often been obtained in research using measures that draw upon the verbal responses to the pictures. But if this is to be the primary approach used with the PAT, why not use verbal rather than picture stimuli, thus obtaining more responses (items) for the same investment of time?

Origins of the MSCS Form H

Form H (for hierarchic) is the original measure, known simply as the MSCS for many years until the other forms were developed. The items have not been changed in any way since the original publication in 1961, and the scorable items have not changed since the inception of the instrument in 1957. There have been pressures to adapt to changing times and culture patterns, but to do so would undermine the cumulative nature of the data and research findings.

Training Evaluation at the Atlantic Refining Company

The MSCS came about because, shortly after joining the personnel research division at Atlantic, the writer was asked to teach a management development program in-house for research and development managers at the Philadelphia refinery. R and D management had emerged from a round of appraisals with a less than satisfactory record, largely because too many individuals were more committed to their engineering and scientific specialties than to the managerial work expected of them. The training need was to create or develop an interest in managing, something that we later came to label "motivation to manage," in people whose preferences were for other types of activities. In order to determine whether the course that was designed to deal with this need (Miner 1963, 1975) had achieved its ends, some measure of managerial motivation was required. An extensive literature search at that time yielded nothing of value.

Initial efforts to deal with this problem focused on the development of a special supervisory interest scale for the existing Kuder Preference Record. To a degree these efforts were successful, but the validities, though significant, were low, and there was a lingering concern about the extent to which scores could be influenced by self-interest (Miner 1960b).

Ultimately a decision was made to develop a sentence completion measure. A projective instrument seemed the most appropriate way to eliminate or at least reduce self-interest bias and to get at unconscious motives. We considered these factors particularly important in this instance because hierarchic managing is an activity about which our democratic society as a whole is decidedly ambivalent and which is by no means always viewed as socially desirable. For reasons noted previously, other projective measures were considered less attractive than a sentence completion approach. With such in instrument it would be possible to focus on a limited set of variables and obtain responses to a sizable number of items, thus, it was hoped, obtaining sufficient reliability.

Item Writing and Subjective Item Analysis

For purposes of item selection, 60 items, largely based on the writer's personal impressions of managerial values in the company involved, were written. The underlying model at this point was that of a generalized managerial interest or motive along the lines of the construct embodied in the Kuder measure. Although components of that model were in mind, they were not articulated to the point of specific subscale components. At this stage the theory is best described as one of the Atlantic Refining Company in the late 1950s, as experienced by a young psychologist with a strong psychoanalytic orientation. It became something much more general than that, but that came later.

The 60 items were administered to some 21 members of the company's corporate personnel department who were housed on the same floor as the writer. Given the fact that the hierarchic levels and general perceptions of performance for these individuals were known, it was possible to conduct a rough item analysis against the external criterion of managerial success. The best items were those that elicited a range of responses both positive and negative, were clearly understood by respondents (while operating within the intended construct domain), and discriminated so that successful and less successful managers responded as hypothesized.

In analyzing items along these lines there were two basic sources of variation: the item or stem itself and the particular scoring system applied to it. In traditional item analysis with multiple-choice alternatives, only the items themselves can vary. With projective measures of this kind, a given response to an item can be designated positive, neutral, or negative, depending on the scoring system in use. Everything can vary, and that is what the term "subjective item analysis" implies. One attempts to end with a set of items and a standardized scoring procedure for them that provide a range of responses (large standard deviations), adequate construct measurements, and maximal discriminations against external criteria, but the ultimate test of the adequacy of these judgments comes only from subsequent validation research.

In the case of Form H, the first pass yielded 40 items that seemed to meet the criteria and a scoring system for them. These items were constituted as a single measure of managerial interest or motivation, and were used in a pre-post design with experimental and control groups to evaluate the training program. The results were positive for the program, and indirectly for the instrument (Miner 1960c, 1965). Fortunately, later studies substantiated this initial conclusion.

Subscales and Ties to Bureaucratic Theory

In working with the instrument it became increasingly apparent that the different constructs included could be differentiated in terms of subscales. This was done entirely on a conceptual, not a statistical, basis. Items that appeared to relate to different aspects of the managerial role were grouped together. There was one set dealing with authority figures that related to upward hierarchic communications, another set dealt with horizontal relationships in the form of competition, and a third focused on the exercise of power downward to subordinates. Because there were a number of competition items, a decision was made to separate those concerned with games and sports, and treat them as a distinct subscale. The results of these initial differentiations were the Authority Figures, Competitive Games, Competitive Situations, and Imposing Wishes subscales.

Another set of items seemed to relate to the masculinity-femininity variable that was widely included in psychological measures at that time, and still is (see Ghiselli 1971; Hofstede 1980 for examples). Initially this was labeled Masculine Role; somewhat later, with changing values, it became Assertive Role, but the items remained the same. The finding from the University of Michigan leadership research that effective managers behave in ways that clearly differentiate them from their subordinates (Kahn & Katz 1953) provided guidance for the creation of another subscale, Standing out from Group. A number of items dealing with basic communication and decision-making tasks in managerial work constituted the Routine Administrative Functions subscale.

Each of the seven subscales contained five items. An additional five items did not fit meaningfully in any subscale category. These were treated as fillers and not scored. When the MSCS was published in 1961, they were replaced with new items intended to hide the purpose of measurement even further and to provide bases for clinical insights. They remain unscored. The number of items per subscale was held to five so that pattern scoring for rares could be carried out along the lines initially proposed by Tomkins (Tomkins & Miner 1957). In an era when computers were not in widespread use, the prospect of developing norms for scoring through hand tabulations of item combinations numbering more than five was singularly unattractive.

The subscales were titled as they were to avoid the implication that unitary motives were involved. Conceptually we had six types of role prescriptions considered to be important for managerial work in general, and corresponding motivational forces that might be expected to energize those roles. Since the starting point was roles rather than motives, and the subjective item analysis utilized an external rather than an internal criterion, a number of motives could combine to produce scores (ranging from -5 to +5) on any subscale. Thus, a high score on Authority Figures could reflect a very positive orientation toward people in general or toward those in positions of authority only. For the purposes at hand it did not matter.

At the time the MSCS was developed and the subscales were identified, the writer had very little knowledge of bureaucratic theory as proposed by Weber (1968) and extended by sociologists such as Selznick (1949), Gouldner (1954), Merton (1940), and Blau (1974). The basic stimulus in choosing items came from the Atlantic Refining Company as the writer experienced it, a clearly very hierarchic organization. That this company turned out to have much in common with other bureaucratic systems was in fact fortuitous, although those with a broader comprehension of the (particularly sociological) literature would certainly have predicted it. In any event the MSCS Form H, has turned out to be a measure of at least some of the motivational forces that propel managerial work in bureaucratic systems.

Origins of the MSCS Form H (Multiple-Choice Version)

For a number of years the writer recorded each new response to an item on one of a number of large sheets divided so as to separate the lists of positive, neutral or noncommittal, and negative responses obtained. Under increasing pressure from a publisher who had a test in print, but no possible way of responding to requests for information on what to do with it, the sheets finally became a scoring guide (Miner 1964).

The RPI Research

Although the writer remained firmly committed to the traditional free-response sentence completion format, others became somewhat impatient with it. Learning to score according to the guide took some time, and certain people never did seem to become very good at it. Even with substantial experience a record usually took about ten minutes to score. All in all, the free-response approach seemed excessively cumbersome, especially when it would be so easy to develop multiple-choice answer alternatives.

This line of reasoning led a group at Rensselaer Polytechnic Institute to construct a forced-choice form of the MSCS (Steger, Kelley, Chouiniere, & Goldenbaum 1975). Three alternative answers were provided, in most cases "like," "indifferent," and "dislike." Also, 8 of the 35 stems were altered to varying degrees, to make them more student-oriented. This instrument yielded a total score correlation with the original MSCS of .68. Subscale correlations ranged from .33 to .74, with a median of .40. Not surprisingly, the loss of the projective element inherent in the new format produced a sizable inflation of scores on all the subscales that totaled an increase of almost ten points overall. When the alternatives were so clearly presented, respondents no longer selected negative answers with the same frequency.

Instrument Development

Prodded by these results, the writer began work on a multiple-choice MSCS of his own. In an attempt to hold down score inflation, actual responses of a positive, neutral, and negative nature taken from previously obtained records were used, rather than the like-indifferent-dislike format. There were two responses of each type, making a total of six for each stem. The six were randomized. No changes in the MSCS, other than the addition of the six alternatives to each stem, were made.

Subsequent findings indicate that score inflation remains a problem with this multiple-choice version of the MSCS, but not nearly to the extent found in the RPI study. The amount of inflation varies in different groups, ranging from something over $+1$ to over $+5$ (Miner 1977a). Total score correlations between the two versions of .38, .56, and .68 have been obtained. Subscale correlations have varied from sample to sample, but the research to date provides no basis for concluding that the Imposing Wishes and Routine Administrative Functions subscales of the multiple-choice MSCS measure the same thing as subscales in the parent measure (Butler, Lardent, & Miner 1983). For the remaining five subscales, correlations ranging from .29 to .63 have been obtained. In general, this attempt to construct a multiple-choice measure from sentence-completion origins appears to have produced much the same type of results as have other similar efforts (Shouval, Duek, & Ginton 1975). A supplement to the original MSCS scoring guide has been developed to provide information on scoring the multiple-choice version (Miner 1977b).

Origins of the MSCS, Form P

Experience with the original MSCS clearly indicated that its effectiveness was limited to a very specific domain, the managerial component of bureaucratic organizations (Miner 1978a). At the same time it was apparent that not all organizational contexts are bureaucratic. In fact, Weber (1968) described certain other forms, including patrimonial or traditional structures, such as kingdoms and family enterprises, and charismatic systems of a quasi-religious nature. This suggested that it might well be fruitful to develop motivational measures for contexts beyond the hierarchic.

Theoretical Efforts

In the modern world three additional types of systems occur with sufficient frequency to justify developing measures for them. Professional systems as found in professional firms and professional components of larger bureaucratic organizations are one. Task systems of the kind entrepreneurs and commission sales people operate in are another. Group systems, such as many voluntary organizations and the autonomous work groups of sociotechnical systems theory, are the third.

In 1975 the writer began to devote himself to creating theories of the key role requirements of these systems. Here, in contrast with the original MSCS, comprehensive theory definitely did precede instrument development. The results of this theoretical effort evolved rather slowly (Miner 1977a, 1980b, 1982). They did, however, provide an underpinning for the creation of additional MSCS forms.

The Oliver Organization Description Questionnaire

At various points, as research with Form H developed, questions arose as to whether a particular organizational context was within the theoretical domain of the instrument. Such matters came to the forefront as theory development spread to other types of organizational systems. As a result, research was undertaken by John Oliver, in connection with his doctoral dissertation at Georgia State, to develop a means of determining the extent to which a particular situation was characterized by each of the four types of structures.

Working from theory, he developed multiple-choice items descriptive of aspects of the four systems and administered them to groups of people whose organizational environments seemed to represent prototypes of the four ideal types. Through item analysis, responses were identified that best discriminated one type from the other three. The resulting scales were then cross-validated on new samples (Oliver 1981, 1982). As a result of this research, it is now possible to establish whether a domain appropriate to each of the various MSCS forms is present. The four organizational system-type constructs are operationalized as variables with possible scores ranging from 0 to 15 in the OODQ. The reliabilities of these measures are in the .80s.

The Development of Form P

The professional theory specifies five major role requirements for professionals working in professional systems. One of these obviously relates to the acquisition of knowledge, since it is the essence of being a professional that the person has developed specialized technical capabilities. Professional norms also require that decisions be made independently, on the basis of expertise; without this requirement there would be no assurance that the specialized knowledge acquired would be put to use. Also, for usage to occur, clients must be obtained. Professionals must achieve sufficient status so that people are attracted to them and want to avail themselves of their services. Furthermore, the client relationship is supposed to be a helping one. It is the duty of professionals to act in ways that serve their clients' best interests. Finally, concepts such as that of a lifetime career imply a strong commitment to the profession that binds a person to the work and to the professional norms that govern it. These five role requirements are activated by motivational patterns appropriate to them. Acquiring Knowledge, Independent Action, Accepting Status, Providing Help, and Professional Commitment are the subscale names.

Working from this theoretical base, 12 items were written as candidates for each of the five subscales. The resulting 60-item measure was completed by 20 faculty members and advanced doctoral students in the management department at Georgia State. As in the personnel department at Atlantic, the writer had information on success indexes such as academic rank, publications, professional reputation, and the like for these individuals. Thus the data needed to carry out subjective item analyses were present. When these analyses were done, it proved possible to construct subscales containing eight items each that appeared to discriminate between more and less successful professionals. These items were randomized to produce the 40-item Form P. No filler items were included in this instrument.

Subsequent research on a much larger group of management professors provided evidence that the initial item selection process had worked as anticipated (Miner 1980c). The scoring guide for Form P was constructed by using responses obtained from the faculty samples (Miner 1981). As yet no multiple-choice version of Form P has been developed. Experience to date has been limited to university faculties, and it is felt that a broader range of experience with professionals of all types is needed to select alternatives.

Form T and Beyond

Form T, dealing with the task domain, has been developed but has not yet been cross-validated. Form G, dealing with the group domain, has not yet been constructed. When it is created, the developmental work will in all likelihood focus on the autonomous work groups of sociotechnical theory. In fact, certain preliminary work has already been done in that area.

Form T and Achievement Motivation Theory

The theoretical underpinning for Form T comes from McClelland's (1961, 1962) concept of the achievement situation. The theory states that there are five situational characteristics that elicit achievement striving from those with a strong need for achievement, thus producing successful performance in an entrepreneurial context. These characteristics serve the same function as did role prescriptions and norms in the hierarchic and professional contexts.

First, the situation is one where people can attain success through their own efforts and experience a feeling of personal accomplishment. In the original theory the second situational aspect was the presence of a moderate degree of difficulty and risk, where people can feel they have accomplished something without the chances of success being so poor that achievement satisfaction is unlikely. Atkinson and Raynor (1974) argue, however, that there is likely to be a general tendency to risk avoidance because achievement-motivated individuals want to be sure of staying in the achievement situation. A series of studies by Brockhaus (1980a, 1980b) and Brockhaus and Nord (1979) indicate that entrepreneurs who succeed are not high risk takers. On the evidence to date, therefore, we are inclined to take the view that risk avoidance is the more likely phenomenon. The third requirement is that the situation provide clear and unambiguous feedback on the degree of success the person's efforts have produced.

In addition to these three major aspects of the achievement situation, two others play a less significant role. The presence of an opportunity for innovation makes it possible for people to clearly identify and be identified with their own work. A requirement for thinking ahead, planning, and anticipating future possibilities constantly stimulates the achievement need.

Developing Form T

The objective in constructing the MSCS Form T was to tap motivational patterns relevant to these five situational requirements via the sentence completion method. The subscales are Self-Achievement, Avoiding Risks, Feedback of Results, Personal Innovation, and Planning for the Future. The major research focus has been on entrepreneurs, although of course other occupational groups fall in the task domain (see Oliver 1981).

Preliminary research indicated that Form H was not applicable to entrepreneurs, although the Authority Figures and Assertive Role subscales did show some relationships to the development of adaptive, growth-oriented firms (Smith & Miner 1983). Thus, the need for a different measure was apparent. Also, there have been some prior efforts to use sentence completion measures to study achievement motivation (Singh 1979). The results of these efforts have been mixed, but in no case has an instrument focused on the full spectrum of the achievement situation as Form T attempts to do.

While forms H and P emerged out of extended organizational experiences of the writer, this type of experiential background was available only to a very limited degree for the development of Form T. Feeling somewhat less certain in constructing possible items for Form T, the writer started out with more of them, as a hedge against the possibility that many might prove rather poor. The preliminary measure contained 75 items, 15 for each subscale.

This instrument was completed by 17 entrepreneurs, most of whom had survived and prospered in that role. Because the group as a whole was quite successful, it was not possible to carry out subjective item analyses within this group. Accordingly, comparisons were made with a group of 20 students in entrepreneurship and business policy classes who were known to be currently employed in positions that clearly did not fit in the task domain. This comparison sample averaged 28 years of age, much younger than the entrepreneurs, and this fact may have introduced some confounding. Nevertheless, the less successful people in prior analyses to develop forms H and P were also younger. In any event, five subscales of eight items each were constructed. Discriminations appear to be very good for Self-Achievement, Avoiding Risks, Feedback of Results, and Personal Innovation; they are somewhat less good for Planning for the Future. So far, at least, the data support a risk-avoidance rather than risk-taking hypothesis for the entrepreneurs.

Arrangements are now in process to carry out cross-validation research with the new Form T. No formal scoring guide is currently in existence, and any multiple-choice version must await much greater experience with the measure.

Beyond Form T

Oliver (1981, 1982) found that autonomous work groups describe their organizational context as that of a group-based system. Theoretical work has been done to specify some of the relevant role requirements and motivational patterns for such a system (Miner 1980b). However, other research suggests that the development of Form G may not be a straightforward matter.

A study by Beldt (1978) in which the multiple-choice Form H was administered to all managers in two sociotechnically organized and two traditional bureaucratically organized plants in the same company reveals some unexpected results. There was evidence that the sociotechnical plants were more effective and that they had fewer managers, as the underlying theory would anticipate, but, as shown in Table 5.1, they also had managers with

TABLE 5.1
MSCS Form H (Multiple Choice), Scores for Managers in
Sociotechnical and Traditional Plants in the Same Company

MSCS Measures	SocioTechnical Plants (N = 9)	Traditional Plants (N = 26)	Significance of Difference
Total score	9.00	3.04	< .05
Authority figures	1.44	.04	< .05
Competitive games	2.33	1.31	< .05
Competitive situations	1.44	.77	—
Assertive role	1.00	.04	—
Imposing wishes	.33	.12	—
Standing out from group	1.56	.81	—
Routine administrative functions	.89	.12	—

Source: Adapted from Beldt 1978.

higher Form H scores. Thus the hierarchic superstructure above the autonomous work groups was characterized by stronger motivation to manage in those plants that in an overall sense were characterized by less bureaucracy. A number of hypotheses can be advanced to explain this finding, but at the moment we do not know with any certainty why it occurred.

However, this same study yielded some additional unexpected conclusions regarding the values of autonomous work group members using the Personal Values Questionnaire (England 1975; England, Olsen, & Agarwal 1971). In these groups, company owners and stockholders were valued less than in the traditional plants, but blue-collar workers and labor unions also were valued less. Not surprisingly where multi-skilling is in effect, skill was valued more in the sociotechnical context, but compassion and tolerance were valued less—contrary to most organization development values. Individuality and risk were valued less in the group context, but success was valued more. These findings suggest a more complex set of dynamics in group-based systems than might have been anticipated from much that has been written in this area to date. The need for new research and new measures—among them, it is hoped, Form G—is apparent.

HOW GOOD ARE THE MSCS MEASURES?

The instruments that have been developed are very similar in format. All three scales were constructed in much the same way and utilize structured stems of a kind that have been found to be particularly productive in research on sentence completion measurement (Turnbow & Dana 1981). There are some variations in the number of scorable items and items per subscale that might well operate to make forms P and T somewhat more reliable than Form H. Since most of the research is on Form H, it may be appropriate to anticipate somewhat better results with the newer instruments. Nevertheless, in an overall sense it seems likely that all the MSCS forms will turn out to have similar psychometric properties. The exception, where this need not be the case, is validity. The scales are intended to measure different properties and the items differ accordingly.

Validity Considerations

The great majority of validity research has involved Form H and was conducted without benefit of the OODQ. Thus decisions as to whether a particular study was conducted within an appropriate domain are to some degree problematic. Nevertheless, on balance, Form H does appear to have been applied within hierarchic systems in a large number of cases. There were also some cases where the context was clearly not hierarchic and where, therefore, validity would not be expected to be obtained.

Results of Individual Studies

Table 5.2 summarizes 26 validity studies with the MSCS Form H that are believed to have been conducted within an appropriate domain. The results are consistently significant in the predicted direction for total scores. The median validity coefficient in those instances where correlations are reported is .35. A number of the studies contain aspects, such as subjects taken from many different organizations and somewhat suspect criteria, that would be expected to lower this median figure. Total score correlations in the .40s can be expected from sound validations carried out among managers within a single firm.

TABLE 5.2
Validation Within the Theoretical Domain

N	Criterion	Design	Total MSCS Score	Authority Figures	Competitive Games	Competitive Situations	Assertive Role	Imposing Wishes	Standing out from Group	Routine Administrative Functions
1. R and D managers-oil company-Miner (1965)										
100	Grade level	concurrent	<.01	<.01	—	<.01	—	—	—	—
81	Performance rating	concurrent	<.05	<.01	—	<.05	—	<.01	—	—
81	Potential rating	concurrent	<.01	<.05	<.05	<.01	—	<.05	<.01	—
2. R and D managers-oil company-Miner (1965)										
49	Grade level change	predictive	<.05	<.01	<.05	—	—	—	<.01	—
3. Marketing managers-oil company-Miner (1965)										
81	Grade level change	predictive	<.01	<.01	—	<.01	—	<.01	—	—
4. R and D and marketing managers-oil company-Miner (1965)										
61	Performance rating	predictive	<.01	<.01	<.05	<.01	<.01	<.01	—	—
5. Managers-department store-Miner (1965)										
70	Grade level	concurrent	<.01	—	—	<.05	—	<.05	—	<.05
70	Performance rating	concurrent	—	not reported		—	—	<.05	—	<.05
70	Potential rating	concurrent	<.05	—	—	—	—	<.05	—	<.05
6. School administrators-large city-Miner (1967)										
82	Grade level	concurrent	—	—	—	—	—	—	—	<.05
82	Compensation	concurrent	<.05	<.05	—	—	—	—	<.05	<.01
82	Performance rating	concurrent	<.01	<.05	<.05	<.01	<.01	—	<.05	—
82	Potential rating	concurrent	<.01	—	—	<.01	<.05	—	<.05	—
7. Graduate students in business-University of Oregon-Miner (1968)										
106	Choice of managerial career	concurrent	<.01	<.01	<.05	<.01	<.01	<.01	<.05	<.01
8. Undergraduate students in business-University of Oregon-Miner & Smith (1969)										
108	Choice of managerial career	concurrent	<.05	—	—	<.01	—	—	—	—
9. Scientists and engineers-government R and D laboratory-Gantz, Erickson, & Stephenson (1977)										
117	Peer rating-supervisory potential	concurrent	<.01	not reported		—	—	—	—	—
10. Scientists, engineers, and managers-government R and D laboratory-Lacey (1974)										
95	Promotion into management	predictive	<.05	—	<.05	.05	—	<.05	—	—
11. Female managers-department store-Miner (1974a)										
44	Grade level	concurrent	<.05	—	—	—	—	<.05	<.05	<.05
12. Undergraduate students in a simulated bureaucratic organization-Western Michigan University-Miner, Rizzo, Harlow, & Hill (1974)										
415	Promotion into management	concurrent	<.01	—	<.05	<.05	—	—	<.05	<.01

Table (continued). Studies of managerial motivation — validity findings for the Miner Sentence Completion Scale. Significance levels reported for each subscale.

#	N	Sample / Measure	Type							
13.		Undergraduate students–RPI–Steger, Kelley, Chouiniere, & Goldenbaum (1975)								
	40	Selection as fraternity president	concurrent	—	.05	—	—	.05	—	.05
14.		Personnel and industrial relations managers–Miner (1976)								
	142	Position level	concurrent	.01	.05	—	—	.05	—	—
15.		Managers–various companies–Miner (1976)								
	395	Position level	concurrent	.01	.01	.01	.01	—	—	.05
16.		Personnel and industrial relations managers–Miner & Miner (1976)								
	101	Composite success measure	concurrent	.01	.01	—	—	—	—	—
17.		Undergraduate students–Georgia State–Singleton (1976)								
	190	Selection for student office	concurrent	.01	—	.05	—	.01	—	.05
18.		Managers–textile company–Southern (1976)								
	50	Grade level	concurrent	.01	not reported	—	—	—	—	—
19.		Managers–textile company–Southern (1976)								
	37	Grade level	concurrent	.05	not reported	—	—	—	—	—
20.		Graduate students in business–Georgia State–Miner (1977a)								
	47	Promotion into management	concurrent	.05	not reported	—	—	.05	—	—
21.		Hospital chief executive officers–Black (1981)								
	729	Compensation	concurrent	.05	—	.01	—	.05	—	—
22.		Graduate students in business–Georgia State–Miner & Crane (1981)								
	56	Managerial orientation	concurrent	.05	—	—	—	—	—	—
23.		Army officer candidates–Butler, Lardent, & Miner (1983)								
	251	Graduation from Officer Candidate School	predictive	.01	—	—	.05	.05	.05	.05
24.		U.S. Military Academy students–Butler, Lardent, & Miner (1983)								
	502	Graduation	predictive	.01	—	.05	.05	—	.05	—
25.		Managers–numerous firms–Miner & Berman (1983)								
	140	Promotion to top level mostly (CEO)	concurrent	—	.05	—	.05	—	—	.01
26.		Undergraduate students–Clemson–Stahl, Grigsby, & Gulati (1983)								
	57	Selection as fraternity or sorority president	concurrent	.01	—	.01	.05	.01	.01	.05
			not reported	—	—	.01	.01	—	—	.01

Notes: Findings reported only if significant and then as p <.05 and <.01.
Significance levels reported are for correlation coefficients or for comparisons between group means, as appropriate.
Source: Adapted from Miner 1978a.

It should be noted that one study (Quigley 1979) was not included in Table 5.2 in spite of the fact that a total score correlation as high as .34 and three significant subscale correlations were obtained within a domain that appeared to be appropriate for Form H. It was a concurrent study conducted in various district offices of a state health agency. There was an obvious mixing of hierarchic and professional systems involved, and without some measure such as the OODQ to differentiate the two, it seems best not to give too much weight to these data. In fact, the Quigley study was a major factor prompting the conduct of the OODQ research.

Generally, in Table 5.2 significance is obtained with a specific subscale less frequently than for the total score, and the correlations are somewhat lower for the subscales. The most consistent subscale validities are obtained with Competitive Situations and Imposing Wishes. Next come Authority Figures and Routine Administrative Functions, followed by Competitive Games, Assertive Role, and Standing out from Group. No subscale yields significance (p < .05) in less than 29 percent of the instances where its score is related to a criterion. The two most effective subscales double this figure.

Although most of the research is concurrent, there are six predictive studies included. In general the predictive studies are just as likely to yield substantial validity as the concurrent ones. Also, several studies employed the multiple-choice version of Form H (Black 1981; Butler, Lardent, & Miner 1983; Stahl, Grigsby, & Gulati 1983) or some other multiple-choice approach (Steger, Kelley, Chouiniere, & Goldenbaum 1975). The validities in these instances are much better than the writer would have anticipated from the correlations obtained between free-response and multiple-choice versions.

Studies conducted outside the theoretical domain with Form H have, almost without exception, failed to yield significant results in a positive direction. Many of these studies have been done among members of professional systems, such as university faculties and a consulting firm structured to emulate the major law firms. However, much the same pattern of results (or, rather, lack thereof) has also been obtained in group systems, in task systems, and in the nonmanagerial components of hierarchic systems—among sales personnel, for instance. Occasionally these validity studies outside the domain yield significant subscale correlations, but no significant total score relationships have been found. When the subscales do produce significance, it appears to be a random event; there is no evidence of clustering on any particular subscale.

Table 5.2 does not contain the results of the one validity study carried out with Form P (Miner 1980c). In this instance 21 criteria, covering various aspects of compensation, academic rank, publications, participation in professional organizations, and position type, were used. Significant positive total score correlations with 17 of the criteria were obtained, the median value being .35. In general the nonsignificant values involved minor criteria. Total professional compensation was correlated .55, and academic rank .51, with Form P. All of the subscales yielded significant correlations with over 33 percent of the criterion measures. In contrast, when Form H was employed against the same criteria, there were only two significant total score correlations—one positive and one negative—and a smattering of subscale relationships.

Comprehensive Evaluations

A review of validity research concludes that projective techniques have fared poorly (Reilly & Chao 1982). However, this review appears slanted toward mental ability tests, relies heavily on Kinslinger (1966) for its assessment of research with projective techniques, and is very incomplete in its coverage of more recent research on projectives, including the MSCS. A much more comprehensive analysis by Cornelius (1983) presents a totally different picture. Cornelius analyzes the pre-1966 research in detail and finds that the great majority of the methodologically sound studies (16 of 20) report positive results, many with substantial validity coefficients. His review of subsequent research is equally favorable, and focuses on the particularly positive findings with the MSCS, as did Korman (1968). Even the Guion and Gottier (1965) review, which covers roughly the same period as Kinslinger (1966), concludes favorably for projectives in the personnel research context.

Perhaps more important is an analysis of the MSCS research using validity generalization techniques carried out by Nathan and Alexander (1982). This analysis was restricted to the free-response version of Form H and did not include studies that used undergraduates as subjects. As a result the number of studies within and outside the domain included in the analysis was less than what is usually found in validity generalization research. Nevertheless, the total score, Competitive Situations, and Imposing Wishes measures showed strong validity in the manner posited by the theory. Authority Figures and Competitive Games also evidenced strong validity, although the support is slightly less pronounced. Routine Administrative Functions provides somewhat ambiguous results; the subscale operates in a manner that is basically consistent with the theory, but the data are insufficient to reach definite conclusions. Assertive Role and Standing out from Group proved to be valid both within and outside the domain in these studies. Although not identical with the subscale conclusions derived directly from Table 5.2, these findings provide additional support for the validity of the MSCS Form H and for the theory underlying it.

Reliability Considerations

There are three aspects of the reliability question that need to be considered: scorer reliability, test-retest, and internal consistency. Since with projective techniques each of these indexes raises a different set of issues, each is considered separately.

Scorer Reliability

Table 5.3 presents the correlational results of all formal scorer reliability studies known to the writer; all involve Form H. In the case of the analyses involving experienced scorers, both members of the pair had received training in scoring the MSCS (or, in the case of the writer, had developed the scoring system). In the other six cases it appears that there was no training other than study of the scoring guide. Training normally emphasized feedback on results and discussion of the rationales for scoring difficult items. In some instances the training was given face-to-face, and in other instances there was a written exchange. Both appear to work equally well.

Among the experienced scorers the coefficients for the total score range from .86 to .97, with a median of .92. The two values in the .80s involve the same individual. It appears that some people find it easier to reach and maintain accurate scoring levels than do others. As in most things, individual differences do operate. Because of a lack of data, it is difficult to make a direct total score comparison for the less experienced scorers, but a median coefficient of around .80 seems likely. The median subscale value for the experienced scorers is .91 and for the less experienced, .76.

What this says is that scorers can, and should, obtain agreement levels reaching into the .90s. This conclusion is consistent with findings with other sentence completion instruments (Fuller, Parmelee, & Carroll 1982; Rootes, Moras, & Gordon 1980; Waugh 1981). Although in formal studies with the MSCS this has been accomplished most frequently with some training beyond study of the scoring guide, the writer's experience is that some individuals can achieve similar levels simply by intensive study of the rationales and examples provided. In fact, several of the scorers in Table 5.3 noted as experienced achieved total score correlations in the .88 to .92 range prior to receiving any feedback at all. There is reason to believe,

TABLE 5.3
MSCS Scorer Reliability Data

Source	N	Both Scorers Experienced	Total MSCS Score	Authority Figures	Competitive Games	Competitive Situations	Assertive Role	Imposing Wishes	Standing out from Group	Routine Administrative Functions
Miner (1976)	15	X	.91	.84	.86	.96	.94	.81	.79	.87
Brief, Aldag, & Chacko (1977) a)	101		not	.71	.85	.72	.74	.71	.58	.69
b)	101		report-	.77	.91	.60	.81	.66	.68	.76
c)	101		ed	.77	.86	.66	.79	.70	.65	.71
Miner (1978b) a)	12	X	.95	.92	.98	.89	.86	.83	.94	.96
b)	12	X	.91	.98	.95	.95	.91	.66	.90	.97
c)	10	X	.88	.76	.88	.91	.82	.84	.82	.88
d)	10	X	.97	.96	.94	.91	.97	.78	.97	.97
e)	10	X	.86	.86	.95	.89	.91	.85	.90	.90
Quigley (1979)	10	X	.97	.96	.92	.98	.98	.81	.90	.97
Bartol, Anderson, & Schneier (1980, 1981)	25		not reported	range from not reported	.61 to .91- (only one	average .83 value below	.75)			
Miner & Smith (1983)	23		.80	not reported						
Butler, Lardent, & Miner (1983)	20		.94	.89	.86	.90	.88	.91	.73	.81
Miner & Berman (1983)	140	X	.94	.83	.93	.87	.90	.82	.91	.90

Source: Prepared by author.

however, that self-teaching may in some cases fall short of what is possible. This becomes evident as one looks more closely at the results for certain of the presumed less experienced scorers as given in Table 5.3.

What appears to happen is that certain individuals check less with the scoring guide and come to introduce a positive bias into their scoring. In essence the scorer does what the multiple-choice approach often does: he or she introduces a certain amount of score inflation. Negative scorings are not given as often as they should be. In Table 5.3 the Brief, Aldag, and Chacko (1977) data exhibit total score inflations for one scorer over the other two of +3.87 and +3.62. The Bartol, Anderson, and Schneier (1980, 1981) inflation is +2.35, using the experienced scorer data from Miner and Smith (1983) as a base. The Butler, Lardent, and Miner (1983) inflation is +2.60, despite the total score reliability coefficient of .94. All of these differences are statistically significant. When both scorers are experienced, no significant differences of any kind have been found.

How this inflation can lead to serious misinterpretation is illustrated by one of the Bartol, Anderson, and Schneier (1980) studies. The results obtained were interpreted as indicating a reversal of the decline in motivation to manage that had been found among business school students over the period from the early 1960s to the early 1970s (Miner 1974b, 1974c). This reversal was dated 1977. At the same time Miner and Smith (1982) found only a leveling off of the decline, not a reversal, as of 1980. When 23 records from the Bartol, Anderson, and Schneier data bank were rescored by the writer, the total score correlation of .80 and mean score inflation of +2.35 previously noted were found (Miner & Smith 1983). It was possible to assess the effects of the score inflation on certain data available from the University of Maryland over a nine-year period (see Table 5.4). When the appropriate correction is made, no reversal, only stabilization, is apparent, thus putting the Bartol, Anderson, and Schneier (1980) data in complete accord with those of Miner and Smith (1982).

Bartol, Anderson, and Schneier also found a sizable and significant sex difference in scores favoring males was reported, something that prior research on business students had also indicated (Miner 1974b). But by 1980 Miner and Smith (1982) no longer found such a difference. Within the scorer reliability sample of 23, the original total scores were +.31 for the females and +1.80 for the males—consistent with the overall finding of a substantial sex difference. Yet on rescoring, the writer found values of -1.15 for the females and -1.70 for the males (Miner & Smith 1983). This suggests that for some reason the score inflation was over twice as great for the males, producing an artificial sex difference. Correcting the scores ac-

TABLE 5.4
Shifts in MSCS Total Scores at the University of Maryland Without and With Correction for Scoring Inflation

	Total MSCS Score				
	1969 (N = 122)	Significance of Difference	1972 (N = 73)	Significance of Difference	1977 (N = 108)
1977 data Uncorrected	.80	<.05	-.96	<.01	1.90
1977 data Corrected	.80	< .05	-.96	NS	-.45

Source: Prepared by author.

cordingly puts the Bartol, Anderson, and Schneier (1980) data once again in complete accord with those of Miner and Smith (1982). Clearly, the fact that the MSCS can be scored with a very high level of consistency does not mean that it always is.

Test-Retest Reliability

Many of the data on test-retest reliability derive from control groups employed in studies carried out to evaluate training programs intended to raise levels of motivation to manage (Miner 1965). For this reason the intervals between administrations are longer than might otherwise be desired for a reliability study, approximately ten weeks. In different samples the total score reliability coefficients range from .68 to .84, with a median of .83. Subscale coefficients range from .44 to .63, with a median of .48.

In contrast, the test-retest correlations obtained among experimental subjects (whose mean scores were raised by the training) were consistently lower, often significantly so. This same type of finding has emerged from work with Fiedler's (1967) Least Preferred Coworker measure (Rice 1978). On the evidence it now appears that reliability is not adequately determined when certain kinds of training experiences intervene between testings.

The findings noted previously are all for the free-response Form H. Stahl, Grigsby, and Gulati (1983) conducted a similar analysis with the multiple-choice version, the retest occurring at a more appropriate, three-week interval. The subscale correlations range from .41 to .69, with a median of .63. The total score figure is .78. Whether the somewhat better subscale performance of the multiple-choice version is due to the shorter time between testings, and thus the decreased opportunity for valid change, or some aspect of the test itself is not known.

In any event the test-retest reliability of the MSCS measures as a whole appears to be entirely satisfactory, consistent with the scorer reliability data and the number of items used, 35. In contrast, the five-item subscales appear suitable primarily for group analyses. Without supporting data from other sources, the subscale reliabilities are not sufficient to justify individual, clinical interpretations of specific scores.

Internal Consistency Reliability

Cornelius (1983), in discussing sentence completion measures, notes that good internal consistency reliability can be, and often is, obtained. For example, Waugh (1981), using a sentence completion index of ego development, found corrected split-half coefficients of .91 and .79 in two different clinical samples. Yet it appears certain that internal consistency reliability of this kind is not characteristic of the MSCS measures.

An analysis of the corrected odd-even reliability of Form P yielded a total score value of .59 and subscale coefficients ranging from .02 to .43, with a median of .31 (Miner 1980c). Stahl, Grigsby, and Gulati (1983), working with the multiple-choice version of Form H, found subscale coefficient alpha values of .00 to .41, with a median of .16. The total score figure is .57. There is no reason to believe that other samples and MSCS measures would yield substantially improved results. One reason is that the item selection process concentrated on discrimination between external criterion groups, rather than between high-scoring and low-scoring groups on the internal measures themselves. In short, the measures have been constructed with reference to external validity but not internal consistency. It is not surprising that the overall outcome reflects this same distribution of foci.

Traditional psychometric considerations lead to the conclusion that internal consistency reliability is a necessary condition for validity. However, there is an increasing body of evidence and theory indicating that this is not the case (Atkinson 1977, 1982; Brody 1980; Cornelius 1983). At least for projective techniques, there are good reasons to believe that internal consistency reliability is not an essential condition for construct validity. In fact, it could inhibit validity by reducing the number of facets of a construct that are tapped.

Perhaps most convincing of all is the fact that MSCS instruments lacking internal consistency reliability have yielded substantial empirical validity with marked consistency, as noted in Table 5.2. In that table the Stahl, Grigsby, and Gulati (1983) study found a total score of 10.65 for campus leaders and 4.85 for nonleaders, as well as significant differences on four subscales in the face of minuscule coefficient alphas. In the Miner (1980c) study of management professors, the highest Form P validities for the total score and each successive subscale were .66, .35, .53, .39, .36, and .50 (all p < .01), in spite of the inadequate odd-even reliability findings. Unfortunately, the problems with internal consistency reliability are not widely recognized at the present time and, accordingly, instruments are frequently evaluated erroneously.

Equal Employment Opportunity Considerations and Adverse Impact

A final issue involves the extent to which the MSCS measures might produce effects that could operate to the disadvantage of various population groups, specifically women and minorities.

Data for the Free-Response Form H

Among actual managers no differences in total score means or validity coefficients have been found between males and females (Miner 1974a, 1977a, 1977c). There are occasional differences on certain subscales that favor one group or another, but these cancel each other out in the total score findings.

In student samples the results have been much the same for education majors (Miner 1965, 1977a). Occasional subscale differences offset each other to produce no differences in total scores. In earlier analyses, during the 1960s and early 1970s, male business administration students scored higher than females. However, by 1980 this disparity seems to have disappeared, thus eliminating a potential source of adverse impact (Miner & Smith 1982).

These empirical findings are important because there are those who have concluded, on the basis of face validity, that the MSCS must discriminate against females. In part this is due to the wording of some of the items, and in part it appears to be related to an assumption that any test copyrighted in 1961 must be unfair. Some users have considered it necessary to alter items in order to make them appear less discriminatory against women. To the extent that this increases the scores of females, while leaving those of males unaltered, there is a substantial risk of introducing reverse discrimination. Where changes of this kind are made in order to deal with face validity problems, it is essential that research be carried out to determine exactly what the empirical consequences are.

Research on minorities is much less extensive than for women. In one instance black male managers obtained a total score of 5.26, while white female and male managers in similar positions in the same company had scores of 1.81 and 2.81, respectively (Miner 1977c). Only the comparisons involving the minority males were significant (both p < .05). What evidence we have, then, indicates no adverse impact against minorities—quite the contrary.

It should be noted, however, that Bartol, Anderson, and Schneier (1980), working with business student samples, did find sex differences in favor of males in 1977; Bartol, Anderson, and Schneier (1981) report higher scores for both males and whites, also in 1977. Given the scoring problems noted in Miner and Smith (1983), and discussed earlier in this chapter, it appears appropriate to hold any conclusions derived from these data in abeyance at the present time. It is hoped that future research will resolve the issues involved.

Problems with the Multiple-Choice Form H

As previously noted, one study found a pattern of higher scores on the free-response Form H for minority male managers than for either white males or females (Miner 1977c). Many of these subjects subsequently completed multiple-choice versions of the test. The consequences of shifting to a multiple-choice format proved to be different within the three groups. The minority males increased their total scores by 21 percent, the females by 91 percent, and the white males by 152 percent (Miner 1977a). The net effect was to eliminate the previous superiority of the minority males; no significant total score differences remained. For some reason the minority males, and to a lesser extent the females, did not take advantage of the opportunity for score inflation that the multiple-choice format provides. This effect could be interpreted as a type of adverse impact associated with multiple-choice measurement. In any event, it appears to call for additional research both with sentence completion instruments and with measures of other kinds that use the multiple-choice format.

CONCLUSIONS

Where does all this leave us with regard to the sentence-completion approach? Clearly there are a number of pluses that stand out:

1. Very good scorer agreement can be obtained, so this factor need not be a detriment in the use of sentence-completion measures.
2. Good test-retest reliability can be expected if the measures are long enough. Ideally, for individual interpretation of scores, the subscales of the MSCS would contain more items than they currently do.
3. It appears that unconscious motives are tapped, given the score inflation with a shift to multiple-choice measurement, and even the multiple-choice version of Form H appears to be independent of meaningful social desirability bias (Stahl, Grigsby, & Gulati 1983)
4. Most important of all, the approach works (yields validity) as hypothesized by the underlying theory, and has continued to do so for a number of years. That is the basic reason why the writer became involved in a program of research extending over a professional lifetime. Each new success seems to open up a whole new set of questions.

With these pluses there are some minuses:

1. It has not been possible to devise a scoring guide that in itself assures adequate scorer reliabilities. Some people cannot obtain an acceptable level, and some simply do not. Training does appear to help, but as long as a scoring guide cannot guarantee success, there are going to be some failures in data interpretation.
2. On the subscales we are currently caught between practical usefulness and desirable levels of reliability. At present a much longer measure would meet considerable resistance, but longer subscales offer substantial psychometric advantages.
3. Like all projectives, sentence completion methods remain somewhat cumbersome, because they have to be scored. Resorting to multiple-choice alternatives solves one set of problems, only to introduce a new set. A great deal needs to be learned in this area.

On balance, however, the future looks much better for this type of measure than many would have guessed in 1960.

REFERENCES

Atkinson, J.W. Motivation for achievement. In T. Blass (ed.), *Personality variables in social behavior*. Hillsdale, N.J.: Erlbaum, 1977.
_____. Motivational determinants of thematic apperception. In A. Stewart (ed.), *Motivation and society*. San Francisco: Jossey-Bass, 1982.

Atkinson, J.W., & Raynor, J.O. *Motivation and achievement.* Washington, D.C.: Winston, 1974.

Bartol, K., Anderson, C.R., & Schneier, C.E. Motivation to manage among college business students: A reassessment. *Journal of Vocational Behavior,* 1980, *17,* 22–32.

_____. Sex and ethnic effects on motivation to manage among college business students. *Journal of Applied Psychology,* 1981, *66,* 40–44.

Beldt, S.F. An analysis of values in traditional organizations and nontraditional organizations structured using socio-technical systems design. Ph.D. dissertation, Georgia State University, 1978.

Berman, F.E. & Miner, J.B. Motivation to manage at the top executive level: A test of the hierarchic role motivation theory. *Personnel Psychology,* in press.

Black, C.H. Managerial motivation of hospital chief administrators in investor-owned and not-for-profit hospitals. Ph.D. dissertation, Georgia State University, 1981.

Blau, P.M. *On the nature of organizations.* New York: Wiley, 1974.

Brief, A.P., Aldag, R.J., & Chacko, T.I. The Miner Sentence Completion Scale: An appraisal. *Academy of Management Journal,* 1977, *20,* 635–643.

Brockhaus, R.H. Risk taking propensity of entrepreneurs. *Academy of Management Journal,* 1980, *23,* 509–520. (a)

_____. Psychological and environmental factors which distinguish the successful from the unsuccessful entrepreneur: A longitudinal study. *Academy of Management Proceedings,* 1980, 368–372. (b)

Brockhaus, R.H., & Nord, W.R. An exploration of factors affecting the entrepreneurial decision. Personal characteristics vs. environmental conditions. *Academy of Management Proceedings,* 1979, 364–368.

Brody, N. Social motivation. *Annual Review of Psychology,* 1980, *31,* 143–168.

Butler, R.P., Lardent, C.L., & Miner, J.B. A motivational basis for turnover in military officer education and training. *Journal of Applied Psychology,* 1983, *68,* 496–506.

Cornelius, E.T. The use of projective techniques in personnel selection. In K.M. Rowland & G.D. Ferris (eds.), *Research in personnel and human resources management.* Greenwich, Conn.: JAI Press, 1983.

England, G.W. *The manager and his values.* Cambridge, Mass.: Ballinger, 1975.

England, G.W., Olsen, K., & Agarwal, N. *A manual of development and research for the Personal Values Questionnaire.* Minneapolis: Industrial Relations Center, University of Minnesota, 1971.

Fiedler, F.E. *A theory of leadership effectiveness.* New York: McGraw-Hill, 1967.

Fuller, G.B., Parmelee, W.M., & Carroll, J.L. Performance of delinquent and nondelinquent high school boys on the Rotter Incomplete Sentence Blank. *Journal of Personality Assessment,* 1983, *46,* 506–510.

Gantz, B.S., Erickson, C.O., & Stephenson, R.W. Measuring the motivation to manage in a research and development population. In J.B. Miner (ed.), *Motivation to manage: A ten-year update on the Studies in Management Education research*. Atlanta: Organizational Measurement Systems Press, 1977.

Ghiselli, E.E. *Explorations in managerial talent*. Pacific Palisades, Calif.: Goodyear, 1971.

Gouldner, A. *Patterns of industrial bureaucracy*. New York: Free Press, 1954.

Guion, R.M., & Gottier, R.F. Validity of personality measures in personnel selection. *Personnel Psychology*, 1965, *18*, 135–164.

Hofstede, G. *Culture's consequences: International differences in work-related values*. Beverly Hills, Calif.: Sage, 1980.

Kahn, R.L., & Katz, D. Leadership practices in relation to productivity and morale. In D. Cartwright & A. Zander (eds.), *Group dynamics: Research and theory*. Evanston, Ill.: Row, Peterson, 1953.

Kinslinger, H.J. Applications of projective techniques in personnel psychology since 1940. *Psychological Bulletin*, 1966, *66*, 134–150.

Korman, A.K. The prediction of managerial performance: A review. *Personnel Psychology*, 1968, *21*, 295–322.

Lacey, L. Discriminability of the Miner Sentence Completion Scale among supervisory and nonsupervisory scientists and engineers. *Academy of Management Journal*, 1974, *17*, 354–358.

McClelland, D.C. *The achieving society*. Princeton, N.J.: Van Nostrand, 1961.

_____. Business drive and national achievement. *Harvard Business Review*, 1962, *40* (4), 99–112.

McClelland, D.C., Atkinson, J.W., Clark, R.A., and Lowell, E.L. *The achievement motive*. New York: Irvington, 1976.

Merton, R.K. Bureaucratic structure and personality. *Social Forces*, 1940, *18*, 560–568.

Miner, J.B. A study of the alcoholic personality utilizing the Thematic Apperception Test. Bachelor of Arts thesis, Princeton University, 1950. Available from author.

_____. Illusory motion: An exploratory study. Master of Arts thesis, Clark University, 1952. Available from author.

_____. Motion perception, time perspective, and creativity. *Journal of Projective Techniques*, 1956, *20*, 405–413.

_____. The concurrent validity of the Picture Arrangement Test in the selection of tabulating machine operators. *Journal of Projective Techniques*, 1960, *24*, 409–418. (a)

_____. The Kuder Preference Record in management appraisal. *Personnel Psychology*, 1960, *13*, 187–196. (b)

_____. The effect of a course in psychology on the attitudes of research and development supervisors. *Journal of Applied Psychology*, 1960, *44*, 224–232. (c)

_____. The validity of the Picture Arrangement Test in the selection of tabulating machine operators: An analysis of predictive power. *Journal of Projective Techniques,* 1961, *25,* 330–333.

_____. Conformity among university professors and business executives. *Administrative Science Quarterly,* 1962, *7,* 96–109. (a)

_____. Personality and ability factors in sales performance. *Journal of Applied Psychology,* 1962, *46,* 6–13. (b)

_____. *The management of ineffective performance.* New York: McGraw-Hill, 1963.

_____. *Scoring guide for the Miner Sentence Completion Scale.* Atlanta: Organizational Measurement Systems Press, 1964.

_____. *Studies in management education.* Atlanta: Organizational Measurement Systems Press, 1965.

_____. *The school administrator and organizational character.* Eugene: University of Oregon Press, 1967.

_____. The early identification of managerial talent. *Personnel and Guidance Journal,* 1968, *46,* 586–591.

_____. Personality tests as predictors of consulting success. *Personnel Psychology,* 1971, *24,* 191–204.

_____. The management consulting firm as a source of high-level managerial talent. *Academy of Management Journal,* 1973, *16,* 253–264.

_____. Motivation to manage among women: Studies of business managers and educational administrators. *Journal of Vocational Behavior,* 1974, *5,* 197–208. (a)

_____. *The human constraint: The coming shortage of managerial talent.* Atlanta: Organizational Measurement Systems Press, 1974. (b)

_____. Student attitudes toward bureaucratic role prescriptions and the prospects for managerial talent shortages. *Personnel Psychology* 1974, *27,* 605–613. (c)

_____. *The challenge of managing.* Philadelphia: Saunders, 1975.

_____. Levels of motivation to manage among personnel and industrial relations managers. *Journal of Applied Psychology,* 1976, *61,* 419–427.

_____ (ed.). *Motivation to manage: A ten-year update on the Studies in Management Education research.* Atlanta: Organizational Measurement Systems Press, 1977. (a)

_____. *1977 supplement: Scoring guide for the Miner Sentence Completion Scale.* Atlanta: Organizational Measurement Systems Press, 1977. (b)

_____. Motivational potential for upgrading among minority and female managers. *Journal of Applied Psychology,* 1977, *62,* 691–697. (c)

_____. Twenty years of research on role-motivation theory of managerial effectiveness. *Personnel Psychology,* 1978, *31,* 739–760. (a)

_____. The Miner Sentence Completion Scale: A reappraisal. *Academy of Management Journal,* 1978, *21,* 283–294. (b)

_____. *Theories of organizational behavior.* Hinsdale, Ill.: Dryden, 1980. (a)

_____. Limited domain theories of organizational energy. In C.C. Pinder & L.F. Moore (eds.), *Middle range theory and the study of organizations.* Boston, Mass.: Martinus Nijhoff, 1980. (b)

_____. The role of managerial and professional motivation in the career success of management professors. *Academy of Management Journal,* 1980, *23,* 487–508. (c)

_____. *Scoring guide for the Miner Sentence Completion Scale-Form P.* Atlanta: Organizational Measurement Systems Press, 1981.

_____. The uncertain future of the leadership concept: Revisions and clarifications. *Journal of Applied Behavioral Science,* 1982, *18,* 293–307.

Miner, J.B., and Crane, D.P. Motivation to manage and the manifestation of a managerial orientation in career planning. *Academy of Management Journal,* 1981, *24,* 626–633.

Miner, J.B., & Culver, J.E. Some aspects of the executive personality. *Journal of Applied Psychology,* 1955, *39,* 348–353.

Miner, J.B., & Miner, M.G. Managerial characteristics of personnel managers. *Industrial Relations,* 1976, *15,* 225–234.

Miner, J.B., Rizzo, J.R., Harlow, D.N., & Hill, J.W. Role motivation theory of managerial effectiveness in simulated organizations of varying degrees of structure. *Journal of Applied Psychology,* 1974, *59,* 31–37.

Miner, J.B., & Smith, N.R. Managerial talent among undergraduate and graduate business students. *Personnel and Guidance Journal,* 1969, *47,* 995–1000.

Miner, J.B., & Smith, N.R. Decline and stabilization of managerial motivation over a 20-year period. *Journal of Applied Psychology,* 1982, *67,* 297–305.

Miner, J.B., Smith, N.R., and Ebrahimi, B. Further considerations in the decline and stabilization of managerial motivation: A rejoinder to Bartol, Anderson, and Schneier (1980). *Journal of Vocational Behavior,* in press.

Nathan, B.R., & Alexander, R.A. Establishing construct validity through the application of validity generalization: The Miner Sentence Completion Scale. Unpublished manuscript, University of Akron, 1982.

Oliver, J.E. *Scoring guide for the Oliver Organization Description Questionnaire.* Atlanta: Organizational Measurement Systems Press, 1981.

_____. An instrument for classifying organizations. *Academy of Management Journal,* 1982, *25,* 855–866.

Piotrowski, Z.A., & Rock, M.R. *The perceptanalytic executive scale: A tool for the selection of top managers.* New York: Grune & Stratton, 1963.

Quigley, J.V. Predicting managerial success in the public sector: Concurrent validation of biodata and the Miner Sentence Completion Scale in the Georgia Department of Human Resources. Ph.D. dissertation, Georgia State University, 1979.

Reilly, R.R., & Chao, G.T. Validity and fairness of some alternative employee selection procedures. *Personnel Psychology,* 1982, *35,* 1–62.

Rice, R.W. Psychometric properties of the Esteem for Least Preferred Coworker (LPC) Scale. *Academy of Management Review,* 1978, *3,* 106–117.

Rootes, M.D., Moras, K., & Gordon, R. Ego development and sociometrically evaluated maturity: An investigation of the validity of the Washington University Sentence Completion Test of Ego Development. *Journal of Personality Assessment,* 1980, *44,* 613–619.

Selznick, P. *TVA and the grassroots.* Berkeley: University of California Press, 1949.

Shouval, R., Duek, E., & Ginton, A. A multiple-choice version of the sentence completion method. *Journal of Personality Assessment,* 1975, *39,* 41–49.

Singh, S. Relationships among projective and direct verbal measures of achievement motivation. *Journal of Personality Assessment,* 1979, *43,* 45–49.

Singleton, T. A study of managerial motivation development among college student leaders. Ph.D. dissertation, Georgia State University, 1976.

Smith, N.R., & Miner, J.B. Type of entrepreneur, type of firm and managerial motivation: Implications for organizational life cycle theory. *Strategic Management Journal,* 1983, *4,* 325–340.

Southern, L.J.F. An analysis of motivation to manage in the tufted carpet and textile industry of northwest Georgia. Ph.D. dissertation, Georgia State University, 1976.

Stahl, M.J., Grigsby, D.W., & Gulati, A. A comparison of McClelland and Miner: Identifying managerial motivation with the Job Choice Exercise and the Miner Sentence Completion Scale. Unpublished manuscript, Clemson University, 1983.

Steger, J.A., Kelley, W.B., Chouiniere, G., & Goldenbaum, A. A forced choice version of the MSCS and how it discriminates campus leaders and nonleaders. *Academy of Management Journal,* 1975, *18,* 453–460.

Tomkins, S.S., & Miner, J.B. *The Tomkins-Horn Picture Arrangement Test.* New York: Springer, 1957.

———. *Picture-Arrangement Test interpretation: Scope and technique.* New York: Springer, 1959.

Turnbow, K., & Dana, R.H. The effects of stem length and directions on sentence completion test responses. *Journal of Personality Assessment,* 1981, *45,* 27–32.

Waugh, M.H. Reliability of the Sentence Completion Test of Ego Development in a clinical population. *Journal of Personality Assessment,* 1981, *45,* 485–487.

Weber, M. *Economy and society.* New York: Bedminster Press, 1968. (Translated and edited by G. Roth and C. Wittich)

6

Using Clinical Methods in a High-Level Management Assessment Center
Joseph L. Moses

INTRODUCTION

"Judgment" (along with terms such as "intuition," "subjectivity," and "introspection") is a word not widely used today, perhaps because it appears to have a negative, nonscientific connotation. Judgment is an illusive, hard-to-define term. It rests on the training, experiences, and subject matter expertise of the individual. It also requires a willingness (as well as the ability) to make decisions that may have profound and lasting effects on an individual, a community, or an organization.

For some reason, it appears that judgment is missing in much of contemporary industrial/organizational (I/O) practice. Consumed with issues of test fairness and validity generalization, leadership behavior, and motivational theories, the practice of I/O psychology has increasingly emphasized statistical methodology as *the* way to determine whether something "works." The recent explosion of computer hardware and software enables researchers further to quantify data in a never-ending search for truth. Yet, judgment is an integral part of the management decision-making process. Too often, this judgment process is either ignored or simply taken for granted.

The judgment process can be viewed as a continuum.* At one end of this continuum are judgments that are objective in nature. Here, quantifi-

---

*A special debt of gratitude is owed to Sheldon Zedeck, of the University of California at Berkeley, who pointed out the continuum to me.

able indices are used to compare individuals or outcomes. Many of the dependent variables used in psychological research fall into this category. At the other end of the continuum are judgments that reflect inferences, guesses, or predictions. Independent variables often represent this end of the continuum. In addition, a third kind of judgment, describing observations, can be identified. Its place on the continuum varies with the expected outcome. Let us examine each aspect of the judgment process in more detail.

Objective-nomothetic judgments anchor one end of the judgment continuum. These judgments allow one to compare an individual with some normed behavior or outcome (hence the label "nomothetic"). Typically, the judgment process consists of determining whether a score is considered an extreme score. For example, it could consist of evaluating whether an MMPI scale score of 70 was extreme, or whether an SAT score of 670 is considered as a passing score for admittance to a school's undergraduate program, or whether the number and kind of white cells indicate leukemia. It makes no difference whether the normed judgment is based on experience or on a statistical formula. These kinds of judgments frequently are dichotomous (Pass-Fail, accept as typical or view as unusual). The prediction accuracy of these types of judgments is a function of the validity of the measures used and of the nature of the prediction itself. One danger when using objective-nomothetic data as *the* basis for judgment is a tendency to inappropriately attribute judgments made for one purpose to other situations. For example, while SAT scores may predict college academic success, knowledge of SAT scores (or similar ability measures) by a supervisor may totally distort performance appraisals based on normative expectations. The analogy to education has been described by Rosenthal (see Rosenthal & Jacobson 1968), who demonstrated that expectations of the student's classroom performance were significantly influenced by teacher assumptions of IQ scores.

Observation-descriptive judgments fall at some point on the judgment continuum. Depending on the kinds of comparisons that are made, they can be near either end of the continuum. These kinds of judgments describe typical behavior. The judgment process consists of aggregating, in some manner, examples of current behavior and then evaluating the likelihood of a future outcome. The aggregation method used can vary, and can include, for example, a teacher averaging test scores to grade a student, or a supervisor using a critical-incident method to rate the performance of a subordinate. Whether the outcome is a report card or a performance appraisal, observation-descriptive judgments are very useful when description, particularly of typical behavior, is an outcome. The predictive accuracy of these judgments can be very great as long as the prediction is made for similar, observable situations. Therefore, high school grades based on the observation-descriptive judgments of many teachers are generally predictive of college grades. They are less likely to be related to career success. Similarly, performance appraisals are useful tools to describe work performance but are not very meaningful indicators of further potential, particularly when subsequent assignments are not close parallels of the present work assignment.

Inference-predictive judgments anchor the other end of the judgment continuum. Often called "clinical" judgments, they are based on internal norms: the training, experience, and confidence of the rater, evaluator, diagnoser, or judge. The judgment itself is a prediction of subsequent behavior or outcome based on the standards of the rater. The predictive accuracy of these kinds of judgments is a function of many things, including the measurement system used (test scores, lab reports, interviews, projective techniques); the quality of the training and experience of the rater; the confidence of the rater; the management of rating errors and response bias; and the relevance of the judgment itself. For example, while many inferences-predictions can be made from an employment interview, the relevance of these predictions is critical. Knowing that a sales applicant is relaxed, articulate, and poised in an employment interview may be useful, but it may be of absolutely no value in estimating whether this individual can make an effective sales presentation to a large audience. Knowing that a subordinate is bright may be of little practical value in deciding whether to assign this person to an emotionally volatile position.

The preceding discussion may help clarify some of the distinctions of the judgment continuum. Depending on purpose, different judgment processes may be called for. It is possible to integrate many or all of these. Rather than view judgment as an objective-subjective issue, this writer feels that we need to understand the best features of different outcomes, and to apply judgments appropriately.

This chapter will explore a judgment-based behavioral measurement approach (the assessment center method) that attempts to utilize inference-predictive judgments to evaluate further potential. In this context, predicting future potential requires both a rigorous and empirically supported measurement system *and* a system that enables decision makers to exercise judgment in an objective and job-related way.

The assessment center method provides a framework for making these kinds of judgments. Assessment centers are widely used for identifying further management potential. Although its most frequent use is for the selection of entry-level (and in some cases middle-level management) positions, its greatest impact is its application in identifying potential for subsequent executive-level managerial assignments. There has been a change recently in assessment center perspectives. While the traditional (and still major) use is for selection, there is a growing application of this method for placement (particularly in nontraditional assignments), development, and career planning efforts. These are particularly relevant when used in senior management staffing.

When assessment is used at senior levels, motivation, personality, and the ability to cope with ambiguity and uncertainty, for example, are important factors to consider when predicting subsequent success. When these data are coupled with information concerning management abilities that are measured by means of behavioral simulations in a management assessment center (decision making, leadership), the information available is extremely useful in understanding and predicting subsequent behavior in complex, demanding situations. The process of integrating and utilizing information from clinical and behavioral sources is found in the type of assessment center we will describe.

Before doing so, we will first review, for the reader unfamiliar with the assessment center method, some introductory concepts. Next, we will describe an application of a senior-level assessment center, the AT&T Advanced Management Potential Assessment Program. We will describe the dimensions measured, and the behavioral and clinical techniques used in this program. Finally, we will examine the role of clinical methods, particularly those using inference-predictive judgments in the search for executive talent.

THE ASSESSMENT CENTER METHOD

It is significant that the precursor of all assessment centers began with an effort to understand personality. In his seminal book, *Explorations In Personality,* Murray (1938) provided a model for studying personality that uses a variety of clinical experiments, interviews, and projective techniques. In a subsequent interview Murray (1982) described how he applied the clinical practice of "grand rounds" to the Diagnostic Council used at the Harvard Psychological Clinic in the early 1930s. Among his many innovative and creative breakthroughs, Murray saw that experts who could integrate multiple sources of information could use this information to describe complex human behavior, which he systematized in his study of personality.

With the advent of World War II, Murray and members of the Harvard Psychological Clinic staff were given an opportunity to use the research method developed at Harvard to predict behavior—specifically, the identification of spies and other operatives for overseas assignments as members of the Office of Strategic Services (OSS). Adapting simulation techniques used by the Germans to produce military officer effectiveness, Murray and his colleagues (OSS Assessment Staff 1948) described the development of the first assessment center. A recent review of this program (written by Donald MacKinnon, a Murray student and the director of the original OSS assessment center) documents the creativity and the relevance of this talented team to understanding and predicting complex behavior (MacKinnon 1977).

Following World War II, MacKinnon developed an assessment center research program at the Institute of Personality Assessment and Research at the University of California. Researchers here focused on identifying creative potential (MacKinnon 1978). The first applied use of assessment centers was pioneered by Douglas Bray in 1956 as part of AT&T's Management Progress Study (Bray, Campbell, & Grant 1974). The application of this method to other management populations began, and its history is well documented elsewhere (Moses & Byham 1977; Thornton & Byham 1982).

An assessment center is both a place and a process. It is a physical center where managers are evaluated for further potential. Here individuals can demonstrate abilities that are needed in more complex and demanding assignments by indicating skills and behaviors that are not seen or are difficult to measure in a current job. It is also a process that is designed to ensure that the judgments of potential are made in a fair, objective, and job-related way.

While there are many forms of the assessment procedures, the term "assessment center" has a specific meaning. As defined by the Task Force on Assessment Center Standards (1980), an assessment center must meet the following criteria:

1. It must contain an explicit definition of the determinants of managerial effectiveness. Often these are called dimensions, characteristics, or assessment variables. They are identified by means of a variety of job analytic techniques, in order to ensure that the behaviors measured are relevant and critical to higher-level manager success.
2. Multiple measurement techniques, which include simulations, are used. Simulations provide the participant with behavioral stimuli that represent important aspects of job behavior and can include leaderless

group exercises, business games, "in baskets", problem-solving exercises, simulated interviews, and fact-finding problems.

3. Performance behavior is observed and evaluated by a carefully selected, and specially trained, team of managers who are knowledgeable about the target position.

4. Integration of information occurs, after all of the measurement techniques are completed, at a specially conducted assessment evaluation session. Ratings made on specific dimensions are pooled and discussed, and overall predictions of potential are made.

In addition to the identification of potential, there are a number of outcomes that occur as a result of participating in an assessment center. From a participant's perspective, the assessment exercises and techniques provide multiple opportunities to demonstrate specific abilities. Well-designed simulations make possible a rich sampling of behavior in a variety of settings. Both the participants and management can receive intensive feedback on the strengths and weaknesses identified. Such feedback contains a wealth of diagnostic data that can be used for development, placement, and self-insight purposes.

For the management assessors, participating as a member of the assessment center team provides a unique developmental experience. For many assessors this assignment is a powerful management development and training experience. Recent research (Lorenzo 1983) suggests that assessor training and experience have great benefit in enhancing such managerial skills as acquiring, evaluating, and communicating information about people.

Finally, assessment data, when aggregated on a group rather than on an individual basis, provide an excellent organizational diagnosis of the strengths and weaknesses of existing personnel. Such data can be extremely valuable when developing recruiting, selection, training, and staffing strategies for both current and future organizational needs.

THE ADVANCED MANAGEMENT POTENTIAL ASSESSMENT PROGRAM

This program, developed by the author for use by AT&T, has several overlapping purposes. It is designed to do the following:

1. Evaluate the further management potential of carefully selected and highly talented middle managers. Participants in this program are experienced middle managers who are serious candidates for further advancement.
2. Provide intensive personal feedback to all participants. This feedback is geared to helping effective managers become even more effective, by indicating ways individuals can enhance their strengths and minimize their deficiencies.
3. Stimulate career planning efforts for participants, staff, and subordinates. Data from the assessment center can be integrated into personal goal setting to help managers to understand and plan their next step in a developmental plan.
4. Provide developmental opportunities for individual growth. A variety of postassessment seminars and programs that integrate assessment center and developmental strategies are available to participants.
5. Serve as a research laboratory for understanding managerial behavior in complex environments. Often behavioral and research test data are used for research purposes at the center. These data, while not used in the measurement of potential, can serve as a valuable aid for the development of hypotheses and constructs concerning behavior in changing environments.

Assessment Phases

The assessment program consists of three distinct phases: assessment, feedback, and postassessment development. Each of these is briefly described. The actual measurement process occurs in the first phase. This consists of three and a half intensive days of participant assessment. Twelve managers are assessed each week; they participate in group exercises, business games, "in baskets", analysis problems, role-playing interviews, in-depth interviews with a psychologist, a career review interview with a manager, and over a dozen paper-and-pencil measures, including ability tests, projective measures, personality and biographical inventories, and research questionnaires.

These data are observed, recorded, and evaluated by the assessment staff. The staff consists of six senior-level managers who have been carefully selected and trained to participate in this program, two non-Bell clinical psychologists, and three industrial psychologists from AT&T who serve as directors of this program. Graduate student assistants serve as role players and test administrators, and a clerical and administrative staff is present as well. Over 15 people are involved in conducting this program. The high staff-to-assesser ratio (almost 1:1) makes possible an intensive and personal examination of individual capabilities.

The next phase, feedback, is provided in a number of ways. Each participant receives personal, in-depth feedback from the clinical psychologist who conducted the assessment interview and who also was a member of the assessment staff. Additional feedback is provided as needed by the AT&T psychologists. In addition, a written report, prepared by the program director, is provided to the senior personnel officer in the participant's organization. This written feedback is designed to be used for long-term staffing and development needs.

The final phase, postassessment development, has a number of outcomes. Depending on the data from feedback and the personal career plan that is developed, individual developmental strategies can be created and updated annually. A variety of developmental experiences, both on and off the job, are available to many of these managers. Often, specific guidance in the selection of subsequent assignments is provided, either to enhance developmental needs or to match skills to specific business environments. Finally, a number of formal developmental programs are available. These include programs for high-potential managers, to ensure rapid movement and advancement, and a unique developmental seminar for all participants, to assist these managers as they cope with future uncertainty, ambiguity, and change.

Dimensions Assessed

A total of 24 assessment dimensions are measured in this program. They fall into six major categories:

1. Work Motivation: these include measures of managerial motivation, such as advancement needs, work standards, and energy level.
2. Communications Skills: included here are measures of oral presentation skills as well as the ability, when challenged, to defend one's ideas.
3. Interpersonal Skills: this category measures such skills as leadership, interpersonal impact, perceptiveness, and negotiation skills.
4. Management Problem Solving: this area encompasses behaviors related to problem analysis, organizing and planning, decision making, and decisiveness.
5. Coping with Change: included here are dimensions such as risk-taking behavior, creativity, and tolerance of uncertainty.

6. Developmental Potential: this last category helps examine individual differences in potential for further development. Included are assessments of intellectual capacity, self-objectivity, and motivation for personal development.

From an overall perspective the first four categories—Work Motivation, Communications Skills, Interpersonal Skills, and Management Problem Solving—represent the necessary skills and motivation required in senior management assignments. Participants viewed as having further potential typically demonstrate a rich variety of skills and behaviors in these "traditional" management potential areas.

The fifth category, Coping with Change, is extremely helpful when making placement recommendations. Some future senior-level assignments will require the capability to respond to novel and uncertain environments, while others will require the management of traditional functions. Identifying which individuals will perform best in either (or both) of these environments can be particularly helpful for future staffing decisions.

The final category, Developmental Potential, is often very useful in determining the status of a candidate with borderline potential. In some cases the staff may feel that an otherwise borderline candidate is so motivated to develop, that further advancement is clearly warranted.

Behavioral Measures

A variety of behavioral assessment techniques constitute a major source of information for predictions of further potential. Simulations created to reflect complex environments have been described in great detail in Moses and Byham (1977). Six discrete simulations are used in this program. Examples of two of these exercises are provided to give a flavor of the rich behavioral input that is provided to the assessment center staff:

Complex business game: This is a group exercise in which six participants must serve as an investment advisory board for a mutual fund. They receive a wealth of financial data concerning a number of stocks that can be purchased and sold, as well as advisory services and dividend data. The managers must absorb a great deal of information and use it in a fast-paced, changing, and uncertain business market. This exercise takes over two and a half hours to complete, and provides a rich source of information on interpersonal and individual problem-solving behavior in complex business environments.

"In basket(s)": Two different "in baskets", requiring different approaches to problem solving, are used. Each basket is approximately two to three hours long, and is followed by an interview or presentation of materials. The "in baskets" capture different business operating environments and require the participant to be able to distinguish between short- and long-range problem-solving and decision-making approaches.

In addition to these exercises, other group and individual exercises provide rich sources of behavior. These include an additional leaderless group exercise, an analysis exercise, and a fact-finding exercise. The assessment program is scheduled to afford at least two distinct simulations for each dimension measured. The techniques are scheduled on different days during the assessment week, in order to capitalize on maximizing the measurement over an extended time period.

Nonbehavioral Measures

A number of nonbehavioral assessment techniques are used as well. These are classified as projective, pencil-and-paper, interview, and research. In this chapter the description of the projective measure used in this program is emphasized. Space constraints limit the description of the other measures to a more cursory review.

Projectives

We use three different projective techniques in this program. Two are incomplete sentence blanks, the Rotter Incomplete Sentence Blank (Rotter & Rafferty 1950) and the Management Incomplete Sentences Test (Grant, Katkovsky, & Bray 1967). The latter test was designed for Bell System use and has been extensively used in the Management Progress Study. The final projective instrument, the Management Apperception Test (MAT) (Ballard, Calhoun, & Moses 1981) was designed for this assessment program. It was intended to provide stimuli similar to those presented in the Thematic Apperception Test (Murray 1943) by providing contemporary, business-oriented stimuli. One feature of this instrument is its ability to provide useful information on dimensions related to coping with change, particularly issues related to uncertainty and ambiguity.

These instruments (the sentence completions and the MAT) are administered to all assessment participants in group settings. A clinical psychologist then prepares a projective report based on these three sources of data. It is the final piece of information shared at the assessment integration session.

The psychologists preparing the projective report are experienced assessors and provide the management assessors with information that is useful in making predictions on a number of the assessment dimensions noted earlier. Although these reports are prepared in the absence of observed behavioral data, the information provided frequently is a rich supplement to an understanding of a participant's behavior. For example, a management assessor might describe a participant's behavior in a group situation as indicating that the individual being assessed is not very effective in interpersonal situations because he constantly interrupts other speakers, tends to argue over matters that others seem to agree on quickly, and, while task-oriented, is either unable or unwilling to accept the ideas of others or to compromise on a given position. Consequently, despite repeated attempts to lead the group, this person is ignored. The projective report might suggest why the person behaves this way. For example, the psychologist might describe dominance, ambition, or extreme competitiveness when dealing with others as an explanation for this person's approach when dealing with others in interpersonal settings.

Having participated in over 500 evaluations, I would estimate that approximately 80-90 percent of all of the projective reports contain uncanny insights into a manager's personality and style. In the few instances where the projective data are at variance with behavioral data, the assessors rely on the behavioral data when making their ratings and overall predictions.

The projective reports are not viewed as a replacement for the behavioral data. Instead, we treat these data as a valuable supplement to the information available on a participant. There are a number of reasons why projective data used in this manner are so valuable.

First, the clinicians are trained assessors and are familiar with all of the techniques used in this program. They write their reports to stress specific assessment dimensions rather than abstract personality traits. They are focusing their efforts on predicting organizational effectiveness characteristics, rather than on describing pathology. Finally, they must present their ideas in a jargonfree manner, and must be able to communicate their thoughts to both the participants and the management assessors. This requires many unique professional skills, which are present in our very talented clinical staff.*

---

*We have been very fortunate to have had the outstanding professional services of a number of clinical psychologists who have been extremely involved in this program since its inception or during the past several years. They are H. Ted Ballard, Ph.D.; Karen S. Calhoun, Ph.D.; Jodi Kassover, Ph.D.; and Richard Ellmore, Ph.D.

Pencil-and-Paper Measures

Although they are not exclusively "clinical" in nature, we integrate these data in a clinical manner. Three pencil-and-paper measures are administered and are used in the evaluation of potential. These include the Bell System Ability Test, a measure of cognitive effectiveness, and two widely used personality inventories, the Edwards Personnel Preference Schedule (Edwards 1954) and the Gordon Personal Inventory (Gordon 1963). All of these tests have been normed on Bell System middle-management populations and have been shown to be related to aspects of management effectiveness.

Interviews

Two interviews are conducted at the center. The first is with the psychologist who will prepare both the projective report and the individual feedback to each manager. This interview covers relevant life and career themes related to advancement, work and life satisfaction, and development. The interview uses an approach similar to that reported by Rychlack (1982). A second interview, with a management assessor, covers career and work experiences and is used to make placement recommendations regarding subsequent job assignments.

Research Instruments

The final group of instruments is voluntary and is not used for evaluation proposes. It currently includes a variety of measures: a Bell System Position Description Questionnaire; a biographical questionnaire; and several research instruments examining ambiguity, stress, and personal style. These can be compared with both the behavioral and the test data, and are useful as tools for a variety of ongoing research projects conducted by the AT&T professional staff.

THE ROLE OF CLINICAL METHODS IN AN ASSESSMENT CENTER

Assessment centers require the evaluators (whether lay management assessors or professional psychologists) to make numerous judgments. Some writers (Sackett & Dreher 1982; Hinrichs 1969) have argued that a statistical weighting of dimensions in a multiple-regression format suggests that an empirically derived weighting process results in greater assessment "accuracy." Some even suggest that assessment center predictions can be made on the basis of as few as five or six dimensions.

What these writers do not consider is the unique aspects of individual performance. This requires understanding many dimensions of management effectiveness. For some individuals the diagnostic importance of one or two dimensions might be critical in future success. At higher levels the diagnostic feedback and the developmental data provided to both the participant and the sponsoring organization may be of greater value than a specific statement of potential that can be reduced to a single rating number.

If the purpose of the assessment program is only prediction, one could possibly argue the merits of an empirically derived "efficient" measurement strategy. However, if, as noted earlier, the purpose of the assessment center program is to provide additional data to the individual and the organization, then this writer would argue the benefits of an approach that maximizes, rather than minimizes, judgment.

In an assessment center, clinical methods supplement behavioral data. They provide rich sources of unique information not available elsewhere. These data can be very useful for predictions of subsequent behavior and, particularly when fed back to the individual in conjunction with behavioral data, provide opportunities for initiating self-reflection, self-understanding, and, where appropriate, change.

Using clinical psychologists in a senior-level center has a number of distinct advantages. As assessors, who are an integral part of the decision-making process, they provide a unique focus that, in their absence, can be overlooked or ignored. They often serve to crystallize an understanding of observed behavior in a global rather than an atomistic sense. In this context they often complement the data and the interpretation of the management assessors on the evaluation panel.

The clinical psychologists have a direct role in the feedback to the management participants. Assessment at this level can often be a stressful process, particularly when used in a future career decision affecting the individual. Issues of self-esteem and self-worth are raised as an outgrowth of attending this program. All members of the population evaluated are viewed as talented managers. For many of these managers, the feedback session is long remembered as a key life event in his or her career. For this reason special care must be taken to ensure that the data provided to the individual not only are useful but also are presented in a manner minimizing defensiveness while maximizing self-esteem. The clinicians who have worked with us on this program are exceptionally adept at providing a positive feedback climate for all participants.

In a more indirect way, the clinical psychologists have an impact on the behavior of the management assessors. These assessors are senior-level managers carefully selected for this program. Most have had little contact with psychologists other than stereotypes in the press and the entertainment media. Few have worked with psychologists in a peer relationship. Often the interaction of managers and psychologists clearly enriches the perspectives of both parties.

RESEARCH USES

The assessment center method can be an unusually effective research tool. While it is beyond the scope of this chapter to review them in detail, a number of illustrative research examples are provided. Assessment centers have been successfully used as criterion measures in a number of research studies (Bernardin 1984; Moses & Ritchie 1976; Hakel, Lyness, Applebaum, & Moses in press). Assessment centers also provide researchers with unique opportunities to study complex behaviors, including stress (Bunker 1982), career planning (London 1982), and ambiguity (Lyness & Moses 1983). Major issues facing contemporary management behavior can be studied with this technique. Using a judgment-based behavioral measurement system such as the assessment center method can result in a better understanding of complex behaviors.

SUMMARY

This chapter has described the AT&T Advanced Management Potential Assessment Program. All of the predictions made in this program are based on judgments. A great deal of care has been taken to ensure that the judgment process is standardized, behaviorally relevant, and germane to on-the-job behavior.

The judgments made in this kind of program reflect the inference-predictive judgments noted earlier. Not all assessment centers, however, achieve this level of judgment. Often poorly designed, poorly managed centers have improperly trained assessors who make judgments that are not as accurate as those that can be made by using objective-nomothetic judgments. Or they may inaccurately describe behavior, or make inappropriate inferences about subsequent behaviors. Typically these centers are staffed by people with little training in behavioral science or who rely on quantitative systems to ensure rater "accuracy." This frequently results in assessors "agreeing" with one another rather than making judgments that differentiate critical behaviors. Usually this results from poor staff selection, poor training, and a poor understanding of the process.

On the other hand, a well-designed assessment center program can provide both lay and psychological assessors with rich sources of information not available elsewhere that, when integrated with a comprehensive feedback and development system, can provide significant information to the individual in terms of seeking out situations that can help to maximize success, and to the organization in terms of a staffing system that ensures long-term organizational vitality.

REFERENCES

Ballard, H.T., Calhoun, K., & Moses, J.L. *The Management Apperception Test manual.* New York: AT&T Management Selection Research Staff, 1981.

Bernardin, H.J. Black-white differences in job performance: A review of the literature. *Proceedings of the Academy of Management,* 1984, 265–268.

Bray, D.W., Campbell, R.J., & Grant, D.L. *Formative years in business.* New York: Wiley, 1974.

Bunker, K. Personal communication. April 1982.

Edwards, A.L. *Personal Preference Schedule manual.* New York: Psychological Corporation, 1954.

Gordon, L.V. *Manual, Gordon Personal Inventory.* New York: Harcourt Brace, 1963.

Grant, D.L., Katkovsky, W., & Bray, D.W. Contributions of projective techniques to assessment of managerial potential. *Journal of Applied Psychology,* 1967, *51,* 226–232.

Hakel, M.D., Lyness, K.S., Applebaum, L.E., & Moses, J.L. Reliable and impartial ratings of management potential. *Personnel Psychology,* in press.

Hinrichs, J.R. Comparison of real life assessments of management potential with situation exercises, paper and pencil ability tests, and personality inventories. *Journal of Applied Psychology,* 1969, *53,* 425–432.

London, M. Personal communication. February 1982.

Lorenzo, R.V. Assessorship and management development: The effects of serving as a trained member on an assessment center staff. Ph.D. dissertation, New York University, 1983.

Lyness, K.S., & Moses, J.L. Measurement strategies, ambiguity, uncertainty, and change: A theoretical view. Paper presented at annual convention, American Psychological Association, Anaheim, Calif., August 1983.

MacKinnon, D.W. From selecting spies to selecting managers. In J.L. Moses & W.C. Byham (eds.), *Applying the assessment center method.* New York: Pergamon, 1977.

_____. *In search of human effectiveness.* Buffalo, N.Y.: Creative Education Foundation, 1978.

Moses, J.L., & Ritchie, R.J. Supervisory relationships training: A behavioral evaluation of a behavior modeling program. *Personnel Psychology,* 1976, *29,* 337–343.

Moses, J.L., & Byham, W.C. (eds.). *Applying the assessment center method.* New York: Pergamon, 1977.

Murray, H.A. *Explorations in personality.* New York: Oxford University Press, 1938.

_____. *Manual: Thematic Apperception Test.* Cambridge, Mass.: Harvard University Press, 1943.

_____. *Pioneers in assessment.* Audiocassette interview with J.L. Moses, March 1982. (available from author)

O.S.S. Assessment Staff. *Assessment of men.* New York: Rinehart, 1948.

Rosenthal, R., & Jacobson, L. *Pygmalion in the classroom.* New York: Holt, Rinehart, & Winston, 1968.

Rotter, J.B., & Rafferty, J.E. *Manual for the Rotter Incomplete Sentences Blank.* New York: Psychological Corporation, 1950.

Rychlack, J.F. *Personality and life style of young male managers.* New York: Academic Press, 1982.

Sackett, P.R. & Dreher, G.F. Constructs and assessment center dimensions: Some troubling empirical findings. *Journal of Applied Psychology,* 1982, *67,* 401–410.

Task Force on Assessment Center Standards. Standards and ethical considerations for assessment center operations. *Personnel Administrator,* 1980, *25* (2), 35–38.

Thornton, G.C., & Byham, W.C. *Assessment centers and managerial performance.* New York: Academic Press, 1982.

7

The Use of Personality Measures in a Management Development Program

David Campbell and
Ellen Van Velsor

Since 1973 the Center for Creative Leadership has offered a one-week course called the Leadership Development Program. Roughly 3,000 individuals have attended. As part of this course, each person takes an extensive battery of psychological tests. As far as we know, we are currently the only institution in the world routinely testing "effectively functioning adults," as opposed to job applicants, military recruits, sophomores, prisoners, patients, or candidates for promotion.

In this chapter we would like to explain what we do, how we do it, why we do it, the problems we encounter, and the benefits we see, and present some of the data that we have been collecting.

THE PARTICIPANTS

First, a description of the participants. Although the course is open to anyone who wishes to come, several factors operate to keep our student body from being a random sample of the population:

1. The course is expensive; the tuition for the week is $2,500, plus travel expenses.
2. The course requires a full workweek, plus a Sunday, plus travel time.

3. The content and marketing of the course are oriented toward people "in charge of something"—leaders, managers, executives, administrators.

Consequently, the attendees tend to be "leadership-oriented" people of whom some organization thinks enough to send them to learn about the art and science of managing others.

One of the main strengths of the course is the variety of people in it. We work hard to attract a diverse student body, encouraging attendance by both men and women, by people of various ethnic backgrounds, and by people from a range of ages, organizations, occupations, status levels, and geographic locations.

Table 7.1 lists the basic demographic characteristics of our population for the years 1979–1982, when roughly 1,000 people attended the course. You will have your own opinion of how successful we were in achieving diversity, the sample being 86 percent male and 92 percent white. All we can say in defense is that had we done nothing, both of those numbers would be much closer to 100 percent.

Our foreign involvement is grossly understated here because these figures include only our public programs in Greensboro. Most of our overseas programs have been contract programs done within a single company, and data from these programs are not included here.

These individuals came from about 150 different organizations, but the "sponsoring organization" distribution was highly skewed, with both the mode and median distribution equaling 1.0. The U.S. Army was the organization sending the most individuals (N = 87) the majority of whom were newly appointed brigadier generals.

CONTENT OF THE COURSE

The course consists of ten stand-alone but complementing modules, each approximately half a day in length, roughly following this sequence:

1. Presentation of a theoretical model covering some leadership/management topic.
2. An interactive exercise or case study to demonstrate the model.
3. Debriefing of the exercise or case study, emphasizing the model.
4. Feedback on a psychological test particularly relevant to the issues under discussion.

The days are organized as follows:

Day 1. The first day is devoted exclusively to the assessment process. More about this later.

Day 2. During the morning, a model for the creative leadership process is presented. This elegant and useful model was developed by Robert Dorn, who also was responsible for the design of the entire course.

The afternoon session covers a model concerned with the issues involved in sharing decision making with subordinates: when to do it, what factors to consider, and what the probable outcome of various approaches will be. This model is based primarily on the work of Vroom and Yetton (1973). As part of this session, participants receive their scores on the Myers-Briggs Type Indicator (MBTI), along with a brief discussion of the relevance of their scores for issues covered by the Vroom-Yetton model. They also are given a report based on their responses to the Leadership Decision Styles Survey (LDSS). The LDSS compares each individual's responses in hypothetical decision-making situations with those responses suggested by the model. It is not a report of "right or wrong" answers but, rather, "how well do you fit the model?"

Day 3. The morning of day 3 covers a situational leadership model based primarily on the work of Hershey and Blanchard (1982) and Reddin (1970). This model suggests how subordinates with differing levels of experience and motivation should be supervised in different types of situations.

As part of this session, each individual is given his or her report on the Leadership Style Indicator (LSI), a questionnaire developed by Robert Bailey.

The LSI report form includes a summary of the responses of three to six selected peers or subordinates concerning the participant's leadership style, organized around the factors from the Hershey-Blanchard model. It also includes the individual's self-report on the same factors. Thus, it allows a quick comparison between the way individuals view themselves and how they are viewed by their peers or subordinates. The decision as to which peers or subordinates fill in the LSI is left up to the individual, but the responses are tallied in such a way as to maintain each respondent's anonymity.

Although this form is psychometrically untidy, its impact on the individual is undeniable. When the reports from subordinates or peers are passed out, the classroom becomes very quiet, then often bubbles with nervous laughter. The data are hard to ignore because the individual personally selected the peers or subordinates who responded.

TABLE 7.1
Demographic Characteristics of the Leadership Development
Program Attendees, 1979–1982 (N = 1,036)

		Mean	S.D.
Age		41	8

		Percent
Sex	male	86
	female	14
Race/ethnic origin	white	92
	black	3
	Oriental	1
	Spanish	2
	American Indian	1
	other	1
Educational level	1-3 years high school	0.4
	high school graduate	3
	1-3 years college	11
	college graduate	30
	some graduate work	13
	M.A. level degree	29
	Ph.D. level degree	11
	other	2
Type of organization	business/industry	65
	education	8
	public service	3
	government	18
	other	5
Level within organization	top executive	22
	upper-middle manager	37
	lower-middle manager	33
	first-level manager	6
	hourly employee	1

	Mean	S.D.
Years of management experience	5	6

	Percent

Gross income (1982 data only)

	Percent	
$0-10,000	1	
10-20,000	3	
20-30,000	8	
30-40,000	20	
40-50,000	27	
50-60,000	20	
60-70,000	10	
70-80,000	3	
80-90,000	4	
90-100,000	1	
100-125,000	1	
125-150,000	1	
$150,000 +	1	median = $46,677

Country	N
U.S.	986
Mexico	25
United Kingdom	8
Canada	7
France	3
Hong Kong	2
Brazil	1
India	1
Malaysia	1
West Germany	1
West Indies	1

Source: Prepared by authors.

The afternoon is devoted to a section called "Utilizing Group Resources," which explains how groups can most effectively use their resources to arrive at better solutions to problems. As part of this session, the participants are given a problem to solve individually, then are assigned to a group and asked to solve the same problem as a group. The eventual comparison between the individual's score and the group score is an assessment both of how effective the individual was in solving the problem, and how much influence he or she was able to exert on the group solution.

Day 4. The morning of day 4 focuses on creativity, with a presentation that describes the forces that block creativity in organizations. This module includes many "nuts-and-bolts" suggestions for more effective, creative problem solving, at both the individual and the group level. Each person receives his or her score on the Kirton Adaptation Inventory, a short inventory related to personal styles of creative problem solving.

The last half of the day is a presentation on appraising the performance of other people, explaining how to pass that appraisal on to them and emphasizing the emotional factors involved. This is in preparation for the next day.

Day 5. The fifth day is feedback day. Each person is given all of the results from the various tests, all of the ratings made on during the assessment exercises, and any other personal data that have been collected in the course. The two major activities of the day are a two-to-three-hour interview with one of our professional staff members, reviewing all of this data in a one-to-one setting, and a three-hour peer feedback process, in which each person hears from a fellow participant a summary of the group impression of him or her, and prepares and delivers a similar summary to someone else.

For the majority of participants, this day is the most powerful part of the week. The staff feedback interview is seen as especially useful. On the postprogram questionnaire, it is always rated as the most valuable part of the week.

This session is definitely not a therapeutic interview but, rather, a personal, informative feedback session. Three of its major goals are to knit the extensive information available on each person into a coherent pattern, to answer any specific questions the person might have about the tests and ratings, and to deal with any anxieties that may have arisen during the course. The session is highly structured and proceeds in an ordered, preordained pattern. Within this pattern each staff member is free to follow his or her professional instincts about how the information should be presented. Because these are individual, idiosyncratic data, personal issues do emerge. Job dissatisfaction, marital turbulence, problems with children, the frustrations of being in a dead-end job, and similar topics come up, and are handled in a professional, sympathetic manner. Often the session ends up focusing on what the individual intends to do about the future, which is a good lead into the last day.

Day 6. The final day is devoted to goal setting. Each individual is led through a planning process designed to focus on what he or she wants to have happen next in terms of career, community involvement, family, and personal lives. Each person designs a plan for immediate implementation, complete with checkpoints and timetables. We collect a copy of each plan and contact the individual on the timetable that he or she has outlined, to see if progress is being made. In follow-up surveys, roughly 90 percent of our participants have completed the goals they set for themselves or are still involved in carrying them out.

THE ASSESSMENT TECHNIQUES

The course has a heavy emphasis on the assessment of the individual. For this process we use the following:

1. A wide range of psychological tests.
2. Observation in standardized exercises by professionals.
3. Observation in "normal" activities by peers.
4. Videotapes.

Psychological Tests

Table 7.2 lists the psychological tests and inventories that we use. Most of them are mailed to the participants several weeks ahead of time. A few—those starred in the table—are filled in after the person arrives at the Center.

TABLE 7.2
Tests Used in the Leadership Development Program Assessment

Biographical questionnaire
California Psychological Inventory (CPI)
"Current situation" questionnaire
Fundamental Interpersonal Relations Orientation-Behavior (FIRO-B)
Hidden figures*
Kirton Adaptation Inventory (KAI)
Managerial Job Satisfaction Questionnaire (MJSQ)
Myers-Briggs Type Indicator (MBTI)
Shipley Institute of Living Scale*
Strong-Campbell Interest Inventory (SCII)

*Completed while at Center.
Source: Prepared by authors.

The specific instruments were chosen to cover a broad spectrum of psychological variables, yet at the same time to be overlapping, so as to provide a more reliable picture of the individual. Here is a brief description of each of them.

Biographical questionnaire. A short questionnaire covering areas such as age, education, current job situation, level in the organization, size of the organization, and annual pay.

"Current situation" questionnaire. A form with open-ended questions about topics such as the person's family situation, books recently read, hobbies, and an informal evaluation of personal strengths and weaknesses. This information is used in a clinical manner by the Center staff member responsible for conducting the staff feedback session. It helps to treat the individual more personally than would be possible in an otherwise brief interview.

The California Psychological Inventory (CPI). A long inventory (480 questions) with 18 scales providing scores on what the author, Harrison Gough, called "folk concepts," such as Dominance, Self-acceptance, and Flexibility. It provides a general overview of the person's psychological makeup.

The Fundamental Interpersonal Relationship Orientation-Behavior. A short inventory (54 questions) that asks the individual to report how he or she feels and acts toward other people on three dimensions: Inclusion (I), Control (C), Affection (A). The scores help individuals understand why they function as they do in work groups.

The Hidden Figures Test. A geometric test asking a person to locate a particular pattern imbedded within a larger field. It is a measure of field dependence/independence, and the results are useful in helping people understand their propensity to focus on either analyzing data or understanding people, on either isolating specific problems from the environmental context or seeing relationships between apparently separate problems.

The Kirton Adaptation Inventory. A short, one-scale inventory (33 questions) that positions each respondent along a dimension of "adaptive versus innovative" problem-solving orientation. This is helpful in emphasizing that each person has the capacity to be creative, though in different ways.

Leadership Style Indicator. A series of 48 adjectives that the individual checks to describe his or her leadership style. The same adjectives are presented to four to six subordinates to use in describing the same individual's style. The report form contains the individual's self-report, along with a summary of the subordinates' report.

The Managerial Job Satisfaction Questionnaire. A work-related inventory (25 questions) reporting the degree of satisfaction with five different aspects of work: Work Itself; Supervision; Pay; Colleagues; and Opportunity for Promotion. It has been normed on a managerial population.

The Myers-Briggs Type Indicator. An inventory (166 questions) providing scores on four bipolar dimensions based on the psychological theory of Carl Jung. It is especially helpful in understanding managerial work styles.

The Strong-Campbell Interest Inventory. A vocational interest inventory (325 questions) used to help the individual understand his or her occupational focus, and also to help make sense of the "total person" by displaying an occupationally oriented psychological profile.

The Shipley Institute of Living Scale: A short (40-item) test of mental agility. Half of it covers vocabulary; the other half, abstract reasoning. It correlates about .8 with longer IQ measures, and provides a rough but useful estimate of the individual's mental prowess. Comparisons between the verbal and abstract scores also provide a crude screen of brain damage, which turns up in our population more often than you might think, usually as a result of alcoholism.

Behavioral Ratings

During the first day of the program, each person participates in two group exercises, during which he or she is observed by Center staff members and rated on the dimensions listed in Table 7.3. For each dimension the person is rated from 10 to 50. In the lower half of Table 7.3 is an example of how the dimensions are defined.

After each exercise participants are asked to rank-order all of the group members on their overall effectiveness; these data are used to calculate both peer rankings and self-rankings. The ratings and rankings are done twice, using two different exercises to give a rough check on the reliability of the data for each person. The two exercises are not exactly alike, but both are "leaderless," that is, no one is in charge and the group has to make its own way. The nature of the exercises places a premium on outgoing, extraverted behavior, which, as we shall see later, is reflected in the personality patterns of those who do well.

These behavioral assessment ratings have worked well for their intended training and development purposes. They have good face validity, and the individuals assessed accept them as useful. The exercises are run early in the program sequence, and they clearly are seen as a slightly stressful challenge. This initial activity tends to build group cohesiveness in the "baptism of fire" sense: "They, the staff, have made things difficult for us, but we have been through this together and survived, so we must be OK people."

TABLE 7.3
Ratings and Rankings, Group Exercises, Day 1

Ratings	Rankings
Activity level	Observer ranking
Led discussion	Peer ranking
Influenced others	Self-ranking
Problem analysis	
Task orientation	
Motivated others	
Interpersonal skills	
Verbal effectiveness	

Rating Points for the "Activity Level" Dimension

50   Always active in process; wants a summary; reviews; questions; keeps at it; never allows group to take the easy way; a hard driver; likely to stick with activity until he/she has exhausted all possible information

40   Maintains high level of interaction, but loses interest in details at end or in specific intermediate activities; seldom allows group to take the easy way

30   Keeps active, but level of interest varies; may come and go during discussion

20   Occasional participation in group activity; not involved in 50% of group activity; answers questions without elaboration

10   Quiet; nondynamic; sometimes appears bored; speaks or acts only when asked; noninvolved

Source: Prepared by authors.

Although the ratings are useful in training, they do have some imperfections. These flaws are not sufficient to invalidate the data, but they suggest caution in making absolute statements about the behavior under study. There are three main problems. First, some of the ratings are made by observers who will eventually be responsible for presenting feedback to the observed individuals. Consequently, there may be some tendency for the rater to think, "I'm going to be reporting these ratings to this individual, and it's a lot more pleasant to report a high rating than a low rating, so I think I'll just ease this rating up a few points."

The raters doubt that this happens very often, and we haven't yet had an opportunity to arrange the data in a way that tests for it. There are several reasons for believing that the bias is not large: not all of the ratings are made by the person who will be reporting them; each rater has to reconcile his/her ratings with one other observer; the summary ranking is a forced-distribution, so that some people have to be ranked high and others ranked low; the raters have been specifically trained in making these ratings; and stereotypes and other kinds of rater biases have been reviewed with them. Consequently, the possibility of bias is only a nagging concern, not a major problem.

One immediate question is why these people are doing the ratings. Why not have unbiased observers? The reason is that the main purpose of collecting these data is to help the participant understand how he or she comes across to other people in a committeelike problem-solving group. The best person to aid in that process is someone who has actually observed the group, rather than a stranger working with secondhand data. In this sense the ratings serve as a conversational catalyst for the discussion of the person's performance in the feedback session.

The second, larger problem is that the raters have trouble making the discriminations called for by the various rating variables. For example, they have trouble distinguishing between the dimensions Activity Level and Influenced Others. This problem is evident in Table 7.5, which reports the intercorrelations between the ratings. Most of the correlations in that table are high, demonstrating that the raters are not distinguishing between the dimensions.

In the best of all worlds, these correlations should be low, we should be dealing with independent dimensions, and each dimension should be providing new and unique data. Yet some of the redundancy is desirable, in order to increase the reliability of the ratings. Just as we wouldn't use only one problem in an algebra test, so we shouldn't use just one rating as a performance measure. The correlated dimensions provide better coverage, just as correlated algebra problems make a better test, as long as we recognize that we actually are dealing with only two or three factors, not eight discrete dimensions.

The third problem, a more complicated technical one, stems from the relative nature of the ratings. They are based on the characteristics of the people who happen to be in a particular exercise. Within the group some are going to be rated high, and others are going to be rated low. Although, in theory, all participants could rate either high or low, it doesn't work out that way in practice.

The problem can best be illustrated by imagining two groups of participants, one drawn from among top performers—fluent, imaginative, diplomatic, personally effective—the second drawn from some problem category—disorganized, passive, confused, ineffective. In both groups some people would be rated high, some low, with the group means similar, even though the true group difference would be substantial.

In our "public" programs, for which anyone can sign up and the participants are drawn from a wide array of personal situations and formal occupations, this problem should not be serious, since the impact is spread randomly across many people. It may be a larger problem in "contract" programs (run by contract for one organization), in which the participants are more homogeneous. As yet, we don't know the magnitude of the problem.

There is nothing dishonest or misleading in reporting such assessments to the individual, as long as the relative nature of the ratings is made clear. The format of our report to the participants emphasizes this by giving, along with the individual's score, the mean, maximum, and minimum values of the particular class that the individual was in.

Peer Appraisal

We use a careful, closely orchestrated process of peer observation and feedback. It is intended to be a model of how to provide constructive suggestions to colleagues and subordinates. Because the process does not produce any quantifiable data, there is no way to document it here.

Videotapes

We have experimented with a variety of ways of using videotapes in the program, usually in conjunction with the assessment portion. The usual way is to videotape some of the training exercises, explain something about effective and ineffective group problem-solving methods, and then have the group watch the tape, discussing their behavior in the context of these methods.

Although this is not assessment in the usual sense, the process does give each person some informative feedback on his or her behavior in a group problem-solving session. Usually this channel of feedback dovetails quite nicely with the information from the tests, behavioral ratings, and peer reports.

RESULTS FROM THE ASSESSMENT PROCESS

Table 7.4 contains the mean ratings on the behavioral assessment variables. These scales range from a low of 10 to a high of 50, with 30 being the "typical" score. In our groups the means range in the mid-30s.

Because our collection of data includes both paper-and-pencil inventories and observational ratings of actual behavior, we have the unusual opportunity to compare behavioral rating data with psychological test scores. This has been done by including in each test profile table the average scores for the individuals ranked at the top in the group exercises versus those ranked at the bottom.

The high-ranked sample includes those participants who were ranked either 1 or 2 by the staff observers, their peers, and themselves; the low-ranked sample includes those who were ranked 4 or lower by all three observers. (The rankings ranged from a high of 1 to a low of 5, 6, or 7, depending on how many people there were in the small group.) Table 7.5 presents the correlation matrix for the behavioral assessment measures.

Tables 7.6-7.8 include summary statistics for the roughly 1,000 people participating in the Leadership Development Program from 1979 to 1982. Scanning these tables gives an idea of our average participant.

On the CPI the highest mean scores (and they are quite high) are on the Dominance, Self-acceptance, Achievement via Independence, Psychological-Mindedness and Social Presence scales. There are no low means.

On the Myers-Briggs the most frequent types are the ISTJs, ESTJs, ENTJs, and INTJs, as shown in Table 7.9. These are management and leadership types, and include both people who are practical, efficient doers (the ISTJs and the ESTJs) and the visionary dreamers (the ENTJs and the INTJs).

On the Strong-Campbell the highest mean scores are on the Business Management and Military Activities scales, with moderately high scores

TABLE 7.4
Behavior Ratings for Total Sample, and for High- and Low-Ranked Subsamples

	Exercise I								Exercise II							
	Total CCL[a] Sample (N = 1,036)		High[b] Ranked (N = 134)		Low[c] Ranked (N = 202)		Mean Difference/ Total S.D.		Total CCL[a] Sample (N = 1,036)		High[b] Ranked (N = 134)		Low[c] Ranked (N = 202)		Mean Difference/ Total S.D.	
Variable	Mean	S.D.	Mean	S.D.	Mean	S.D.			Mean	S.D.	Mean	S.D.	Mean	S.D.		
Activity level	36	6.4	41	3.3	29	6.3	1.9		36	6.0	40	4.6	33	6.7	1.2	
Led the discussion	34	7.0	41	3.1	26	6.4	2.2		34	6.5	38	4.7	30	7.0	1.2	
Influenced others	35	6.7	41	3.1	28	6.4	1.9		35	6.3	38	4.8	31	7.1	1.1	
Problem analysis	36	5.7	40	4.0	31	6.4	1.6		36	5.7	39	4.7	33	6.8	1.0	
Task orientation	36	5.6	41	3.2	31	5.3	1.8		37	5.4	40	4.6	34	5.9	1.1	
Motivated others	33	6.7	38	4.9	27	6.8	1.7		34	6.3	37	4.2	30	7.1	1.1	
Verbal Effectiveness	37	4.9	40	3.5	34	4.6	1.2		37	4.5	39	3.4	35	5.2	0.9	
Interpersonal skills	34	4.9	36	5.6	32	3.3	0.8		34	4.3	35	4.6	33	3.9	0.5	
Observer rating	3.5	1.6	1.4	0.5	5.2	0.8	-2.4		3.5	1.6	2.7	1.5	4.3	1.5	-1.0	
Peer rating	3.2	1.4	1.6	0.5	4.7	0.8	-2.2		3.3	1.4	2.6	1.1	3.9	1.4	-0.9	
Self-rating	3.2	1.4	1.7	0.5	4.8	0.8	-2.2		3.3	1.4	2.6	1.2	4.1	1.3	-1.1	

[a] All participants in CCL-LDP public programs (1979–1982).
[b] "High" = Individuals ranked 1 or 2 in Exercise 1 by observers, peers, and self.
[c] "Low" = Individuals ranked 4 or lower in Exercise 1 by observers, peers, and self.
Source: Prepared by the authors.

TABLE 7.5
Correlations Among Behavioral Assessment Measures for the Total Sample (N = 968)

	Exercise I											Exercise II										
	Act.	Led	Inf.	Ana.	Task	Mot.	IpS.	Verb.	ObsR	Peer	SelfR	Act.	Led	Inf.	Ana.	Task	Mot.	IpS.	Verb.	ObsR	Peer	SelfR
Exercise I																						
Activity level	1.00																					
Led discussion	.92	1.00																				
Influenced others	.87	.90	1.00																			
Problem analysis	.77	.74	.79	1.00																		
Task orientation	.83	.84	.81	.76	1.00																	
Motivated others	.74	.76	.74	.71	.71	1.00																
Interpersonal skills	.37	.36	.40	.49	.35	.62	1.00															
Verbal effectiveness	.68	.65	.70	.74	.64	.60	.48	1.00														
Observer rating*	.70	.75	.74	.59	.69	.65	.42	.56	1.00													
Peer rating*	.53	.56	.54	.42	.49	.43	.22	.41	.58	1.00												
Self-rating*	.53	.55	.55	.44	.50	.46	.26	.38	.59	.51	1.00											
Exercise II																						
Activity level	.47	.47	.46	.42	.42	.38	.23	.45	.39	.37	.37	1.00										
Led discussion	.48	.49	.48	.42	.44	.39	.23	.45	.41	.39	.39	.91	1.00									
Influenced others	.45	.46	.45	.40	.41	.37	.23	.44	.38	.37	.35	.89	.90	1.00								
Problem analysis	.37	.38	.39	.38	.35	.33	.23	.39	.31	.31	.28	.76	.82	.82	1.00							
Task orientation	.45	.45	.44	.39	.42	.33	.21	.42	.37	.32	.32	.84	.82	.83	.78	1.00						
Motivated others	.44	.43	.44	.40	.39	.38	.26	.42	.39	.35	.35	.82	.84	.85	.78	.80	1.00					
Interpersonal skills	.25	.22	.25	.25	.21	.29	.35	.29	.23	.20	.22	.48	.50	.53	.53	.47	.66	1.00				
Verbal effectiveness	.44	.43	.46	.46	.43	.39	.30	.54	.37	.33	.33	.72	.73	.77	.75	.72	.72	.56	1.00			
Observer rating*	.36	.37	.35	.31	.32	.28	.19	.33	.37	.37	.35	.73	.76	.74	.68	.70	.73	.49	.59	1.00		
Peer rating*	.30	.29	.29	.26	.28	.22	.13	.28	.25	.38	.23	.56	.59	.57	.50	.51	.53	.32	.45	.57	1.00	
Self-rating*	.28	.29	.28	.23	.23	.22	.14	.24	.28	.25	.41	.55	.58	.54	.45	.48	.50	.27	.39	.60	.48	1.00

*For consistency, the algebraic signs of these correlations have been reversed.
Source: Prepared by the authors.

TABLE 7.6
Psychological Test Scores for Total Sample, and for
High- and Low-Ranked Subsamples

Test	Total CCL[a] Sample (N = 1,036)		High[b] Rated (N = 132)		Low[c] Rated (N = 199)		Mean Difference/ Total Sample
	Mean	S.D.	Mean	S.D.	Mean	S.D.	S.D.
Shipley Institute of Living Scale							
Verbal	35	3.4	35	3.0	34	3.7	0.3
Abstract	33	5.2	34	4.8	31	5.8	0.6
Total (IQ)	119	7.4	120	6.9	117'	8.0	0.4
Kirton Adapta- tion-Innova- tion Inventory	105	16.2	109	15.8	98	15.1	0.7
Hidden Figures	17	7.7	18	8.2	15	7.9	0.4
FIRO-B							
Expressed inclusion	3.7	2.1	3.7	2.1	3.2	2.0	0.2
Wanted inclusion	2.9	3.2	3.0	3.2	2.4	3.1	0.2
Expressed control	4.9	2.6	6.0	2.4	4.3	2.6	0.7
Wanted control	3.1	1.9	2.9	2.0	3.3	2.0	-0.2
Expressed affection	3.1	2.0	3.3	2.2	2.7	1.9	0.3
Wanted affection	4.8	2.2	4.9	2.3	4.8	2.1	0.0

[a]All participants in CCL-LDP public programs (1979–1982).
[b]"High" = Individuals ranked 1 or 2 in Exercise I by observers, peers, and self.
[c]"Low" = Individuals ranked 4 or lower in Exercise I by observers, peers, and self.
Source: Prepared by the authors.

TABLE 7.7
California Psychological Inventory Scores for Total Sample,
and for High- and Low-Ranked Subsamples

CPI Scale	Total CCL[a] Sample (N = 1,036)		High[b] Rated (N = 131)		Low[c] Rated (N = 194)		Mean Difference/ Total Sample
	Mean	S.D.	Mean	S.D.	Mean	S.D.	S.D.
Dominance	63	9.6	67	8.1	58	9.6	0.9
Capacity for status	55	8.8	58	7.5	51	8.8	0.8
Sociability	53	9.4	56	7.8	50	9.4	0.6
Social presence	57	10.4	60	8.3	53	10.5	0.7
Self-acceptance	60	9.3	64	8.0	56	9.8	0.9
Sense of well-being	52	9.6	53	8.5	51	9.3	0.2
Responsibility	49	8.8	51	8.5	47	9.4	0.5
Socialization	49	8.8	49	8.8	49	8.8	0.0
Self-control	48	9.7	48	8.7	49	9.0	-0.1
Tolerance	52	8.6	54	7.2	50	8.4	0.5
Good impression	48	9.5	49	9.4	46	9.7	0.3
Communality	55	7.2	55	7.0	56	6.7	-0.1
Achievement via con-formance	55	8.6	57	7.7	52	8.4	0.6
Achievement via inde-pendence	58	8.4	59	7.5	56	8.7	0.4
Intellectual efficiency	52	9.6	54	7.8	49	9.5	0.5
Psychological-mindedness	58	9.2	59	8.9	56	9.1	0.3
Flexibility	54	10.4	53	10.0	52	10.4	0.1

[a]All participants in CCL-LDP public programs (1979–1982).
[b]"High" = Individuals ranked 1 or 2 in Exercise I by observers, peers, and self.
[c]"Low" = Individuals ranked 4 in Exercise I by observers, peers, and self.
Source: Prepared by the authors.

TABLE 7.8
Strong-Campbell Interest Inventory Scores for Total Sample,
and for High- and Low-Ranked Subsamples

SCII Scale	Total CCL[a] Sample (N = 1,036)		High[b] Rated (N = 132)		Low[c] Rated (N = 196)		Mean Difference/ Total Sample
	Mean	S.D.	Mean	S.D.	Mean	S.D.	S.D.
General occu-pational themes							
Realistic	55	11.0	54	11.2	57	11.2	-0.3
Investigative	51	9.4	52	9.4	51	9.9	0.1
Artistic	47	10.8	48	10.5	45	10.6	0.3
Social	48	9.7	48	10.3	48	9.8	0.0
Enterprising	53	9.4	54	9.9	52	8.9	0.2
Conventional	50	8.6	50	7.6	51	8.2	-0.1
Special scales Academic comfort	44	13.5	45	13.2	42	13.8	0.2
Intraversion/ extraversion	48	10.7	44	9.0	52	11.1	0.7
Basic interest scales							
Agriculture	52	9.8	50	9.4	54	10.5	-0.4
Nature	48	11.1	46	11.4	49	10.9	-0.3
Adventure	54	9.5	56	9.3	53	9.6	0.3
Military activities	56	12.3	58	12.4	55	12.4	0.2
Mechanical activities	53	11.3	52	11.5	55	11.6	-0.3
Science	49	10.1	49	10.0	51	10.6	-0.2
Mathematics	53	10.4	55	9.6	54	10.6	0.1
Medical science	50	10.0	49	10.5	50	10.3	0.1
Medical service	45	7.7	44	7.7	46	8.0	-0.3
Music/ dramatics	47	11.3	47	11.1	45	11.6	0.2
Art	45	11.2	45	10.8	44	11.4	0.1
Writing	47	10.6	48	10.3	44	10.4	0.4
Teaching	47	9.9	48	9.3	46	9.9	0.2
Social service	46	9.4	46	9.8	45	9.5	0.1
Athletics	53	10.1	53	9.5	53	10.0	0.0
Domestic arts	43	9.9	44	9.5	43	10.3	0.1
Religious activities	47	10.1	46	10.1	48	10.0	-0.2

Public speaking	53	9.6	57	8.7	50	9.7	0.7
Law/politics	54	9.4	57	8.0	51	9.2	0.6
Merchandising	52	9.4	53	8.9	50	9.3	0.3
Sales	52	10.2	53	11.2	51	9.9	0.2
Business management	57	8.8	58	7.9	56	9.1	0.2
Office practices	45	7.1	44	6.3	46	7.4	-0.3

[a]All participants in CCL-LDP public programs (1979–1982).

[b]"High" = Individuals ranked 1 or 2 in Exercise I by observers, peers, and self.

[c]"Low" = Individuals ranked 4 or lower in Exercise 1 by observers, peers, and self.

Source: Prepared by the authors.

on Adventure (given the average age of this sample, 42, a mean of 54 on the Adventure scale is quite high, since scores on that scale tend to decline with age), Athletics, Mechanical Activities, Mathematics, and Public Speaking. Our sample has low mean scores on the Art and Social Service scales, and a very low score on the Domestic Arts scale. Some of these results, especially the scores on Mechanical Activities, Art, and Domestic Arts scales, can be explained simply by the predominance of men in our sample.

On the Shipley Scale the group averages 119, a very respectable score. (That scale has a population average of 100, with a ceiling of 140.) On the hidden figures the average is 17, well toward the field-independent end of the dimension.

On the Kirton the group is in the middle, with a slight tilt toward the Innovative end of the dimension, versus the Adaptive end.

On the FIRO-B the most interesting mean is on the Expressed Control scale, a scale reflecting a willingness, an eagerness, perhaps even a determination, to be in charge. The other interesting finding is the high mean score on the Wanted Affection scale. It is indeed lonely at the top.

TEST SCORE COMPARISONS BETWEEN THE HIGH- AND LOW-RANKED GROUPS

The test score data presented in tables 7.6-7.9 provide a comparison between the high- and low-ranked groups. The most important column is the far right-hand one in each table, which shows an estimate of the magnitude of difference between the groups, usually the mean difference divided by the total group standard deviation (SD). (The senior author has long had an abhorrence for the techniques of statistical inference because

TABLE 7.9
MBTI Type Percentages for Total Sample,
and for High- and Low-Rated Subgroups

	CCL Norms (N = 1,022) % (N)	High Ranked (N = 133) % (N)	Low Ranked (N = 201) % (N)	High % ÷ Low %
ISTJ	21(215)	19(25)	31(63)	0.6
ESTJ	18(181)	16(22)	15(31)	1.1
ENTJ	13(135)	18(24)	6(13)	3.0
INTJ	11(110)	8(10)	12(24)	0.7
INTP	7(69)	9(12)	7(15)	1.3
ENTP	6(61)	6(8)	2(4)	3.0
ENFP	4(46)	4(5)	4(8)	1.0
ISTP	4(40)	2(2)	7(14)	0.3
ESTP	4(38)	5(6)	5(9)	1.0
ESFJ	3(31)	4(5)	2(3)	2.0
INFP	3(27)	3(4)	3(6)	1.0
ISFJ	2(21)	3(4)	2(4)	1.5
ENFJ	2(18)	4(5)	1(2)	4.0
INFJ	2(16)	1(1)	1(1)	1.0
ESFP	1(10)	0(0)	2(3)	—
ISFP	—(4)	0(0)	1(1)	—
E's	51(520)	57(75)	36(73)	1.6
I's	49(502)	45(58)	64(128)	0.7
S's	53(540)	49(64)	64(128)	0.8
N's	47(482)	53(69)	36(73)	1.5
T's	83(849)	83(109)	87(173)	1.0
F's	17(173)	19(24)	14(28)	1.4
J's	71(727)	73(96)	70(141)	1.0
P's	29(295)	29(37)	30(60)	1.0
ST	46(474)	42(55)	58(117)	0.7
NT	37(375)	41(54)	28(56)	1.5
SF	6(66)	7(9)	5(11)	1.4
NF	10(107)	12(15)	8(17)	1.5

Source: Prepared by David Campbell, Center for Creative Leadership. Copyright 1983 by David Campbell.

the typical methods reveal nothing about the magnitude of the difference under study. The concept of "number of SDs separating the groups" is much more meaningful; whenever there is a difference of 0.5 standard deviation or more, it is important. A difference of that magnitude is far beyond the usual bounds of statistical significance, especially with large samples, such as we have here.

In Table 7.4 we can see that the two criterion groups differ by over two standard deviations on the rankings that were used to define them, and they differ by almost that much in the other ratings from Exercise 1—no surprise there; those are artificially contrived differences. However, on Exercise II, which can be viewed as validity generalization, the difference between the groups was still quite large, usually about one standard deviation. We are in fact dealing with some durable "truth" here.

In the other tables of data, any differences larger than 0.5 SD are worth noting; and scanning those tables shows a very reasonable pattern of differences between the two groups. They differ on many of the scales of the CPI, usually in predictable ways. The biggest differences are on the Dominance and Self-Acceptance scales (0.9 SD), with other large differences on Capacity for Status (0.8), Social Presence (0.7), Sociability and Achievement via Conformance (0.6 each), and Intellectual Efficiency (0.5). This diffuse pattern of high scores suggests that the CPI may have some of the same characteristics as our group exercise ratings in not being able to discriminate between related "good" behaviors.

Other noteworthy ratio differences are on the KAI score (0.7), FIRO-B Expressed Control (0.7), and the Shipley Abstract Reasoning scale (0.6).

The large differences on the SCII are on Introversion-Extraversion scale and Public Speaking (0.7), and Law/Politics (0.6), a satisfying, sensible pattern. Also on the SCII, in marked contrast with the other tests, the low-ranked group scored higher on some scales, such as Agriculture (0.4) and Nature, Mechanical Activities, and Office Practices (all 0.3). Although these differences are smaller than the others, the interest inventory did pick up the areas where the low-ranked group preferred to be more active than the high-ranked group—the pattern again being quite sensible.

This overall pattern of test score differences between the two groups demonstrates that both the tests and the ratings are working reasonably well. Collectively they describe a believable pattern of differences between people who work well with small groups of strangers and people who are less effective. The former group tends to include outgoing, dominant, energetic, self-confident people who enjoy public speaking and verbal sparring. Organized, methodical, quiet people interested in a tidy world don't come across as well in these settings although they, of course, have their own strengths in other areas.

WHY WE USE THESE TESTS

Without exception, everyone on our staff is an "Intuitive" on the Myers-Briggs. One characteristic of that type is a tendency to make decisions on the basis of intuition and hunches, and then, after the fact, search for some rationale to explain what they did. That is clearly the case here. The tests that we use were chosen at different times for different reasons, including "Let's just try it out and see what happens." In retrospect, the survivors in the test battery have proven useful for some combination of the following reasons:

1. **To demonstrate psychological principles.** This collection of inventories covers a wide range of psychological constructs, such as Dominance, Extraversion-Introversion, and Field Independence. The constructs are explained in the course of the instruction, usually in the classroom, with elaboration as appropriate in the one-on-one test interpretation sessions, in the belief that an understanding of them will lead to a better understanding of one's own behavior and the behavior of others.

2. **To help the individual better understand his or her specific strengths, stresses, and weaknesses.** Most people have a fairly accurate perception of their own psychological characteristics; few are truly surprised by the test results. ("Yes, I've known for years that I'm an introvert.") What they are less certain of is how they compare with other people ("Isn't everyone?"). Some of the scores may pinpoint specific points that are not apparent to someone who does not have normed data available for comparison. The best example of this is probably the Managerial Job Satisfaction Questionnaire. The individual's scores on this reflect satisfaction, or lack of it, in several work-related areas, and the normed scores show each person how he or she falls within the managerial population; this comparison may turn up some sizable discrepancies in self-perception. ("I knew I wasn't thrilled about my work, but my gosh, I didn't realize I was that unhappy," or vice versa.)

People also may have trouble seeing the overall pattern of their psychological makeup; we see our individual trees clearly, but the forest is hard to grasp. The overall picture provided by the summarized information coming from varying directions can be very valuable.

3. **To help people understand the behavior of others.** Being a leader (or manager or executive or administrator or whatever word suits you) involves a heavy dose of daily interaction with others—in fact, that's about all the job really is: how do you arrange the lives of people to keep

them motivated while getting a job done? Good leaders need to understand the motivations of others, their quirks, aspirations, and characteristic modes of thinking. The psychological constructs covered by these tests should add to that understanding.

4. **To help the individual plan a future course of action.** Our course has a heavy component of career planning in it. Career planning is a universal, lifelong concern. No matter what our age, occupational status, level of income, or other achievements, we are all continually trying to figure out what to do with our futures. This is especially true in the life of a "leader." Leadership development is essentially career development, with the good leader continually trying to take on more responsibility, a bigger staff, larger budgets, and more complicated problems. Reviewing this sizable collection of personal information helps each individual to see a clearer picture of the present, and then perhaps to see more clearly into both the near and the distant future. For many of these action-oriented people, this appears to be the first time they have sat down and systematically examined where they are and where they are going.

5. **To emphasize the wide range of psychological diversity in groups.** People are different, and while most of us realize that in principle, accepting it in practice is difficult. One way of dramatizing the diversity is to bring together a group, give it a collection of tests and questionnaires, and display the results in a way that emphasizes the group variability while preserving the anonymity of the individuals involved. Looking at the range of test scores in a small group that has been working together for a week is a marvelous way of emphasizing the diversity. It also increases the credibility of the tests because the members of the group have had some chance to get to know one another's work styles; and the tests usually reflect those individual differences in ways that are eminently reasonable.

6. **To emphasize the unique individuality of each person in the session.** One of the problems in many educational or training sessions is that people do not feel they are being given individualized attention; everyone is treated the same. In contrast, giving each person his or her own test profile, and calling attention to the wide range of differences within the group, is a wonderful way to make each person feel uniqueness. Everyone is indeed different, and the program, with the use of psychological tests, emphasizes that point.

7. **To increase the scientific credibility of the Center and its programs.** This emphasis on assessment and the scientifically established uniqueness and value of the individual is one of the major distinguishing characteristics separating the Center's programs from similar programs of

other organizations. Partially this is an "image opportunity"; psychological tests look scientific, and the good ones are. Using them in professional ways enhances the image of the Center in the eyes of the people who come here. It gives us a well-earned aura of respectability and professionalism, especially since we work hard at making the test results useful to the individual in a gentle, ego-protecting, constructive manner.

8. **To provide enjoyment.** One of the major reasons that we use so many tests is that both staff and participants enjoy using them. Pure enjoyment is not in itself a sufficient primary reason for using tests, but it is a good secondary one. People like to take tests and see their results, and staff members like to be part of that process, partly because of the inherently interesting nature of the activity—you get to see what people are really like—and partly because it gives us a source of "expert" power in our dealings with the group. There is a certain implied "guru" status in the role of test interpreter.

9. **For research purposes, so that reports such as this one can be prepared.** For the Leadership Development Program to continue into its second decade, it needs to be continually under scrutiny. What are we doing? Why are we doing it? What is the impact? These are questions that must always be in front of us. The use of systematic ways of assessing people is a great aid in that process.

REFERENCES

Hershey, P., & Blanchard, K.H. *Management of organizational behavior: Utilizing human resources* (4th ed.). Englewood Cliffs, N.J.: Prentice-Hall, 1982.

Reddin, W.J. *Managerial effectiveness.* New York: McGraw-Hill, 1970.

Vroom, V.H., & Yetton, P. *Leadership and decision making.* Pittsburgh: University of Pittsburgh, 1973.

8

Styles of Cognitive-Personality Functioning
Donald R. Goodenough

In the 1970s McKenney and Keen (1974) published a paper in the *Harvard Business Review*. The paper was about differences in how managers reach decisions. They describe a few specific differences. For example, some managers are said to be systematic, while others are said to be intuitive, in their approach to business problems. But they focus on three more general conclusions. In their view there is no simple, best way of thinking about a problem. The most effective decisions about a given problem may be reached in one way by some people, and in a different way by other people. If that is so, then managers differ in what have been called dimensions of cognitive style.

McKenney and Keen also conclude that stylistic differences in cognitive functioning may reflect more general differences in personality functioning. Finally, they suggest that it is important to recognize problems that are created when work situations are incompatible with an individual's style of cognitive-personality functioning. McKenney and Keen were not the first to suggest these conclusions, but they are a good example, I think, of a growing interest in the application of cognitive-style principles to business problems.

There is a long history of research on stylistic differences, but I believe that the term "cognitive style" was introduced in the 1950s by psychologists who belonged to what was then called the New Look movement in perception. The New Look movement was a loose confederation of theorists who were discontented with traditional treatments of perception and personality as two isolated areas. They shared the view that personality affects the way an individual functions in all areas of life. The term "cognitive styles" was used to describe the dimensions of cognitive-personality functioning that they began to uncover (see Messick 1969).

The New Look movement reached its peak in the mid-1950s, but there has been a recent revival of interest in stylistic dimensions from two new sources. One source involves information-processing psychologists who have been trying to develop detailed models of the way that problems are solved. Their work has uncovered some interesting differences in problem-solving styles. In some cases people differ dramatically in how the problem is solved, without much difference in how well it is solved (see Hunt 1983). The other source involves specialists in business and education who have been studying cognitive styles in industrial and school settings. The work of McKenney and Keen (1974) is an example of this type.

Not much applied research has been done in business settings, so I would like to begin by focusing on the more academic work, where the concepts can be illustrated and documented more fully.

COGNITIVE STYLES FROM THE NEW LOOK TRADITION

The rallying cry for the New Look movement was expressed by Klein and Schlesinger (1949) in a paper entitled "Where Is the Perceiver in Perceptual Theory?" The question emphasized their view that the adaptive needs of a central regulating personality structure are served even by very simple perceptual processes. To answer the question, they reexamined some classical perceptual studies in the hope of finding individual differences that might be related to the personality of the perceiver.

Field-dependence, the most widely studied dimension of this type, is a good example of the New Look approach to cognitive styles. It was discovered by Witkin and Asch (1948) while they were studying the role of visual cues in perception of the vertical direction. A typical experiment involves displays such as those shown in Figure 8.1.

The subject views a rod, like the one at the left of the figure; the problem is to adjust the rod to the vertical position.

The problem seems too trivial to be interesting, and in fact almost everyone can align the rod with the vertical without much error under normal conditions. But it is not so obvious how the judgments are made. One set of proprioceptive cues to the vertical is available from the vestibular,

FIGURE 8.1
Typical Display in Studies of Visual Cues in Perception

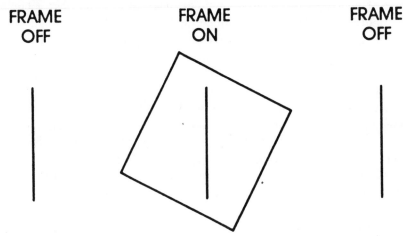

FRAME OFF   FRAME ON   FRAME OFF

Source: Prepared by author

tactile, and kinesthetic senses, and a set of visual cues is normally available in the form of contours that are aligned with the vertical and the horizontal directions. For example, the corners of the walls in this room could be used as cues to the vertical direction. The question was, how important are these visual cues?

To answer the question, Witkin and Asch (1948) designed some tests to create a conflict between the visual and proprioceptive cues. In a rod-and-frame condition the room lights are turned off, and a large square frame is lit up. The conflict is created by tilting the frame, so that the vertical direction indicated by the visual cues is not the same as the vertical direction indicated by the proprioceptive cues. What; the subject sees is illustrated in the center of the figure. The hypothesis was that rod settings would err in the same direction as the frame, to the extent that visual cues are important. The frame is tilted clockwise in the figure, so subjects were expected to set the rod in a clockwise direction if they relied on the frame.

Witkin and Asch found dramatic individual differences. Some people adjusted the rod very much in the direction of the frame, evidently basing their judgments primarily on cues from the visual field. These people were therefore called field-dependent. Other people aligned the rod more or less with the vertical, whether or not the frame was lit, evidently basing their judgments primarily on proprioceptive cues. These people were called field-independent. Most people are located between the two extremes, basing their judgments on a compromise resolution of the cue conflict.

The rod-and-frame test is still used to measure degree of field dependence, under standard conditions where upright observers view a tilted frame. Under these conditions field-dependent people are less accurate than field-independent people. But normally the visual effect has adaptive value when the observer is tilted (Bischof 1974). If you tilt your body to the side, objects appear to maintain a constant orientation in space. But orientation constancy is not complete in the absence of visual cues. If you lie on your side in a dark room, for example, an objectively vertical rod looks slightly tilted in the opposite direction. The illusion can be measured by asking the observer to adjust the rod to the vertical. If that is done, rod settings reveal an error of about 15 degrees in the same direction as the body is tilted, as shown in the illustration at the left in Figure 8.2.

The errors are eliminated if the room lights are turned on. Thus, field dependence helps to maintain visual orientation constancy under these con-

FIGURE 8.2
Illustration of Illusory Error in Adjusting the Rod to Vertical

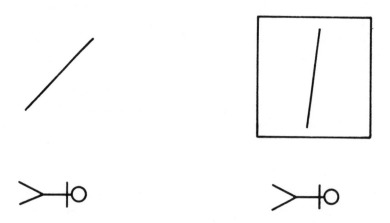

Source: Prepared by author

ditions. If the room lights are turned off, and a vertically oriented frame is substituted, as shown in the illustration at the right in Figure 8.2, the errors are not totally eliminated but are very much reduced. In fact, we recently completed a study suggesting that field-dependent people are more accurate than field-independent people if subjects are lying on their sides while viewing the upright frame. Thus, field-dependent people may be less accurate than field-independent people under some conditions, but more accurate under other conditions. Taking all conditions into account, the field dependence dimension appears to have more to do with *how* the orientation problem is solved than with *how well* the problem is solved.

The fact that people differ in the way they decide which way is up is of limited interest in itself. For most of us, the difference is important only to the extent that it reflects differences in the way a person functions more generally. In the tradition of their time, Witkin and many other New Look psychologists jumped at the question of how the dramatic differences in field dependence might be related to the perceiver's personality (Witkin et al. 1954).

The Educational Testing Service publishes a biannual bibliography of the field dependence literature, which now numbers about 4,000 references (Cox & Gall 1981). It seems clear from this work that the field dependence dimension is related to personality. The differences perhaps can be described most simply by saying that field-dependent people tend to have a more social, *inter*personal orientation to life. In contrast, field-independent people tend to be more abstract, *im*personal, and self-reliant or inner-directed (Witkin & Goodenough 1977). To illustrate the variety of evidence that is currently available to support this conclusion, I would like now to describe, very briefly, some of the different kinds of research that have been done on the question. I should say at the outset that I have not personally been involved in most of this work, but I don't have the time to mention all the authors' names except for a few points that are based on only one study.

The personality correlates of the field dependence dimension have often been studied by collecting ratings from peers or trained observers. Field-dependent subjects have been described as gregarious, affiliation-oriented, socially outgoing, interested in people, knowing many people, and known by many people. Contrasting terms have been used to describe field-independent subjects—for example, individualistic, preferring solitary activities, concerned with ideas and principles, aloof, and cold and distant in relationships with other people (Witkin & Goodenough 1977).

Similar conclusions have been reached by many authors who have recorded the details of social behavior. Some of these authors have worked in naturalistic settings, and others have borrowed techniques from experimental social psychology in which group interactions are observed under controlled laboratory conditions.

The evidence suggests that subjects who prefer to be closely involved with people are more likely to be field-dependent than field-independent. Most studies that have been done in naturalistic settings show that subjects who spend more time in group activities tend to be field-dependent (see Coates et al. 1975). For example, college athletes who participate in team sports such as baseball, football, and hockey tend to be more field-dependent than athletes who participate in individual sports such as wrestling, track, or gymnastics (Schreiber 1972). The evidence from laboratory studies also suggests that field-dependent subjects prefer to be physically near other members of the group while they are interacting with them. For example, studies of interpersonal space show that they stand closer to their conversational partners than do field-independent subjects (see Justice 1969).

There is also a variety of evidence on the importance to field-dependent subjects of information about other people. They produce more social words when asked to say the first thing that comes into their minds (Goldberger & Bendich 1972). Many authors have concluded that field-dependent subjects pay more attention to social information. Most studies show that they spend more time looking at people with whom they are interacting (see Ruble & Nakamura 1972). It is not surprising, therefore, that they acquire more social information. For example, they tend to remember more names and faces of the people in groups to which they belong (Crutchfield et al. 1958; Oltman et al. 1975). Under more controlled laboratory conditions, most studies show that incidental learning of social information is greater among field-dependent subjects than among field-independent subjects (see Eagle, Goldberger, & Breitman 1969). These learning differences are clearly due to motivational rather than intellectual factors, because field-dependent people are no better than field-independent people at intentional learning of social material or incidental learning of nonsocial material (Goodenough 1976).

The greater commerce in personal information among field-dependent people appears to be a two-way street. They not only know more about other people, but detailed analyses of their conversation show that they tell other people more about themselves (Souza-Poza & Rohrberg 1976). This work is consistent with the finding that field-independent people are rated as more reserved, aloof, and impersonal.

To me, at least, some of the most interesting work on the personality correlates of the field dependence dimension involves the degree to which people's behavior can be predicted from the character of the social groups to which they belong. Many authors have concluded that social factors have more effect on the actions, opinions, attitudes, and feelings of field-dependent people than of field-independent people. Some of this work has been done on the effects of ambiguous social situations, in which the roles of the group members are not well defined. Social ambiguity appears to make field-dependent subjects particularly uncomfortable, but it has little effect on field-independent subjects (see Culver et al. 1964; Gates 1971). Many laboratory studies of social conformity have been reported. They suggest that field-dependent subjects are more likely to change their judgments to agree with the opinions of other people in the groups to which they belong (Linton 1955). In contrast, field-independent subjects are less likely to change their opinions, even when they are led to believe that other people are more knowledgeable or even that their judgments are more accurate (Mausner & Graham 1970). In sum, the experimental work on interpersonal influence suggests that the properties of social groups are better predictors of behavior for field-dependent than for field-independent people.

As we look at the evidence on personality correlates, it is tempting to say that field-dependent people are very socially dependent. And in some sense, I suppose they are. But they do not show all of the behaviors that have sometimes been considered signs of emotional dependency. No consistent relationships have been found with emotional dependency when measured by personality inventories, or with hypnotizability or responsiveness to placebos (Morgan 1972; Freund et al. 1972). Nor does approval seeking seem to be particularly characteristic of field-dependent subjects. For example, they are no more likely than field-independent people to volunteer for worthy causes (Soat 1974). And, although incentives evidently do have a greater effect on the behavior of field-dependent than field-independent people, incentives in the form of material rewards seems to be as effective as social approval (see Steinfeld 1973).

Of course, it is possible to interpret conformity with group pressure in terms of a need for the approval of other people. But the work of Mausner and Graham (1970) on the relationship between field dependence and conforming behavior suggests a somewhat different interpretation. The subjects of their study were placed in a fairly standard laboratory situation designed to measure social effects on judgments about the rate of alternation of a flickering light. The social pressure is created by having members of a group announce their opinions before the subjects are asked for their own judgments. The work of Mausner and Graham was novel because some subjects were shown that the group opinion was generally less accurate than their own opinion, while other subjects were shown that the group opinion was more accurate than their own. As might be expected, the judgments of the field-dependent subjects shifted more toward their partners when they thought the partners might be more accurate than when they thought the partners might be less accurate. But variations in their partners' competence had very little effect on the judgments of field-independent subjects. The results suggest that relationships between field dependence and conformity may be more a matter of the self-reliance of field-independent people than of a need to be agreeable among field-dependent people.

One of our own studies of opinion change in groups suggests, I think, a similar flavor of extremely individualistic behavior among some field-independent people (Oltman et al. 1975). The subjects in our study were assigned to two-person discussion groups that were given the task of reaching a compromise agreement on an issue about which they had initially disagreed. We found that compromises were almost always reached when the groups were composed of two field-dependent subjects. But when the groups were composed of two field-independent people, more than a third failed to reach any compromise solution. Here again, the evidence suggests to me that some field-independent people are unwilling or unable to accommodate their views to meet the reasonable requirements of a task.

The way I read the experimental work on social behavior, field-independent people are regulated more by internalized values and standards than by the immediate social environment. Witkin reached a similar conclusion in a more clinical study of therapy transcripts in which field-dependent patients were judged to be regulated more by socially induced feelings of embarrassment or shame, while field-independent patients were regulated primarily by feelings of guilt when they violated their own standards of conduct (Witkin et al. 1968).

While it seems clear that personality is related to field dependence in orientation perception, it is not so clear how these relationships can best be understood. Witkin offered two alternative explanations. At an early stage of his work, he suggested that field-dependent people are more global, and field-independent people are more analytical, in their approach to life (Witkin & Asch 1948). He developed an embedded-figures test to measure analytical approaches to the location of a camouflaged target. The embedded-figure test has been widely used as an economical alternative to the rod-and-frame test to measure field dependence (Witkin & Asch 1948).

At a later stage Witkin was more impressed by the gross analogy between the attentiveness of field-dependent subjects to visual cues in orientation perception that are judged to come from the inanimate environment, and their attentiveness to other people in the immediate social environment. He thought that behavior on the rod-and-frame test and in social situations might reflect a common outer-directed orientation to life (Witkin & Goodenough 1981), and that the embedded-figures test measured an entirely different, but related, dimension.

Field dependence is clearly related to a variety of standard measures of visualization ability, and not just to the embedded-figures test (Vernon 1972; Linn & Kylonnen 1981). It is not yet clear, however, what kind of field dependence theory can accommodate these ability and personality correlates most effectively. One might argue that the differences in cognition are a consequence of personality functions, or that the personality correlates are a consequence of the differences in cognitive functioning. But the pros and cons of various theoretical alternatives may be less interesting to the business practitioner than the question of how important the field-dependence dimension may be when it is transported from the laboratory to everyday life. On this latter point, there is some evidence to suggest that the dimension is at least very salient in ordinary commerce among people.

For me, at least, the most persuasive evidence about the salience of the dimension comes from findings that interpersonal attraction is higher among people who are similar in degree of field dependence than among people who are dissimilar. Among residents of a college dormitory, for example, one study found that field-dependent students tended to be chosen as friends by their field-dependent roommates, and field-independent students tended to be chosen as friends by their more field-independent roommates (Wong 1976). It is not surprising that people choose friends who are similar to themselves, but it is noteworthy, I think, to find that the rod-and-frame test taps a dimension that is important enough to have a detectable effect against the background of similarities and differences among people in many other personal characteristics.

COGNITIVE STYLES FROM THE INFORMATION-PROCESSING TRADITION

I'd like to turn now to the cognitive-style issues that have arisen in the more recent experimental work on problem solving. The traditional approach to intelligence testing has focused primarily on individual differences in problem-solving effectiveness. But, particularly in current information-processing research, the primary emphasis has shifted to questions about the way people transform the problem information to arrive at their solutions. By focusing on how, and not just on how well problems are solved, one might expect problem-solving styles to be discovered, if they exist. In fact, as information-processing models have been tested in detail, it has sometimes been found that one model fits the data from some subjects, but a very different model is required to fit the data from others. If contrasting groups of people are discovered in this way, the conclusion seems warranted that there are stylistic differences in the way the problem is solved. The work of Hunt and his colleagues on matching sentences and pictures is one of the simplest examples of this type (Hunt 1983; Mathews, Hunt, & McLeod 1980; McLeod, Hunt, & Mathews 1978).

In a typical experiment the subjects are first shown a sentence, and then a picture. For example the sentence might be "The star is above the cross," and the picture might show a star above a cross, or a star below a cross. The problem is to decide whether the sentence describes the picture. The theories are designed to predict differences among people in the time taken to reach a decision.

The problem seems too trivial to be interesting and, in fact, normal adults make very few errors. But it was not so obvious how the decision is reached. Like apples and oranges, the sentence and the picture have very different forms. Evidently the two kinds of information must be translated into some common form in order to make the comparison.

Hunt concluded that one of two forms may be used. For some people the common form appears to be verbal. The picture is translated into linguistic terms for comparison with the sentence. For other people the common form appears to be visual. The sentence is translated into an image of a star and a cross for comparison with the picture.

For most of us, the fact that people differ in the way they reach a decision in so simple a problem is of limited importance in itself. But the difference may be interesting if it reflects more general styles of solving problems. In the case of sentence-picture comparisons, there is some reason to believe that a variety of problems may be solved by either visual or linguistic strategies (see Sternberg & Weil 1979). There is also reason to believe that individual differences in the way the comparison is made may reflect more pervasive tendencies to approach problems visually or verbally.

The idea that some people may approach problems more visually and others more verbally is an old one, of course, and its current popularity may be due primarily to recent research on hemispheric specialization that shows that the right hemisphere of the brain is normally more specialized for processing figural material and the left hemisphere for processing verbal material. But Hunt's work on sentence-picture matching is a good example of the kind of research that I suspect will become increasingly important in the attempt to characterize people in terms of their problem-solving style.

The cognitive styles that are beginning to appear in the information-processing literature differ in some ways from the earlier styles of the New Look movement. The New Look dimensions were often continuous variables. It may be convenient to talk about the contrasts between field-dependent and field-independent subjects, for example, but the terms refer to extremes of the dimension, and not to discrete types of perception or types of people. But visual and verbal ways of solving problems are qualitatively different from each other. The New Look dimensions also are often very stable and hard to change. But visual and verbal ways of comparing sentences and pictures appear to be more a matter of strategy choice. Although a given person may typically use one of these two methods, most college students can easily shift from one to the other (Mathews et al. 1980).

Although the method used may be largely a matter of strategy choice, the choice is not trivial, because the subject may be able to solve the problem more effectively by one method than by the other. Hunt has argued persuasively that a visual strategy requires different abilities than does a linguistic strategy. For example, when sentences are compared with pictures visually, the time taken to reach a decision is particularly related to standard tests of visualization ability. But when pictures are compared with sentences linguistically, speed is related particularly to verbal ability. So a person who is higher in verbal than in visual abiilty may work more effectively by using a linguistic strategy, and a person who is higher in visual than in verbal ability may work more effectively by using a visual strategy.

These findings raise a question about whether a person's choice of strategies is based on his or her pattern of abilities. In Hunt's terms, it would be interesting to know whether people lead from their strength. In the case of sentence-picture matching, there is some evidence that they do tend to use the method that works best for them. But the correspondence between strategy choice and ability patterns is far from perfect (MacLeod et al. 1978; Mathews et al. 1980). So it may be important to distinguish between cognitive styles in the sense of the way a person typically works, and ability patterns, which may affect how the person works most effectively.

When college students work on the simple problem of comparing sentences with pictures, the choice of strategies doesn't make much difference in problem-solving effectiveness. But there is good reason to believe that people may solve complex problems more effectively by using methods that are most congenial for each individual (Hunt 1983).

In their focus on personality, the New Look dimensions obviously differ from the cognitive styles that are beginning to appear in the information-processing literature. Witkin, for example, was interested in cognitive behavior primarily because he thought it played an adaptive role in the individual's style of life. But this difference may be more a matter of starting points than of final products. If visual and verbal ways of solving problems are pervasive styles of cognitive functioning, then they may play some role in the economy of individual personalities. In fact, if the tendency to choose visual strategies is related to visualization abilities, and the rod-and-frame test is also related to visualization abilities, then there may be some overlap between a visual problem-solving style and field independence. More generally speaking, I suspect that current research on how problems are solved will lead to a renewal of interest in styles of cognitive-personality functioning.

APPLICATIONS

Whatever the differences may be between the older and newer cognitive style traditions, it seems clear that they have attracted the interest of applied psychologists for similar reasons. The interest is due primarily, I think, to the possibility that people may be more satisfied and effective if they are working under conditions that are most compatible with their individual cognitive-personality styles.

It is possible to distinguish three different issues in the cognitive-style literature on compatibility matching. The first issue involves the matching of styles and problems. If there are different ways of solving problems, it seems unlikely that any one would be equally effective for all types of problems. For example, visual strategies obviously work better for some problems, and verbal strategies for others. Ideally, a person would shift from one way to the other, depending on the requirements of each particular problem. But stable individual differences in the preferred way of working may make some problems more compatible than others with a person's stylistic tendencies. The same kind of issue has been raised in the case of the field-dependence dimension. For example, Witkin suggested that working in social-interpersonal contexts may be more congenial for field-dependent people, and working in abstract, impersonal contexts may be more congenial for field-independent people (Witkin et al. 1977a). One question of interest in vocational guidance is whether information about cognitive-personality styles may be of some value in choosing compatible occupations for people.

The second issue involves compatibility matching between people's style of work and how a particular problem is actually solved. In the simple laboratory problem of matching sentences and pictures, the choice of a verbal strategy may be more or less effective than a visual strategy, depending on the person's pattern of abilities. It is easy to imagine business situations in which people are forced to work in a way that is more or less effective for them. If the same job can be done in more than one way, the applied question of interest is whether satisfaction and effectiveness might be improved by allowing or even encouraging people to work in a way that is most congenial for them.

The third issue involves compatibility matching among people. There may be situations in which people with very different styles have difficulty getting along with each other. This possibility is suggested, for example, by the research, mentioned earlier, that suggests that interpersonal attraction is higher if people are similar in degree of field dependence than if they are dissimilar. If two people have very different ways of working, then the applied question of interest is whether job satisfaction and effectiveness can be improved if their stylistic differences are recognized and accepted— to take an obvious example, if a manager can accept the fact that an employee is doing an effective job, even though the job is not being done in the manager's own style.

Cognitive style considerations focus attention on compatibility matching, but these issues have often been addressed without using stylistic concepts. It seems reasonable to ask whether anything is added by formulating the issues in stylistic terms. The answer depends, I suppose, on our ability to identify and measure specific styles that can profitably be applied to problems in the real world. But only a few dimensions have been identified so far, and it is not yet clear how useful they may be.

I'd like to turn now to some of the work that has been done on the applications of compatibility matching in business and education. Each of the three compatibility-matching issues that I mentioned earlier is addressed by McKenney and Keen (1974) in their work on systematic and intuitive managers. They conclude that well-defined problems are more congenial for systematic thinkers, and they suggest that this type of problem is particularly characteristic of occupations like accounting, production management, and managerial science. In contrast, ill-defined and open-ended problems are preferred by intuitive thinkers; problems of this type are more characteristic of specialties like marketing and advertising. I have not been able to find any research on the application of these suggestions to vocational guidance.

McKenney and Keen (1974) also focus on the problem of compatibility matching among people. They discuss at some length the difficulties that systematic and intuitive managers encounter in understanding and working with each other. Although systematic and intuitive people may prefer different kinds of jobs, McKenney and Keen emphasize that many problems can be solved by managers of either style. If you are a systematic manager, but the job can be done effectively in an intuitive way, it would be inappropriate and even harmful, in their view, to change the other person's way of working to suit your own style. McKenney and Keen conclude that it is critically important for managers to be more aware of, and accepting of, differences in the styles of work they encounter.

Similar views have been expressed by some educators who have focused on differences among students in styles of learning. For example, it has been suggested that students may learn more if they are encouraged to learn in a way that is most congenial for them; that problems may develop in the classroom if the teacher's style is incompatible with the student's style; and that teachers should become more aware of, and accepting of, differences in learning styles (Witkin et al. 1977a).

The enthusiasm for these views is probably ahead of the evidence at the moment. But much more applied research has been done in educational settings than in business settings.

Some of this work has involved the field dependence dimension. If field-independent people are more inner-directed, then students of this sort should do well if they are allowed to follow a more independent course of study. But the more field-dependent student should learn more effectively when the teacher is involved in setting the goals and providing the incentives to learn. Because of their greater interpersonal orientation, field-dependent students might also be expected to learn more in group settings.

There is some evidence to support the view that learning is more affected by rewards and punishments among field-dependent subjects than among field-independent subjects (Steinfeld 1973). And there is also some evidence that field-dependent students are more productive when working in groups, and field-independent people are more productive when working alone (Birnbaum 1975).

I would expect field-dependent people to differ in approaching their jobs in ways that are similar to differences in their approach to learning. In other words, field-dependent workers might be more productive in group settings, and extrinsic social or material rewards might be more important for them. In fact, Gruenfeld and Weissenberg (1970) have reported that extrinsic rewards such as salary and job security are highly correlated with job satisfaction among civil service managers who are field-dependent, but not among field-independent managers.

Returning to educational applications, some work has been done to see whether compatibility matching of teachers and students makes any difference in the classroom. I don't know of any evidence that students learn more if they are similar to their teachers in degree of field-dependence. A few studies have found greater student satisfaction and more accurate teacher evaluation of students among matched teacher-student pairs than among mismatched pairs (see Di Stefano 1969; Saracho 1980). But a few other studies have not found a match-mismatch effect of any sort (see Witkin et al. 1977a).

The suggestion has been made that the inconsistent results of studies on match-mismatch effects may be due to the fact that some experienced teachers are able to recognize their students' learning styles, and adapt their methods to the differing needs of their field-dependent and field-independent pupils. This kind of teacher adaptation was observed in a study of classroom behavior by Stone (1981). The teachers in Stone's study did not know the test scores of their students, but they tended to give more personal attention to their field-dependent students, while the field-independent students were more often allowed to work independently.

In another study, by Doebler and Eicke (1979), workshops were conducted to increase teachers' awareness of the educational implications of the field dependence dimension. They report increased student satisfaction with school, presumably because the teachers became more adaptable in their instructional methods.

I suppose that the most visible current applications of cognitive styles in business are workshops designed to increase managers' awareness of individual differences in ways of working. But we are a long way from being sure that the particular styles that have been identified are of any practical importance in either industry or education.

Much more work has been done on the potential applications of the field dependence dimension to problems of vocational guidance. In this case, predictions about compatible occupations have been based on combinations of cognitive and personality characteristics. Since field-dependent people evidently have a more interpersonal orientation and less visualization ability, one might expect them to be found in occupations that deal more with people, such as sales, social work, and teaching. In contrast, field-independent people might favor occupations such as architecture and engineering, which are more impersonal and visual. These hypotheses have been confirmed in many studies (see Witkin et al. 1977). The evidence also suggests that field dependence is related to specialty choices within disciplines. Clinical psychologists, for example, tend to be more field-dependent than do experimental psychologists (Nagle 1967).

A few studies have been done in which young men and women have been tested, and then followed longitudinally in an attempt to predict subsequent academic or vocational choices. In one study by Witkin (Witkin et al. 1977a), field dependence was measured among entering college freshmen, and the students' academic majors was recorded at different stages during their college careers. He found no relationship with the major choices that students made as freshmen. But field-independent students more often graduated with abstract majors, such as physics and math, while their more field-dependent classmates tended to graduate in people-oriented disciplines, such as nursing and education.

The change in results between college entry and graduation was clearly due to a shift in major during their college careers among students who had initially chosen a subject that was predicted to be less compatible for them, to a later subject that was predicted to be more compatible for them. For example, field-dependent people who began in physics often shifted to the humanities before graduation. There was no significant difference in field dependence between students who completed college and those who dropped out, and no significant relationship between field dependence and grade-point averages (Witkin et al. 1977b).

Another longitudinal study covered the period from professional school to professional practice. In this study an attempt was made to predict which specialties would be chosen by doctors who were tested during medical school. Ten years after graduation, the field-dependent students were more often found to be certified psychiatrists, while field-independent students were more often found to be certified surgeons (Goodenough et al. 1979).

It would be important to know, of course, whether the happiest or most successful psychiatrists tend to be more field-dependent, and the happiest or most successful surgeons tend to be more field-independent. But little work has been done so far relating field dependence to job performance or job satisfaction for any occupation.

Returning for a moment to the concepts of McKenney and Keen, when I think about the issues in a systematic way, I can't find much evidence to warrant a decision that dimensions of cognitive personality functioning help to solve applied problems in business or education. When I think about the same issues in a more intuitive way, it seems easy to decide that they have a potential that warrants the continuing interest of educators and businessmen.

REFERENCES

Birnbaum, A.S.G. Social correlates of field articulation in adolescents: The effect upon productivity in the presence of others. Ph.D. dissertation, Hofstra University, 1975.

Bischof, N. Optic-vestibular orientation to the vertical. In H.H. Kornhuber (ed.), *Handbook of sensory physiology, vestibular system,* part 2. New York: Springer-Verlag, 1974.

Coates, S., Lord, M., & Jakabovics, E. Field dependence-independence, social-non-social play and sex differences in preschool children. *Perceptual and Motor Skills,* 1975, *40,* 195–202.

Cox, P.W., & Gall, B.E. *Field dependence-independence and psychological differentiation, supplement no. 5.* Research Report 81-29. Princeton, N.J.: Educational Testing Service, 1981.

Crutchfield, R.S., Woodworth, D.G., & Albrecht, R.E. *Perceptual performance and the effective person.* WADC-TN-58-60. Lackland Air Force Base, Tex.: Personnel laboratory, Wright Air Development Center, Air Research and Development Command, 1958. (ASTIA no. AD-151-039)

Culver, C.M., Cohen, S.I., Silverman, A.J., & Schmavonian, B.M. Cognitive structuring, field-dependence-independence, and the psychophysiological response to perceptual isolation. In J. Wortis (ed.), *Recent advances in biological psychiatry* (vol. VI). New York: Plenum Press, 1964.

DiStefano, J.J. Interpersonal perceptions of field independent and field dependent teachers and students. Ph.D. dissertation, Cornell University, 1969.

Doebler, L.K., & Eicke, F.J. Effects of teacher awareness of the educational implications of field-dependent/field-independent cognitive style on selected classroom variables. *Journal of Educational Psychology,* 1979, *71,* 226–232.

Eagle, M., Goldberger, L., & Breitman, M. Field dependence and memory for social v. neutral and relevant v. irrelevant incidental stimuli. *Perceptual & Motor Skills,* 1969, *29,* 903–910.

Freund, J., Krupp, G., Goodenough, D.R., & Preston, L.W. The doctor-patient relationship and drug effect. *Clinical Pharmacology and Therapeutics,* 1972, *13,* 172–180.

Gates, D.W. Verbal conditioning, transfer and operant level "speech style" as functions of cognitive style. Ph.D. dissertation, City University of New York, 1971.

Goldberger, L., & Bendich, S. Field dependence and social responsiveness as determinants of spontaneously produced words. *Perceptual and Motor Skills,* 1972, *34,* 883–886.

Goodenough, D.R. The role of individual differences in field dependence as a factor in learning and memory. *Psychological Bulletin,* 1976, *83,* 675–694.

Goodenough, D.R., Oltman, P.K., Friedman, F., Moore, C.A., Witkin, H.A., Owen, D., & Raskin, E. Cognitive styles in the development of medical careers. *Journal of Vocational Behavior,* 1979, *14,* 341–351.

Gruenfeld, L.W., & Weissenberg, P. Field independence and articulation of sources of job satisfaction. *Journal of Applied Psychology,* 1970, *54,* 424–426.

Hunt, E. On the nature of intelligence. *Science,* 1983, *219,* 141–146.

Justice, M.T. Field dependence, intimacy of topic and interperson distance. Ph.D. dissertation, University of Florida, 1969.

Klein, G.S., & Schlesinger, H. Where is the perceiver in perceptual theory? *Journal of Personality,* 1949, *18,* 32–47.

Linn, M.C., & Kylonnen, P. The field dependence-independence construct: Some, one, or none. *Journal of Educational Psychology,* 1981, *73,* 261–273.

Linton, H.B. Dependence on external influence: Correlates in perception, attitudes, and judgment. *Journal of Abnormal and Social Psychology,* 1955, *51,* 502–507.

MacLeod, C.M., Hunt, E.B., & Mathews, N.N. Individual differences in the verification of sentence-picture relationships. *Journal of Verbal Learning and Verbal Behavior,* 1978, *17,* 493–507.

Mathews, N.N., Hunt, E.B., & MacLeod, C.M. Strategy choice and strategy training in sentence-picture verification. *Journal of Verbal Learning and Verbal Behavior,* 1980, *19,* 531–548.

Mausner, B., & Graham, J. Field dependence and prior reinforcement as determinants of social interaction in judgment. *Journal of Personality and Social Psychology,* 1970, *16,* 486–493.

McKenney, J.L., & Keen, P.G.W. How managers' minds work. *Harvard Business Review,* 1974, *52,* 79–90.

Messick, S. Measures of cognitive styles and personality and their potential for educational practice. In K. Ingendamp (ed.), *Developments in educational testing.* London: University of London Press, 1969.

Morgan, A.H. Hypnotizability and "cognitive styles": A search for relationships. *Journal of Personality,* 1972, *40,* 503–509.

Nagle, R.M. Personality differences between graduate students in clinical and experimental psychology at varying experience levels. Ph.D. dissertation, Michigan State University, 1967.

Oltman, P.K., Goodenough, D.R., Witkin, H.A., Freedman, N., & Friedman, F. Psychological differentiation as a factor in conflict resolution. *Journal of Personality and Social Psychology,* 1975, *32,* 730–736.

Ruble, D.N., & Nakamura, C.Y. Task orientation v. social orientation in young children and their attention to relevant social cues. *Child Development,* 1972, *43,* 471–480.

Saracho, O. The relationship between the teachers' cognitive style and their perceptions of their students' academic achievements. *Educational Research Quarterly*, 1980, *5*, 40–49.

Schreiber, R.M. Field dependence-independence and athletic team choice. Master's thesis, Boston University, 1972.

Soat, D.M. Cognitive style, self-concept, and expressed willingness to help others. Ph.D. dissertation, Marquette University, 1974.

Sousa-Poza, J.F., & Rohrberg, R. Communicational and interactional aspects of self-disclosure in psychotherapy: Differences related to cognitive style. *Psychiatry*, 1976, *39*, 81–91.

Steinfeld, S.L. Level of differentiation and age as predictors of reinforcer effectiveness. Ph.D. dissertation, Hofstra University, 1973.

Sternberg, R., & Weil, E. *An aptitude strategy interaction in linear syllogistic reasoning*. No. 0001478C0025, ID no. NR 150–457. Washington, D.C.: Personnel and Training Research Programs, Psychological Science Division, Office of Naval Research, 1979.

Stone, K.L. *Teacher adaptation to student cognitive style and its effects on learning*. Ed.D. dissertation, Columbia University, 1981.

Vernon, P.E. The distinctiveness of field independence. *Journal of Personality*, 1972, *40*, 366–391.

Witkin, H.A., & Asch, S.E. Studies in space orientation. IV. Further experiments on perception of the upright with displaced visual fields. *Journal of Experimental Psychology*, 1948, *38*, 762–782.

Witkin, H.A., Dyk, R.B. Paterson, H.F., Goodenough, D.R., & Karp, S.A. *Psychological differentiation*. Potomac, Md.: Erlbaum, 1974. (First published 1962)

Witkin, H.A., & Goodenough, D.R. Field dependence and interpersonal behavior. *Psychological Bulletin*, 1977, *84*, 661–689.

_____. *Cognitive styles: Essence and origins*. New York: International Universities Press, 1981.

Witkin, H.A., Lewis, H.B., Hertzman, M., Machover, K., Meissner, P.B., & Wapner, S. *Personality through perception*. New York: Harper, 1954.

Witkin, H.A., Lewis, H.B., & Weil, E. Affective reactions and patient-therapist interactions among more differentiated and less differentiated patients in therapy. *Journal of Nervous & Mental Disease*, 1968, *146*, 193–208.

Witkin, H.A., Moore, C.A., Goodenough, D.R., & Cox, P.W. Field-dependent and field-independent cognitive styles and their educational implications. *Review of Educational Research*, 1977, *47*, 1–64. (a)

Witkin, H.A., Moore, C.A., Oltman, P.K., Goodenough, D.R., Friedman, F., Owen, D.R., & Raskin, E. Role of field-dependent and field-independent cognitive styles in academic evolution: A longitudinal study. *Journal of Educational Psychology*, 1977, *69*, 197–211. (b)

Wong, K.L. Psychological differentiation as a determinant of friendship choice. Ph.D. dissertation, City University of New York, 1976.

9

Honesty Testing
for Personnel Selection:
A Review and Critique
Paul R. Sackett and
Michael M. Harris

INTRODUCTION

The aim of this chapter is to provide industrial/organizational (I/O) psychologists with an overview of the use of paper-and-pencil predictors of employee theft and other forms of counterproductivity in the work place. We have observed that many I/O psychologists have little or no knowledge of this field and are astonished to discover the extent to which these instruments are used. This is not surprising: little information about these tests finds its way into the mainstream psychological literature. In this chapter we will do several things. First, we will discuss the scope of the problem of employee theft and provide an overview of the various solutions that have been suggested. Second, we will describe a variety of paper-and-pencil measures that have been designed to predict honest/dishonest behavior in the work place. Third, we will examine the implications of two bodies of literature—attitude-behavior and person-situation interaction—for the use of honesty tests. Fourth, we will examine a relatively large number of (mostly unpublished) studies of reliability, validity, and the impact on minority groups of these tests. Finally, a variety of suggestions for future research will be made.

The domain of this chapter will be limited to paper-and-pencil instruments used to measure and/or predict employee honesty in the work place.

Several related measures will not be included. The use of polygraphs and voice stress analyzers will not be reviewed here. They are being excluded for two reasons. First, these instruments are conceptually distinct from paper-and-pencil measures in that while also concerned with identifying individuals with a propensity toward counterproductive behavior, they are not used as measures of what is variously called an attitude toward honesty or a personality trait of honesty. Rather, they are used either as a basis for an examiner's judgment that the examinee has a history of theft or other defalcations or to elicit a confession of such theft. Inferences about future behavior based on past behavior are used to make employment decisions. Second, we see no need for a review of the polygraph and voice stress literature here, since these topics have been treated elsewhere (see Lykken 1981 for an extensive examination of polygraph and voice stress research; see Podlesny & Raskin 1977 for a more favorable view of polygraph validity; see Sackett & Decker 1979 for a review focusing on employment uses of these instruments). Polygraph-based judgments will be discussed with regard to their use as criteria in validity studies of various paper-and-pencil measures.

A second, related topic that will not be treated extensively in this chapter is the use of-paper-and pencil measures to predict deviant behavior in settings other than the work place (such as predicting delinquency in adolescents). This is being done to limit the scope of the chapter to the overall theme, personality assessment in organizations. Much of the research concerning prediction of deviant behavior has been reviewed by Ash (1971). Ash suggested that two approaches have been used: social and familial history, emphasizing early experiences and behavior, and personality tests. The former is exemplified by Glueck and Glueck (1968) and is somewhat like the biodata format in more traditional personnel selection. The latter approach has been employed by a number of authors, including Gough (1965), using the California Personality Inventory; Bechtold (1964), using the Kvaraceus Scale and Checklist; and Clarke and Hasler (1967), using Activity Vector Analysis. In general, these studies have been reasonably successful in differentiating between groups of interest.

A final topic that will not be discussed is the use of instruments designed to predict forms of employee counterproductivity other than theft. Although some of the instruments reviewed include scales to measure characteristics such as drug or alcohol abuse or potential for violence, this chapter will be limited to the honesty scales of these instruments.

EMPLOYEE THEFT: THE PROBLEM AND PROPOSED SOLUTIONS

Extent of the Problem

A survey of the promotional literature distributed by test publishers reveals a wide range of estimates of business losses due to crime, varying from $6 billion to $40 billion per year. At least three reasons can be cited for the wide differences in estimates. First, these figures depend on the particular source used. For example, Jaspan asserts that employees steal about $3 billion a year (*U.S. News and World Report* 1971). The American Management Association (1977) cites a figure of $30–40 billion for losses due to crime. Thus, one reason for the wide range in estimates may be due to the particular time period being described. Second, the manner in which the figure is derived may differ widely, for there is no simple and unequivocal method for determining how much loss is due to employee theft, how much is due to shoplifting, and how much is due to clerical and billing errors (Hollinger & Clark 1983). Finally, the $30–40 billion figure provided by the American Management Association includes all forms of crime against business, including commercial bribery ($3.5–10 billion), securities theft/fraud ($5 billion), embezzlement ($4 billion), burglary ($2.5 billion), vandalism ($2.5 billion), shoplifting and insurance fraud ($2 billion each), arson ($1.3 billion), check fraud ($1–2 billion), credit card fraud ($0.5 billion), and employee theft ($5–10 billion). In reality, then, even the largest estimates place employee theft at no more than $10 billion per year, which is, nonetheless, a significant figure.

Two studies have examined the number of employees stealing. Tatham (1974) found that 50 percent of the workers he sampled in the retail sector had taken merchandise from their employer; however, he had a sample size of only 98. Hollinger and Clark (1983) administered an anonymous questionnaire to employees from 21 hospitals (N = 4,111), 10 manufacturing firms (N = 1,497), and 16 retail store companies (N = 3,567). The percentage of employees admitting to stealing varied widely from company to company. The means were 41.8 percent (SD = 18.3) for the retail sector, 32.2 percent for hospitals (SD = 6.4), and 26.2 percent (SD = 5.9) for manufacturing firms. On the basis of these and other, more specific data, Hollinger and Clark conclude that "Most of the theft reported was not very serious and occurred rather infrequently" (1983, p. 141). In short, the evidence of widespread employee theft is, at best, rather mixed.

Approaches to Reduction of Employee Theft

Various approaches have been used in relation to the cause and prevention of employee theft (Bologna 1981, cited in Jones 1982b). At one end of the continuum are those who advocate greater control and scrutiny of employees and applicants. For example, accountants tend to view such behavior as the result of poor internal accounting control; prevention of employee theft would involve increased auditing and control. Personnel administrators generally consider theft to be due to poor selection procedures, and believe that improved screening techniques can ameliorate counterproductive behavior. Security personnel are apt to view theft as the result of lax security and recruitment standards. Their answer to this problem is tighter security and more effective screening techniques.

Organizational behavior scientists and sociologists fall at the other end of the continuum. They tend to view theft as the result of inappropriate climate and norms. Their solution to counterproductivity would consist of improving job satisfaction, and creating a more positive and honest climate. This chapter will focus on applicant screening as a theft reduction technique.

PAPER-AND-PENCIL PREDICTORS OF HONESTY

Paper-and-pencil honesty testing is a multimillion dollar industry (Tampor 1981). Although test marketers are reluctant to reveal sales figures, aggregating their statements about the number of organizations using their services suggests that at least 5,000 firms are using honesty tests to some extent. Such tests are commonly used in settings where employees have access to cash or merchandise, such as retail stores, financial institutions, and warehouse operations. Tests are used for both low-level jobs, such as clerks, tellers, cashiers, and security guards, and for higher-level positions, such as managers and police officers.

Paper-and-pencil tests of honesty have largely been developed as alternatives to polygraph screening; many tests are marketed by security firms specializing in polygraph investigations. They are less costly, and they can be used in states where preemployment polygraph examinations are illegal. Lykken (1981) notes that 16 states prohibit requiring preemployment polygraph examinations; three more states have done so since 1981. The Minnesota law, prohibiting the use of "any test purporting to test the honesty of any employee or prospective employee" (Lykken

1981), appeared also to ban paper-and-pencil measures; however, a recent Minnesota Supreme Court decision interpreted this as applying only to tests purporting to measure physiological changes in the subjects tested (*State of Minnesota* v. *Century Camera, Inc.* 1981). Thus there are at present no state laws prohibiting the use of paper-and-pencil honesty tests.

The development of paper-and-pencil tests for predicting employee honesty is a phenomenon that has taken place largely outside the mainstream of psychological testing. Many of the instruments are relatively recent, and published information about these tests is minimal. Accessible information in mainstream psychological journals is available for only two tests, the Reid Report and the London House Personnel Selection Inventory (Ash 1971; Jones 1980; Jones & Terris 1983; Terris & Jones 1982); the *Eighth Mental Measurements Yearbook* mentions two tests, the Reid Report and the Keeler Pre-employment Opinion survey. Other reviews to date cover three or fewer tests (Bickman et al. 1979; Lykken 1981; Sackett & Decker 1979). Thus there was no readily accessible source of information for identifying commercially available honesty tests.

The primary means of identifying tests for inclusion in this review was a mail survey of over 1,000 retail organizations. This survey was designed to obtain information about what types of psychological tests were being used for entry-level selection. Marketers of tests identified by this survey were contacted and asked to provide any published or unpublished evaluative studies regarding their tests. In phone conversations with these test marketers, inquiries about competitors served to identify additional tests for inclusion. A total of 24 tests was identified. Evaluative studies were obtained for ten of these; descriptive but no evaluative information was obtained for three others. Six marketers had gone out of business or moved with no forwarding address, and the remaining five did not respond to our inquiries. (A note on the number of test marketers who could not be located: a common observation from established test marketers is that there is a recurring problem with pirated versions of existing tests being marketed, only the name of the test being changed. Legal action or threat thereof is used to put a stop to these operations.) We concede that it is not at all unlikely that we failed to uncover some honesty tests. However, our sample includes what are acknowledged in the field to be the most widely used tests and represents the range of types of instruments being used to predict honesty in the work place.

Table 9.1 contains some basic descriptive information about the ten tests for which evaluative information was obtained. Most undisguisedly inquire into a job applicant's attitudes toward theft and other defalcations;

TABLE 9.1
Description of Tests Included in the Review

Test	Theft Attitudes	Theft Admissions	Distortion Scale	Other Scales	Length
Keeler Pre-employment Opinion Survey	yes	no	no	none	40 items
London House Personnel Selection Inventory	yes	yes	yes	drug abuse violence	102 items
Milby Profile	yes	yes	yes	longevity job performance hostility alcohol drugs	134 items
Personal Outlook Inventory	no	no	no	none	37 items
Phase II Profile	yes	yes	yes	alcohol/drug abuse (sold separately; not included in item count)	116 items
Pre-employment Analysis Questionnaire	yes	yes	yes	none	111 items
Reid Report	yes	yes	no	none	158 items
Stanton Survey	yes	yes	no	none	66 items
Trustworthiness Attitude Survey	yes	no	no	none	135 items
Wilkerson Pre-employment Audit	yes	yes	yes	none	100 items

Source: Prepared by authors.

items probing beliefs about frequency and extent of theft in our society (such as "What percentage of people take more than $1.00 per week from their employer?" or "Do you think the average person would cheat if he thought he could get away with it?") are common. Punitiveness toward theft is commonly examined (for instance, "Should a person be fired if caught stealing $5.00?"). Questions dealing with consideration of theft (such as "Have you ever thought about taking company merchandise without actually taking any?"), perceived ease of theft (such as "How easy would it be for a dishonest person to steal from an employer?"), likelihood of detection (such as "What percent of employee thieves are ever caught?"), knowledge of employee theft (such as "Do you know for certain that some of your friends steal from their employer?"), and rationalizations about theft (such as "An employer who pays people poorly has it coming to him when employees steal") are also common. Finally, assessments of one's own honesty are frequently included (for instance, "compared to other people, how honest are you?").

The Wilkerson Pre-employment Audit claims to disguise its purpose by embedding items of the above types among nonthreatening items (for instance, "Radio, television and printed news is boring") in an attempt to reduce the possibility of faking. The Personal Outlook Inventory is significantly different from the others in that there is no obvious reference to theft. This test was developed by empirically identifying standard personality items that differentiate between individuals known to be dishonest (such as employees fired for theft) and those assumed to be honest (such as employees with no record of theft).

Finally, a variety of projective tests are being marketed for purposes of predicting employee honesty. These include the Draw-a-Person test, a color preference test, and handwriting analysis. While descriptive promotional material was obtained for these tests, no objective evaluative data were available. Thus, these measures will not be considered further.

In addition to theft attitude and/or personality items, many tests include questions directly seeking admissions of theft (for instance, "What is the total value of cash and merchandise you have taken from your employer in the past year?"). Some include in-depth questioning about other criminal activity and drug use (for instance, "Which of the following list of activities have you engaged in, in the past 5 years?") Admissions are either clinically integrated with the attitude portion of the test to form a hiring recommendation or reported separately along with the score on the attitude portion.

A number of tests include social desirability or "lie" scales, which involve counting the number of socially desirable but implausible responses (such as responding "no" to questions such as "have you ever told a lie?").

Scores on these scales are either clinically or statistically combined with attitude scores or reported separately.

As indicated in Table 9.1, a number of tests include scales to measure characteristics other than honesty. As noted earlier, these will not be discussed in this chapter. They are listed simply for descriptive purposes. In addition, their inclusion in the table aids in understanding why test lengths can not be directly compared. Which items constitute the honesty scale and how those items are weighted are typically viewed as proprietary by the test marketers; the number of items constituting the honesty scale cannot be accurately determined by examining the tests themselves because of the inclusion of distortion scales, other scales such as drug abuse, and the use of filler items. Thus, test length is reported for the entire test and not for the honesty scale.

ATTITUDE-BEHAVIOR RELATIONSHIPS, PERSON-SITUATION INTERACTIONS, AND EMPLOYEE HONESTY

Some honesty tests make no claims to measure an underlying construct; they are seen simply as empirical correlates of polygraph examination results or of future employee theft. Most, however, claim to measure a predisposition toward theft, viewed either as an attitude or a personality trait (for instance, criminality). Prior to examining the empirical research studies dealing with honesty testing, two important bodies of research will be briefly reviewed: research on the relationship between attitudes and behavior, and the debate regarding the relative importance of dispositional and situational determinants of behavior, an issue in which the Hartshorne and May (1928) studies of honesty have played an important part.

Attitude-Behavior Research

In light of contemporary attitude-behavior research, the reported relationship between honesty and theft is somewhat surprising. Most researchers have found only limited evidence for a strong relationship between attitudes and behavior (see Wickert 1969 for an overview). Ajzen and Fishbein (1977) have proposed that attitudes will predict behavior when the two correspond in action, target of action, context, and time. Of these four elements, the match between target and action seems most critical. An examination of employee honesty tests suggests that most examine the action (for instance, "Would you steal?"), rather than the target (for instance, "Would you steal from the company you are applying to?"). In studies employing measures corresponding in action elements only, Ajzen and Fishbein found that five out of ten reported nonsignificant relations; the remaining five obtained "relatively low but significant attitude-behavior relations" (1977, p. 896).

Two of the studies reviewed by Ajzen and Fishbein deserve special attention because of their similarity to the present topic. Corey (1937) and Freeman and Ataov (1960) examined the relationship between attitudes toward cheating and actual cheating on tests by university students. Corey developed an "attitude toward cheating" questionnaire (unfortunately, no examples of items are provided) with an apparently respectable reliability (corrected $r = .913$). For the criterion measure, Corey had the subjects take five objective classroom tests over a five-week period. Tests were surreptitiously scored, then returned to the students for grading. The differences between the actual scores and the students' self-report scores were used to assess the amount of cheating. The relationship between attitude and sum of the cheating scores was nonsignificant ($r = .024$) In addition, a "temptation to cheat" index was computed. this measured the difference between the actual score and the maximum possible score; the relationship between this index and the amount of cheating was significant ($r = .46$). Corey concluded that, at least in this case, attitudes do not predict behavior. The results do, on the other hand, suggest that the situation is the best predictor of cheating, although Corey does not suggest this.

A similar study was conducted by Freeman and Ataov (1960). They devised a somewhat different attitude questionnaire, involving three types of items. One group of items asked about the number of students cheating on exams (for instance, "What is the percentage of students who cheat in an average college class with the honor system?"). The second group of items concerned perceptions of whether students described in a hypothetical case were cheating (for instance, "One student is whispering to the student next to him"). The final class of items concerned hypothetical situations of cheating about which subjects were to judge whether they were fact or rumor (for instance, "A set of students developed a code such that by coughing they were able to communicate the answers"). In addition, the questionnaire contained a direct item: "Have you ever cheated on an exam?" As in Corey (1937), the criterion involved a surreptitious scoring of the tests and these scores being compared with the scores reported by the students marking their own papers. Using Kendall's tau, a measure of association between two ordinal variables, Freeman and Ataov found that none of the predictors had a significant relationship to the criterion. The direct question also had an insignificant relationship to cheating. Considering other relevant research, then, claims of a strong relationship between theft attitudes and theft demand careful scrutiny.

The Person-Situation Debate

A major controversy in psychology concerns the extent to which behavior is determined by internal dispositions or by situational factors (a more extensive discussion of the implication of the debate for honesty research can be found in Sackett 1983). Advocates of traits or internal dispositions have sought evidence of behavioral stability across situations, while situationists have sought evidence of situational specificity of behavior. Within these two paradigms various positions are possible. In the most extreme version of the trait position, an individual should be as likely to manifest a behavior (such as stealing) in one situation (such as Company A) as in another situation (such as Company B). In other words, behavior would be constant across situations. However, there would be differences between individuals (for instance, Joe may be more likely to steal than Jim). A less extreme trait position would allow the situation to make a difference. Specifically, some settings may be more conducive to theft (such as low-security firms) than others (such as high-security firms). However, the rank ordering of individuals in terms of their likelihood of stealing may remain the same. While both Joe and Jim are more likely to steal in the low-security company, in both instances Joe is more likely to steal than Jim.

In contrast with the pure dispositional approach is an extreme situationist position. Such an approach posits differences in situations (for instance, individuals are more likely to steal in low-security firms than in high-security firms), but that all individuals behave the same way in a given situation.

A third position, the person-situation interaction, maintains that both internal disposition and situation affect behavior. In other words, the rank order of persons in terms of likelihood of steaing may vary from situation to situation. One would therefore need to know both the situation and the trait in order to make a valid prediction.

Much empirical research has been done concerning this area. A variety of subject populations have been used, ranging from infants to adults; myriad behaviors have been examined, including cheating, drinking, and smoking; and a number of different research methodologies have been employed, such as experiments, passive observational designs, and self-reports. Bowers (1973) averaged findings across 19 studies and found that an average of 12.71 percent of variance was due to the person, 10.17 percent to situations, and 20.77 percent to the person-situation interaction. In addition, findings varied widely across studies. Compelling evidence for either the trait position or the situation position has yet to appear. Moreover, conclusive evidence for either approach is unlikely to be found in the near future. As shown above, at least some variance can be accounted for by the person, the situation, and the person-situation interaction. The actual amount of variance attributable to each source may depend heavily upon design factors (O'Grady 1982), leading some to conclude that research questions such as "Which accounts for more variance in C , A or B?" are futile (Campbell, Daft, & Hulin 1982).

Hartshorne and May's Research on Honesty

Hartshorne and May's *Studies in Deceit* (1928) represents one of the best-known studies in psychology. Not only does this research relate to the person-situation debate, but it has implications for the general issue of honesty as well. Hartshorne and May's study was one component of a five-year project, labeled the Character Education Inquiry, funded by the Institute of Social and Religious Research. The overall aim of this project was to examine the effects of religious education on character development. The specific goal of the Hartshorne and May investigation was to develop a set of situations in which dishonesty could be objectively measured. A large number of schoolchildren, mainly in grades 5 and 8, from a large number of schools were employed as subjects. A total sample of 10,865 was used, representing 23 different schools. Thirty-three different tests, or opportunities for deceit, were devised.

In developing these tests, Hartshorne and May attempted to meet the following objectives: create a natural situation; allow all students equal opportunity to exhibit the behavior; minimize the students' suspicion as to the real aim; provide a quantitative measure; and avoid any uncertainty as to the outcome. The tests varied on a number of dimensions, including setting (classroom, athletic performance, homework, and party games), type of deception involved (cheating with no consequences to others, cheating with consequences to others, lying, and stealing), and method of detecting deception (direct observation versus inference based on improbable achievement).

The underlying hypothesis examined by Hartshorne and May was the prevalent notion at the time: that honesty was a unified, inherent trait. On the basis of this hypothesis, one would expect a virtually perfect correlation between honesty in different situations, between repeated measures of the same situation, and between different tests in the same situation.

The results, as explicated by Hartshorne and May, demonstrated little support for this thesis. The average test-retest for two test types was .569 and .566. Further, average correlation between tests for the same type (for instance, three different chances to grade one's own test) ranged from .440 to .696. Finally, the average intercorrelation between tests of different types ranged from -.003 to .400.

A second set of findings described by Hartshorne and May further supports the rejection of the hypothesis that honesty is a unified trait. They observed that the percentage of subjects engaging in dishonest behavior varied across test types. An extreme trait position would contend that subjects should be either honest or dishonest in all situations. The results showed that only 10.2 percent of the subjects were either honest or dishonest in all situations.

Finally, Hartshorne and May speculated that honesty may be a matter of degree, rather than a discrete (honest/dishonest) trait. Accordingly, they assumed that if honesty was a continuous variable, tests could be scaled on a continuum representing the difficulty of being honest. Thus, an individual cheating on one test should also cheat on tests in which cheating is less difficult. However, Hartshorne and May were unable to construct such a scale, and concluded that viewing honesty as a single, continuous variable is untenable.

On the basis of these data, then, Hartshorne and May assert that "Honesty or dishonesty is not a unified character in children of the ages studied, but a series of specific responses to specific situations" (1928, bk. II, p. 243).

Despite Hartshorne and May's rejection of a pure trait approach, the data also fail to support a pure situationist position; since varying percentages of subjects were dishonest in any given test, the situation alone does not completely explain behavior. Hartshorne and May assert that "The point is that deception is a matter of the situation as much as, if not more than, the nature of the child" (1928, bk. II, p. 218).

In summary, given the initial hypothesis, Hartshorne and May are led to reject a trait position. However, they do not deny the value of dispositions in explaining behavior but, rather, contend that "This common factor is not an inner entity operating independently of the situations in which the individuals are placed but is a function of the situation in the sense that an individual behaves similarly in different situations in proportion as these situations are alike, have been experienced as common occasions for honest or dishonest behavior, and are comprehended as opportunities for deception or honesty" (1928, bk. I, p. 385).

That the Hartshorne and May data do not reject dispositional factors has been reemphasized in reanalyses of the data by Eysenck (1953) and Burton (1963). Thus, these data do not justify rejecting attempts to predict employee honesty on grounds that honesty is situationally determined. The data highlight the need to consider situational as well as dispositional factors in attempting to predict employee honesty.

RESEARCH FINDINGS: VALIDITY, RELIABILITY, AND ADVERSE IMPACT VALIDATION STRATEGIES

A wide variety of validation strategies have been used in attempts to demonstrate the usefulness of paper-and-pencil honesty tests. A conceptual overview of some of the most common is provided in Figure 9.1. The model presented reflects the sequence of developments leading to the current state of affairs in the field of honesty testing. On the basis of the notion that past behavior is a good predictor of future behavior, the polygraph, which had originally been used primarily for criminal investigations, came to be commonly used to determine whether a job applicant had a history of theft or other defalcations. To combat state laws forbidding the use of polygraphs for employment purposes, paper-and-pencil tests were devised as a surrogate for the polygraph. Thus, a commonly used validation strategy, represented by arrow A in Figure 9.1, was to compare test scores with the hire/no hire recommendation made by a polygrapher.

Note the inferences made in presenting a correlation with a polygraph as an indicator of honesty test validity: that the polygraph is a perfectly accurate measure of past dishonest behavior and that past dishonest behavior is a perfect predictor of future dishonest behavior. Noting these inferential leaps, honesty researchers began attempting to validate directly against measures of past behavior, typically relying on self-reports (arrow B), or against direct measures of dishonesty on the job (arrow C). While validating against on-the-job behavior may seem clearly to be the most appropriate strategy, reasons for the relative rarity of its use can be noted. It is argued that theft on the job is rarely detected. Without a reasonably accurate way of determining who is and is not engaging in theft or other dishonest behavior on the job, this strategy cannot meaningfully be used. Speculation abounds as to whether those employee thieves who are caught are a random

Figure 9.1
Validation Strategies in Honesty Test Research

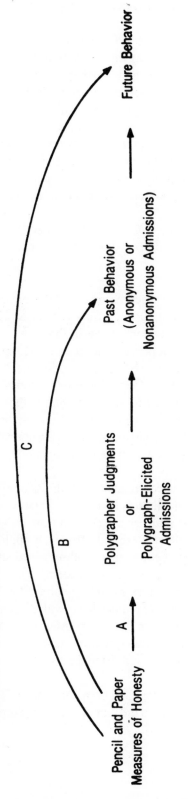

Source: Prepared by authors.

sample of all employee thieves or whether they differ in some manner, thus limiting the generalizability of research using this validation strategy.

Note that in some cases, tests were created as paper-and-pencil surrogates for a polygraph exam; thus the heavy reliance on polygraph comparison as a validation strategy. An employer who has been using and is satisfied with a polygraph-based screening procedure will be seeking evidence that lower-cost paper-and-pencil tests yield the same results. On the other hand, an employer who has rejected polygraph screening on the basis of concerns about its accuracy will be seeking evidence that paper-and-pencil tests are related to criteria other than polygraph-based employment decisions.

Five major categories of validity studies have been identified. The characteristics of each will be discussed briefly prior to summarizing research using each strategy:

1. Polygraph comparisons. Honesty test scores are correlated either with polygrapher judgments about an applicant's trustworthiness or with admissions of theft or other defalcations made in the course of the polygraph exam. Correlations with polygrapher judgments represent attempts to document the extent to which the paper-and-pencil test can be substituted for the polygraph exam. Correlations with admissions in the course of the polygraph exam are more compelling to those who question the validity of polygrapher judgments. An important issue not addressed in most polygraph comparison studies is the potential effects of an anticipated polygraph exam on paper-and-pencil test performance.

2. Admissions. Honesty test scores are correlated with admissions of past thefts or other defalcations. Typically this involves correlating scores on the attitude portion of the test with criteria derived from the admissions portion. Some studies collect these data from job applicants; others reason that applicants may be reluctant to admit past dishonest behavior and thus do not administer the tests in preemployment settings but, rather, in settings where subjects can be assured anonymity.

3. Future behavior. Honesty test scores are correlated with measures of job behavior collected at some time in the future. Measures include being discharged for theft and the number of working days on which there was a cash shortage. Tests are administered either to job applicants or to current employees.

4. Shrinkage reduction. Using this strategy, an organizational unit (such as a store), rather than an individual, is the unit of analysis. Storewide

shrinkage or loss measures are monitored for a period of time prior to introduction of an honesty testing program. As noted earlier, it is virtually impossible in many instances to ascertain the amount of shrinkage that is attributable to various sources, such as employee theft, shoplifting, and accounting errors. Shrinkage rates after introduction of the testing program are compared with rates prior to its introduction.

5. Contrasted groups. This strategy contrasts mean test scores of two groups, one of which is presumed to be dishonest (such as convicts) and the other representing the general population. A finding of mean differences in the predicted direction is taken as evidence both of the validity of the test and of its resistance to attempts to fake "good," as convicts are presumed to be motivated to do, to beat the test in order to increase their chances for early parole.

It should be noted that the tests vary as to whether high or low scores indicate dishonesty. To simplify interpretation of results, signs will be reversed for those tests where low scores indicate dishonesty. Thus, for all tests, positive correlations represent results in the hypothesized direction— for instance, high dishonesty scores being associated with high theft admissions or judgments that the applicant is a poor employment risk. Also, wherever possible, results are presented in correlational terms; at times we computed these indices ourselves on the basis of data in the research reports.

Polygraph Comparisons

The results of 14 validity studies using polygrapher recommendations or admissions made in a polygraph exam are summarized in Table 9.2 and discussed below.

A correlation of .48 is reported between test scores and a rating obtained from the polygraph examination for the Keeler Pre-employment Opinion Survey (P.O.S. Corporation n.d.). No data about the subject population or the conditions of test or polygraph administration are provided. An earlier study is also mentioned, with a reported correlation of .38 based on 757 cases. It is not clear whether these are two independent samples or whether additional cases were added to the original data base for the more recent study.

Three polygraph comparison studies using the London House Personnel Selection Inventory are reported. The first (Terris 1982) correlated honesty scale scores with admissions of theft of money or merchandise ob-

TABLE 9.2
Summary of Polygraph Comparison Studies

Test	Sample	Predictors	Criteria	Results
Keeler Pre-employment Opinion Survey (P.O.S. Corporation n.d.)	N = 1,047 (unspecified)	not specified	not specified	$r_{bis} = .48$
London House Personnel Selection Inventory (Terris 1982)	N = 439 ("applicants for positions of trust")	honesty scale	dollar value of theft admitted	$r = .56$
London House Personnel Selection Inventory (Terris & Jones 1981)	N = 80 (applicants for retail management positions)	multiple cutoff: honesty, drug abuse, and violence scales	score on rating form completed by polygrapher	$r_{phi} = .41–.59$, depending on cutoffs used (mean $r = .48$)
London House Personnel Selection Inventory (Moretti, Jones, & Terris 1983)	N = 179 (applicants for bank jobs)	multiple cutoff: honesty, drug abuse, and violence scales	polygrapher recommendation	$r_{phi} = .27$
Phase II Profile (Phase II Profile 1982)	N = 660 (unspecified)	composite of attitude items, admissions, and lie scale	pass or fail polygraph, with failure confirmed by subsequent admissions	$r_{pbis} = .77$
Reid Report (Ash 1970)	N = 1,159 whites 360 blacks (applicants for positions of trust)	78-item subset of honesty items	polygrapher recommendation	$r = .43$ (whites) $r = .38$ (blacks)
Reid Report (Ash 1971)	N = 254 (unspecified)	honesty scale	polygrapher recommendation	$r = .43$

Reid Report (Ash 1972)	N = 1,230 (795 white male, 233 black male, 147 white female, 55 black female; job unspecified)	70-item subset of attitude items	polygrapher recommendation	$r = .62$ (total) $r = .62$ (white male) $r = .61$ (black male) $r = .51$ (white female) $r = .36$ (black female)
Stanton Survey (Klump 1980)	N = 930 (applicants for wide variety of jobs)	composite of attitude items and admissions	admissions during polygraph exam	$r_{bis} = .86$
Stanton Survey (Klump 1980)	N = 1,806 (applicants for wide variety of jobs)	composite of attitude items and admissions	admissions during polygraph exam	$r_{bis} = .80$
Stanton Survey (Reed 1982)	N = 259 (unspecified)	composite of attitude items and admissions	recommendation based on admissions during the polygraph exam	$r_{bis} = .72$
Trustworthiness Attitude Survey (Personnel Security Corp. n.d.)	N = 400 (unspecified)	honesty scale	polygrapher recommendation	$r_{phi} = .53$
Trustworthiness Attitude Survey (Personnel Security Corp. n.d.)	N = 600 (unspecified)	honesty scale	polygrapher recommendation	$r_{pbis} = .76$
Wilkerson Pre-employment Audit (Wilkerson 1980)	N = 820 (unspecified)	composite of attitude items, admissions, and biographical data	not specified	$r = .75$

Source: Prepared by authors.

tained in the course of a polygraph examination. While the job(s) for which the subjects were applying were not specified, demographic data are provided, indicating that the sample was quite heterogeneous with regard to race, sex, age, and education. A correlation of .56 was obtained. The second (Terris & Jones 1981) used applicants for retail management positions. A strong point of the study is that while the applicants were taking the test, they were unaware that they would be polygraphed, thus eliminating the possibility that test responses were affected by the threat of a polygraph. (Reed 1982, for example, found that slightly more admissions of past theft were made on the Stanton Survey when respondents expected that a polygraph exam would follow.) However, the study uses as the predictor a pass-fail decision based on scoring above a cutoff not only on the honesty scale but also on the drug abuse and violence scales. Phi coefficients range from .41 to .59, depending on which cutoffs are used for the pass-fail decision. The third study (Moretti, Jones, & Terris 1983) also used the composite prediction based on honesty, violence, and drug abuse scales to predict polygrapher recommendations in a sample of applicants for bank jobs, with a resulting phi coefficient of .27. Twenty-three percent of the subjects passed the polygraph but failed the paper-and-pencil test; the authors suggest that individuals predisposed to theft but with little or no job experience are likely to pass a polygraph; thus, polygraph comparison is not a true measure of the predictive power of the paper-and-pencil test. This observation is consistent with Figure 9.1, which highlights the inferential leaps that need to be made in using polygraph comparison studies as estimates of predictor validity.

A polygraph comparison study is also reported for the Phase II Profile (Phase II Profile 1982b), which compares test scores of a group of 330 subjects (no further information provided) who had passed a polygraph exam with those of a group of 330 who had failed a polygraph exam and subsequently admitted to theft activities. A point-biserial correlation of .77 was found between test scores and group membership. It should be noted that the predictor used in this study was a composite of attitudinal items, the theft admissions portion of the instrument, and the lie scale. Thus the ability of the attitudinal measure alone to predict polygraph results cannot be determined, and the magnitude of the correlation, compared with other studies, is at least in part due to the inclusion of theft admissions in the predictor.

Three polygraph comparison studies are reported for the Reid Report (Ash 1970, 1971, 1972). The studies are similar in design, and all use a polygrapher recommendation as the criterion. Relatively large samples permit validation separately by race (Ash 1970) and sex (Ash 1972). Validities range from .36 to .62, with the lowest validities found for a small sample of black females. Ash (1972) notes that test score differences by race and sex are not significant. In two studies, subsets of items providing optimal prediction were used, thus limiting generalizability to operational use of the entire scale.

Three large-sample studies are reported for the Stanton Survey (Klump 1980; Reed 1982). As in the Phase II Profile discussed above, the predictor used is a composite of attitude items and admissions. Theft admissions, a common element of both predictor and criterion, contribute to the high correlations found using this strategy (r = .86, .80, .72) and prevent the determination of the predictive power of the attitude items alone.

Little descriptive information is provided about two studies using the Trustworthiness Attitude Survey (Personnel Security Corporation n.d.). In the first, 200 applicants who had passed the test and 200 who had failed were polygraphed; a phi coefficient of .53 was found between the dichotomous test recommendation and polygrapher judgments. In the second, a point biserial correlation of .76 was reported between test scores and polygrapher judgments.

Finally, a study with a sample of 820 job applicants using the Wilkerson Pre-employment Audit (Wilkerson 1980) was reported. Attitude items, admissions, and biographical data questions form the basis for the test prediction; whether polygrapher judgments or admissions were used as the criterion was unspecified. A correlation of .75 was found.

At first glance there appear to be substantial variations in findings across tests. However, by dividing the studies into two groups, findings become somewhat more consistent. In the first group, five studies used both attitude items and admissions to form the predictor; for these studies correlations averaged .78, with a range from .72 to .86. In the second group, nine studies used only attitude items to form the predictor; for these studies correlations averaged .49, with a range from .27 to .76. Correlations based on different tests are not directly comparable, since differences may be due to a variety of factors, including sampling error, differences in subject populations, and differences in criteria. In sum, honesty scale scores are consistently found to correlate with both polygrapher judgments and admissions made during a polygraph exam. Not surprisingly, higher correlations are obtained when admissions are incorporated into the predictor as well as the criterion.

Future Behavior as Criteria

The results of seven studies predicting subsequent on-the-job behavior are summarized in Table 9.3 and discussed below.

Four predictive validity studies using the London House Personnel Selection Inventory (PSI) have been reported. The first (Jones & Terris 1981b) examined the relationship between honesty scale scores of 61 convenience store job applicants and managerial ratings, obtained three months later, on whether the employee had been caught stealing or disciplined for cash or merchandise shortages, and whether the employee had been suspected of theft. The honesty test had been used in the hiring decision; however, 11 individuals who had failed the test had been hired because of managerial latitude in making hiring decisions. Six of the 61 employees were caught stealing or were disciplined; 3 of these had passed the test and 3 had failed. The difference in percent caught or disciplined among those passing and failing the test was significant at the .05 level. Suspicion of theft, however, proved unrelated to test score.

The second (Jones & Terris 1981b) involved 80 seasonal employees hired by the Salvation Army as "kettlers." These are minimum-wage employees who work an eight-hour shift, ringing a bell to solicit donations at Christmas time. The PSI was administered at time of hiring but not used in the hiring decision. Average daily take was the primary criterion. Kettlers were assigned to various locations; past experience allowed these to be classified as high-, average-, or low-profit locations (for instance, prestige department store versus grocery store in lower-class neighborhood). Location was treated as a covariate. A correlation of .28 was found between honesty scale scores and average dollar take: mean daily take was $81.00 for those recommended by the test and $62.77 for those not recommended. Analysis of covariance indicated that location was not a significant covariate. The authors' inference is that dishonest kettlers were stealing money from their collections each day. Possible alternative explanations not discussed by the authors include unauthorized work breaks as a determinant of lower daily take and the issue of whether differences in physical attractiveness or in solicitation technique are related to honesty scale scores. Also, as in the first study, supervisory ratings of suspicion of theft proved unrelated to honesty scale scores.

In the third study (Terris & Jones 1982a), the PSI was administered to 527 applicants for jobs in a department store chain who were hired regardless of their test score. Thirty-two were subsequently discharged for theft or other offenses. Mean honesty scale scores for those discharged were significantly lower than for those not discharged. It should be noted that while

TABLE 9.3
Summary of Predictive Validity Studies

Test	Sample	Predictors	Criteria	Results
London House Personnel Selection Inventory (Jones & Terris 1981)	61 convenience store job applicants	honesty scale	caught stealing or disciplined for cash/merchandise shortages	% caught or disciplined greater for those failing test ($Z = 2.1$; p<.05)
London House Personnel Inventory (Jones & Terris 1981)	80 Salvation Army "kettlers"	honesty scale	average daily intake	r = .28
London House Personnel Selection Inventory (Terris & Jones 1982)	527 department store applicants	honesty scale	discharged for theft	significantly lower mean test score (p = <.05) for those discharged
London House Personnel Selection Inventory (Jones & Terris 1983)	64 home improvement center applicants	honesty scale	disciplined for mishandling cash/merchandise	r = .23
Milby Profile (Bradley 1980)	gas station/convenience store employees: 83 cashier applicants 101 current cashiers 56 new & current managers	stepwise selection of honesty items	average number of days per two-week period when employee was working & a cash shortage over $5 was found	cashier applicants: r = .82 current cashiers: r = .68 managers: r = .72
Personal Outlook Inventory (Selection Research Publishing 1983)	459 department store applicants	weighted sum based on item analysis	discharged for theft of cash or merchandise	derivation sample: r = .48 cross-validation sample: r = .39
Reid Report (Ash 1975)	140 bank job applicants	honesty scale	discharged for theft	only 2 individuals discharged; r = .06

Source: Prepared by authors.

28 of the 32 discharged failed the PSI, 342 of the 495 not discharged also failed the test. The authors assert that many of those who failed the PSI and were not discharged probably did steal significant amounts of money or merchandise. The difficulty in verifying this assumption is perhaps the largest obstacle to assessing the validity of honesty tests.

The final PSI study (Jones & Terris 1983) correlated honesty scores of 64 home improvement center applicants with a series of managerial ratings obtained eight months later. Seven employees had been disciplined at least once for mishandling cash or merchandise; the correlation between honesty scale scores and frequency of being disciplined was .23. Low, but significant, correlations were also found with tardiness and performance ratings.

Analyses of three employee samples in a gas station/convenience store chain are reported for the Milby Profile (Bradley 1980). All three analyses—cashier applicants, current cashiers, and managers—suffer from the same critical flaw: stepwise item selection was used to generate a multiple correlation for each sample, with no attempt to cross-validate the equations developed in one sample on another sample. When the number of predictors—70 in this case—approaches or exceeds the number of cases—83, 101, and 56 in this case—high multiple correlations are inevitable and most likely artifactual. Cross-validation and/or validation using the scoring system that is used operationally is necessary; the current analyses are not interpretable.

In the largest predictive study reported to date, the Personal Outlook Inventory (Selection Research Publishing 1983) was administered to department store job applicants. Ninety-one individuals discharged for theft and 188 individuals still employed after nine months served as criterion groups for identifying a set of 35 predictive items. A weighted sum of these items produced an r of .48 with group membership. Applying this scoring scheme to a holdout sample of 86 individuals discharged for theft and 184 individuals still employed produced an r of .39. This study is unique in terms of the number of individuals caught stealing; the frequency of detected theft is much lower in most studies.

A predictive study using the Reid Report (Ash 1975) was attempted. A sample of 140 applicants for positions in a bank were hired without reference to test scores. Only 2 of the 140 were terminated for theft. Thus, meaningful analysis of the data is not possible. The reported correlation of .06 should not be interpreted as evidence that the test is invalid because of the lack of criterion variance.

Reviewing attempts at predictive validation of honesty tests reveals recurring problems in detecting theft on the job. With the exception of the one study using the Personal Outlook Inventory, a limited number of employee thieves were identified. The cash shortage measure used by Bradley (1980) and the dollar "take" measure used by Jones and Terris (1981b) represent less direct, but perhaps more accessible, criterion measures for future predictive studies.

Admissions

Sixteen studies using admissions of theft as the criterion were found. They are listed in Table 9.4 and described below.

Two basic strategies have been employed. In some studies, applicants for a given job fill out the honesty test along with a questionnaire regarding past theft. In other studies both the honesty test and the admissions questionnaire are filled out anonymously. The criterion may be measured in several different ways; some, in fact, are actually part of the test and are used in the clinical recommendation.

Three admissions studies using the Reid Report were found. Ash (1975) obtained data from 140 job applicants at a large bank, who had been hired without regard to their test scores. The sample was composed primarily of young white females. Correlations, for admissions of total dollar value of merchandise taken and total money taken, with the Reid Report total score, projective score, and punitive score, ranged between .11 and .25. However, only 4 applicants admitted theft; there was little variance in the criterion. Harris (n.d.), using a random sample of 982 applicants from a wide variety of occupations, correlated the Reid Report total score with admissions of monetary value of merchandise taken and total amount of money taken. The correlations were .15 and .07, respectively; the percent of applicants admitting theft was not reported. Finally, Ash (1975) reports a second study in which a sample of 1,230 was used. Of the respondents, 7.8 percent admitted cash theft; 22.4 percent admitted merchandise theft. The correlation between the Reid Report total score and admissions of cash and merchandise theft were .30 and .45, respectively.

One admissions study is reported for the Phase II Profile (Phase II 1982b). One hundred and twenty subjects who had failed a preemployment polygraph examination and subsequently admitted they had lied were combined with 120 subjects judged to be honest. No indication is given as to precisely how the honest subjects were chosen (for instance, were they a random sample?). For the total sample of 240, a correlation of .636 was found between honesty and amount of money stolen (including shoplifting). This relationship is artificially inflated as compared with other

TABLE 9.4
Summary of Theft Admission Studies

Test	Sample	Predictors	Criteria	Results
Reid Report (Ash 1975)	140 bank applicants	honesty score	admitted cash theft admitted merchandise theft	r = .19 r = .25
Reid Report (Harris 1980)	982 applicants	honesty score	value of cash theft admitted value of merchandise theft admitted	r = .07 r = .15
Reid Report (Ash 1975)	1,230 specified respondents	honesty score	value of cash theft admitted value of merchandise theft admitted	r = .30 r = .45
Phase II Profile (1982)	240 applicants	honesty items and admission items	value of cash or merchandise stolen	r = .64
Pre-employment Analysis Questionnaire (Gerhardt n.d.)	100 food store applicants	honesty scale	number of illegal activities admitted	r = .45–.53, at various test cutoffs
Wilkerson Pre-employment Audit (Morey 1981)	605 unspecified respondents	not specified	admission vs. no admission	contingency coefficient = .63
London House PSI (Jones 1982)	89 nurses	honesty scale	$ theft (anonymous)	r = .56

Study	Sample	Predictor	Criterion	Result
(Moretti 1980)	17 warehouse employees / 14 supermarket employees	honesty scale	$ theft (anonymous)	r = .56 / r = .41
(Terris & Jones 1982)	74 department store employees	honesty scale	$ theft (anonymous)	r = .57, .58, .34 in 3 stores
(Moretti 1982)	132 grocery workers / 64 hospital workers	honesty scale	theft index (anonymous)	r = .41
(Jones 1981)	33 nurses	honesty scale	$ theft of drugs & supplies (anonymous)	r = .59
(Terris & Jones n.d.)	37 supermarket employees	honesty scale	$ theft (anonymous)	r = .66, .81 in 2 stores
(Jones 1980)	39 employees, various organizations	honesty scale	$ or merchandise theft (anonymous)	r = .41
(Jones & Terris 1982)	254 department store employees	composite of honesty, violence, & drug abuse scales	admissions of theft or other rule infractions (anonymous)	sig. mean difference between unscreened group and group prescreened with PSI
(Terris 1979)	146 college students	honesty scale	$ theft (anonymous)	r = .63
(Jones 1982)	71 high school students	honesty scale	theft frequency (anonymous)	r = .51

Source: Prepared by authors.

studies, such as those described above, insofar as subjects were chosen from extreme groups rather than being selected at random.

In a study using the Pre-employment Analysis Questionnaire, Gerhardt (n.d.) divided 100 randomly selected applicants from a large food store chain into two groups, on the basis of their "Attitudes Toward Honesty score. For the criterion measure, 12 questionnaire items measuring theft on the job were summed to form a single score. Using several different cutoff scores, the point-biserial ranged between .45 and .53. Forty-four percent of applicants admitted some theft.

Using the Wilkerson Pre-employment Audit, Morey (1981) found significant mean test score differences between Theft Admission and No Admission groups, though no information is given as to what dollar amount of theft was needed to place an individual into the Theft Admission group.

Ten admissions studies were conducted by London House. Unlike the studies reviewed above, these were conducted on an anonymous basis, questionnaires being returned without identifying names on them. Percentages of applicants admitting theft are typically not reported in these studies, because continuous variables such as Dollar Theft Admitted are used as criteria.

Jones (1982a) collected data on 89 nurses from two major Chicago-area hospitals. He found a correlation of .56 between honesty and admissions of theft. Moretti (1980) examined two samples, one of warehouse workers ($N = 17$) and one of supermarket employees ($N = 14$). The correlations between honesty and money and merchandise taken were .56 and .41, respectively. Terris and Jones (1982a) conducted a study using employees from three different department stores. The correlations between the PSI honesty scale and frequency of theft were .53 ($N = 27$), .63 ($N = 19$), and .53 ($N = 28$) for stores 1, 2, and 3, respectively. Correlations between PSI Honesty and total money and value of merchandise stolen were .57, .58, and .34 for stores 1, 2 and 3, respectively. Moretti (1982) collected data on a sample of 132 grocery store workers and a sample of 64 hospital employees. The correlation between the PSI Honesty scale and money taken was .41 for the entire sample. Jones (1981) obtained anonymous data from 33 nurses employed in the trauma emergency room in a major Chicago hospital. He found a correlation of .59 between the PSI and value of merchandise taken. Terris and Jones (n.d.) used a sample of employees from two supermarkets ($N = 27$, $N = 15$). The correlations between the PSI Honesty score and total dollar value of merchandise taken were .66 and .81, respectively. Jones (1980) obtained a sample of 39 subjects employed in a variety of work settings. The correlation between the Honesty scale and value of merchandise taken was .41. Finally, Jones and Terris (1982b) compared anonymous theft admissions, made eight months after hire, of a group of employees who had been screened using the PSI and a group who had not been screened; significantly more admissions were made by the nonscreened group.

Thus, honesty test scores consistently correlate with admissions of past theft made by both job applicants and current employees reporting theft anonymously. The only exceptions are those situations in which only a small proportion of job applicants admitted to previous theft (see Ash 1975); the lack of criterion variance makes a low correlation inevitable. A number of factors are likely to affect the magnitude of reported correlations. First, a multi-item theft index is likely to be more reliable than a single question dealing with theft admissions. Second, some studies include admissions in both the predictor and the criterion. Third, preselecting approximately equal proportions of individuals admitting and not admitting theft will produce higher correlations than random selection of subjects. Fourth, some studies use dollar value of theft admitted as the criterion, while others create a theft-no theft dichotomy. In light of these and other differences, we caution against attempting to draw conclusions about the merits of various tests based on these studies.

Two studies using the PSI were conducted with students. Terris (1979) used 146 college students (66 males and 80 females; 104 white, 36 non-white, and 6 other) for an anonymous study of theft. He found a correlation of .63 with honesty and theft both on and off the job; the smallest subgroup correlation was .54. In addition, Jones (1982b) studied 71 high school students; he found that the PSI Honesty scale correlated .51 with employee theft.

Shrinkage Reduction

One approach to avoiding the criterion problem encountered in predictive validation studies is to move from individual employees to organizational units as the unit of analysis. Terris and Jones (1982) used monthly shrinkage figures for 30 convenience stores as the basis for assessing the impact of the PSI. Although shrinkage measures include shoplifting and inventory control errors as well as employee theft, these aggregate measures are reflective of both detected and undetected employee theft. During a 23-month base period, preemployment polygraph screening was used; the polygraph was replaced by the PSI for the next 19 months. Shrinkage per store per month dropped from $515 during the polygraph phase to $249 during the PSI phase; shrinkage as a percent of sales dropped from 2.35 to .97. The study would have been strengthened substantially by inclusion of a control group or the use of a reversal design, since a variety of explanations for the findings are feasible. These include unmeasured third variables, such as changes in the economy and perceived changes in company policies and attitudes toward theft. This latter explanation is of particular interest, since the reduction in shrinkage was not gradual, but took place within one month of changing from the polygraph to the PSI. Also, the large number of studies showing relatively high agreement between honesty test scores and polygrapher judgments suggests that explanations other than the selection of more honest employees account for the findings. The authors suggest that the polygraph may be less effective with young applicants having limited job histories, and thus limited opportunity to steal from past employers; however, information about applicant age is not provided.

Contrasted Groups

A final approach to validating honesty tests involves comparing mean test scores of a group of incarcerated convicts with scores of job applicants, in a search for evidence that the tests differentiate between honest and dishonest people. This strategy has been used with the Reid Report (Ash 1974), the Personnel Selection Inventory (Jones & Terris 1981a), and the Wilkerson Pre-employment Audit (Morey 1981); all three found large and highly significant mean differences in the expected direction. These studies are used in Reid and Wilkerson literature as evidence that the tests are resistant to efforts to "fake good," based on the assumption that convicts would try to beat the test in order to increase chances of parole. This is sheer speculation; alternative speculative explanations include the views that convicts reasoned that faking would lessen their chances of parole—for instance, they'd look ridiculous asserting that most of their co-workers (fellow prisoners) were very honest people, and that since anonymity was assured, they felt no pressure to "fake good," electing instead to "fake bad" in order to give the researcher the results they thought were wanted. Much more direct approaches to determining whether tests are unfakable are available.

Reliability

Information about test reliability is reported for seven tests. Unfortunately, it is difficult to compare findings, because of differences in the types of reliability estimates used and of gaps in the information provided in the research reports. Three studies used internal consistency indices. A Kuder-Richardson reliability of .91 is reported for the Stanton Survey (Klump 1980); a split half reliability of .95 is reported for the Trustworthiness Attitude Survey (Personnel Security Corporation n.d.); and a Spearman-Brown estimate of .95 is reported for the London House Personnel Selection Inventory (Terris 1982). Two studies report test-retest reliabilities. A ten-day retest reliability is reported for the Phase II Profile (Phase II Profile 1982b); and a reliability estimate of .76 with unspecified time interval is reported for the Pre-employment Opinion Survey (P.O.S. Corporation n.d.). Finally, two reliability studies report reliability estimates without specifying the method by which they were obtained. A reliability estimate of .92 is reported for the Reid Report (Ash 1975), and a reliability estimate of .58 is reported for the Personal Outlook Inventory (Selection Research Publishing 1983). Thus, reliability estimates are generally quite high, regardless of the method used to obtain the estimate. The outlying value of .58 was obtained by using the instrument most different from the others; the Personal Outlook Inventory does not contain questions about theft or theft attitudes.

Adverse Impact

Test performance by race and sex is reported for all tests except the Personal Outlook Inventory (P.O.S. Corporation n.d.; Jones & Terris 1982; Terris 1982; Jones & Terris 1982; Terris & Jones 1982a; Terris 1979; Bradley 1981; Phase II Profile 1982a; Gerhardt n.d.; Ash 1970; Ash 1972; Reed 1982; Personnel Security Corporation n.d.; Morey 1981). Two studies report sex differences in passing rates in favor of females (Ash 1972; Terris 1979); the remaining studies report no sex differences. One study reports slightly higher passing rates for blacks (Ash 1970); the remaining studies report no race differences. Three studies examined the effects of age on test performance (Ash 1972; Morey 1981; Phase II Profile 1982a); all three report that younger applicants are more likely to fail the tests than older applicants. Failure rates are highest for applicants in their teens and early twenties.

These adverse impact studies typically report either means for the groups being compared or percentages of each group falling above or below a certain cutoff. When cutoffs other than the mean or the cut score reported in the analysis are used, differences in passing rates may be found. Only one study (Ash 1970) compares passing rates at a wide range of cut scores.

Other Empirical Studies

Before concluding this section on empirical research dealing with honesty tests, three additional topics will briefly be discussed: the use of lie scales in honesty testing, the relationship between these tests and other constructs, and moving beyond individual-difference variables to the use of organizational variables, such as climate, in predicting theft and other defalcations.

First, as noted earlier, many of these tests include lie scales. Few studies report correlations between Honesty scale scores and Lie scale scores, but the studies reported are provocative. Kochkin (1981) reports a correlation of .42 between Reid Report scores and the "faking good" scale of the 16-PF; Jones and Terris (1981b) report a correlation of -.37 between the Honesty scale of the London House Personnel Selection Inventory and the accompanying Lie scale; Jones and Terris (1982a) report a correlation of -.38 for the Theft Attitudes scale of an instrument similar to the PSI but designed for use with current employees rather than job applicants. These negative correlations indicate that those giving socially desirable responses tend to do well on the honesty test. The Terris and Jones (1981b) study also reports a correlation of -.67 between Lie scale scores and the theft admission portion of the test. This suggests the possibility that validity findings using admissions as the criterion may be at least in part artifactual: both the honesty test predictor and the admissions criterion are correlated with the social desirability score. The inclusion in a study of a group of people who "fake good" on the honesty test and conceal actual theft when asked for admissions of past theft can create a spurious relationship between honesty scores and admissions. Further research partialing out the effects of social desirability and determining the ease and extent of faking honesty tests is needed.

Second, virtually nothing is known about the relationships between honesty, as measured by these tests, and other constructs in the personality and ability domain. Jones and Terris (1982) use both the London House Personnel Selection Inventory and the MMPI as predictors of attitudes toward nuclear crime, but do not report correlations between the two instruments. Both the London House PSI and the Reid Report have been correlated with the 16-PF (Jones & Terris 1983a; Kochkin 1981). Vectors containing correlations between the 16 16-PF scales and honesty test scores were created for both the PSI and the Reid Report, and the correlation between the pattern of 16-PF relationships for the PSI and the Reid was found to be .88. This high degree of similarity between the two tests in terms of how they correlate with the 16-PF serves as indirect evidence of the similarity of the tests. (We are unaware of any direct comparisons of any of these tests by administering two or more to the same group of job applicants. Attempts to compare tests by administering each to different samples in the same organization and comparing validities have, to date, been based on sample sizes too small to warrant confidence in the findings.) These studies indicate that people who do poorly on the honesty tests tend to obtain 16-PF scores indicating that they have low ego strength and weak superego strength, and are suspicious, controlled, and tense. Both studies report only simple correlations between honesty scores and the 16-PF; neither reports how closely honesty scores can be modeled by using a weighted composite of 16-PF scales. No research relating honesty tests to other measures of other constructs has been identified.

Third, the concept of an organization's "climate of honesty" has been investigated as a moderator of the validity of honesty tests. Two different conceptualizations of climate have been used. Cherrington and Cherrington (1983) sought employee perceptions of the presence or absence of a strong company code of ethics, the level of honesty of top management, the adequacy of internal accounting controls, and the discipline and publicity accompanying the detection of employee theft or fraud. Shrinkage in three organizations was examined; greater shrinkage was found in companies where a code of ethics was not well defined, where good internal accounting controls were not present, and where a punitive system of discipline existed—those caught stealing were openly punished as a deterrent to others. A different approach was taken by Jones and Terris (1983), who operationalized honesty climate as the mean honesty test score of present employees. This index was computed for eight home improvement centers and used as a predictor of counterproductive behavior for new job applicants. The climate index proved to be predictive of supervisor ratings of a variety of counterproductive behaviors, such as taking extended work breaks. These studies suggest sorely needed areas for research: an examination of both individual and organizational factors in predicting theft and other defalcations.

DISCUSSION

Interpretation of Validity Findings

As has been seen, a wide variety of strategies have been used to validate honesty tests. How strong is the validity evidence? We will present two contrasting viewpoints on this issue. The skeptic could argue that the validity evidence is very weak on several grounds.

First, comparisons with polygrapher judgments should be dismissed out of hand. A criterion that is seriously questioned in the scientific community cannot serve as the basis for meaningful evaluation of new instruments, such as honesty tests.

Second, studies relying on admissions of past behavior, obtained with or without aid of a polygraph, are flawed. Correlations in such studies are inflated by social desirability, which both inhibits admissions and heightens honesty scores. Some test predictions are based in part on admissions as well as attitudinal items, making the correlation between such predictions and admissions less than surprising. Also, while past behavior may predict future behavior, the relationship between the two is by no means perfect, thus making questionable the use of these correlations as estimates of how well tests predict future behavior.

Third, the time series designs reported to date do not have sufficient control of extraneous factors to attribute shrinkage reduction to the selection of honest applicants. A perceived increase in organizational concern about employee theft is one alternative explanation for the results. Use of control groups or reversal designs is needed.

Fourth, mean test score differences between convicts and applicants are not persuasive evidence of validity or of resistance to faking. Differences may simply be the result of the demand characteristics of the two situations.

Fifth, while true predictive studies are the most persuasive, most studies to date are flawed by the fact that only a very small number of employee thefts have been detected. While the researchers cannot be faulted for this state of affairs, it is nonetheless not very compelling to report that while the detected thieves on average did poorly on the tests, the vast majority of individuals not recommended by the test (25-75 percent of all applicants) were not caught or suspected of stealing. The one study in which large numbers of individuals were caught stealing used a test different from all others (the Personal Outlook Inventory), in that test questions do not directly address theft attitudes. In short, compelling evidence of the validity of honesty tests has yet to be produced.

An advocate of honesty testing could counter the above argument as follows. While it is acknowledged that each of the validity strategies used to date has flaws, what stands out is the consistency of positive findings across tests and across validity strategies. While the difficulty of obtaining sound criterion measures is a problem in all validation research, the problem is particularly acute in the area of honesty testing: employee theft is not easily detected. Hence a variety of alternatives to predictive validity designs are used; each is subject to a different set of flaws, but each contributes to the growing body of evidence that honesty tests correlate with various indices of past or future theft. It should also be noted that validity findings are attenuated by the less-than-perfect reliability of criteria such as polygrapher judgments and dollar-value-of-theft admissions.

The discrepancy between these two positions can be resolved only by research designed to overcome the flaws noted above. Studies using admissions as criteria can be improved by carefully examining the role played by social desirability. Aggregate-level shrinkage reduction studies can be improved by the use of control groups or reversal designs. Predictive studies can augment "caught stealing" criteria with other, less direct measures, such as cash drawer shortages. The ease of, extent of, and ability and personality correlates of fakability of these tests can be examined. Criterion reliability can be assessed. Finally, clear separation of the attitudinal and admission components of honesty tests is needed.

Research Needs

Despite the fairly extensive amount of research regarding the validity of various tests of honesty, there is a dearth of literature concerning some basic issues. Specifically, little is known about the nature and structure of either the honesty construct or the criterion Theft and Counterproductivity. Even less is known about how these factors interrelate. Considering first the honesty construct, there are almost no data regarding its factor structure. For example, the Reid Report consists of punitive and projective scales, which are summed for a total score. Ash (1975) reports a correlation of .56 between the two scales. It remains open to question, however, whether a two-factor structure is most appropriate. Many tests seem to presume that honesty is a unidimensional construct. It is likely that the lack of research regarding the factor structure is due to an early interest in predicting the polygraph decision, rather than in developing scales measuring the latent construct.

A second, related issue concerning honesty tests is scale construction and development. Although the tests developed to date rely on classical test theory, honesty tests could profitably employ modern test theory or item response theory (IRT). This latter approach has several potential advantages for honesty testing: it leads to more accurate measurement; it can be implemented for use in tailored testing, thereby eliminating the need for a testtaker to answer all items; it provides a superior means for assessing bias at the item level; and if items differ from job to job, IRT will enable one to construct different tests with the same underlying scale. In short, IRT may be a superior approach to scale construction.

The criterion of interest has also been virtually ignored. Although the terms "employee theft" and "counterproductivity" were used interchangeably in this chapter, there is little evidence on the dimensionality of this set of behaviors. For instance, Hollinger and Clark (1983) devised questionnaires measuring counterproductivity. Sample items include taking care of personal business on company time, doing slow or sloppy work on purpose, and punching a time clock for an absent employee. No attempt was made to examine the dimensionality of the scale. Thus, while the notion of constructing a reliable and valid criterion measure is a sound one, some basic work needs to be done.

A more fundamental issue is the structure of counterproductivity: Hollinger and Clark (1983) separate this construct into two components, production deviance and property deviance. Although the two are reasonably correlated (approximately .40, depending on the industry), it is not entirely clear how they are structured. Further, no discussion exists on the other end of the continuum, productivity. Do counterproductivity and productivity comprise a single dimension, or is it possible for an employee to be productive and counterproductive at the same time? There is a limited amount of honesty test research showing positive relationships between passing an honesty test and performance ratings (see Jones & Terris 1983b; Bradley 1980). These issues demand closer examination if we are to fully understand counterproductivity.

Turning now to the relationship between the honesty construct and actual behavior, the research described above has relied on individual differences to account for theft. A few attempts have evoked theories to explain theft. Cherrington and Cherrington (1983), for instance, examine climate as a cause of theft; Farrington (1979) describes an interesting application of the Subjective Expected Utility (USE) model in accounting for theft behavior. Although Farrington's research was not conducted in an organizational setting, it may be applicable in the present context. Facet theory (Levy 1982; Shapira & Zevulun 1979) may be a useful tool for studying employee theft. Although an explication of this technique is beyond the scope of the present chapter, a few comments are in order. First, facet theory compels one to develop and articulate a structure of the phenomenon. This serves to reduce the "fishing expedition" nature of much of the research in this area. Second, facet theory emphasizes empirical prediction along with useful hypotheses regarding the phenomenon at hand (Guttman 1954). A number of dimensions have been used in attempting to predict theft: earlier behavior, judgments concerning others' honesty, beliefs about the amount of theft by fellow workers. These dimensions (or facets) may be useful in developing a coherent structure of employee theft.

Finally, the honesty construct needs to be compared with other personality constructs. For example, to what degree does honesty correlate with authoritarianism? The little research available indicates that a substantial relationship exists with social desirability. Comparisons between various honesty tests would be useful as well. In short, studies examining convergent and discriminant validity are necessary for ascertaining the nature of honesty tests.

Ethical Concerns

The use of honesty tests has been questioned on ethical grounds. Extensive questioning about theft attitudes and previous theft behavior is seen by some as offensive and as an invasion of the privacy of the job applicant. This may be true: concern for company image is often cited as a reason why some organizations do not use honesty tests. It is also pointed out that, depending on which test cutoff an organization chooses to use, anywhere from 25 to 75 percent of job applicants will fail an honesty test. Given less than perfect validity, innocent people will be misclassified and wrongly denied jobs. In response it can be argued that, given an employer's legitimate interest in hiring employees who will not steal, inquiries about honesty are unethical only if the test is invalid, and that selection procedures with modest validities are the best that psychology has been able to devise; thus, selection errors are made with any test.

While honesty testing may be useful for institutional prediction (that is, a higher percentage of those scoring below a cutoff may steal than of those scoring above), we caution against placing a high degree of confidence in individual scores, and particularly against communicating test results to the rejected applicant. Of particular concern is the use of honesty tests with current employees rather than job applicants. A formerly trusted employee may unjustly lose a job or a promotion, or be constantly viewed with suspicion as a result of such a test. In trying to draw a fine line between employer interests and employee rights, we argue that the infringement on individual rights is much greater in the case of a current employee than of a job applicant. Being rejected for a job is an unpleasant but not uncommon part of a job search; however, the impact of the loss of one's job, status, or reputation due to a test classification error leads us to object to the use of honesty test predictions, unsubstantiated by actual admissions of theft, with current employees.

CONCLUSION

We have reviewed a fairly extensive body of literature, much of its unpublished, on the use of paper-and-pencil honesty testing for personnel selection. We have attempted to identify research needs at a variety of levels, including test construction, criterion development, developing a conceptual understanding of the concept of counterproductivity, and the examination of both individual and situational factors relating to counterproductivity. We have pointed out the different validation strategies used by various test developers, and noted that differences between studies on a number of dimensions—including sample selection, conditions of test administration, nature of the predictor and criterion used, and the statistical procedure used for analysis—make direct comparisons of validity coefficients for various tests misleading. Finally, we have noted the increase in the number of honesty tests being marketed and in the extent to which these tests are being used. Despite being a topic of concern to many organizations, honesty in the work place has not been closely examined by industrial/organizational psychologists; we encourage greater involvement by I/O psychologists in this area.

REFERENCES

Ajzen, I., & Fishbein, M. Attitude-behavior relations: A theoretical analysis and review of empirical research. *Psychological Bulletin,* 1977, *84,* 888–918.

American Management Association. *Crimes against business project: Background and recommendations.* New York: American Management Association, 1977.

Ash, P. Validation of an instrument to predict the likelihood of employee theft. *Proceedings of the 78th Annual Convention of the American Psychological Association.* 1970, 579–580.

———. Screening employment applicants for attitudes toward theft. *Journal of Applied Psychology,* 1971, *55,* 161–164.

———. Attitudes of work applicants toward theft. *Proceedings of the XVIIth International Congress of Applied Psychology.* 1972, 985–988.

———. Convicted felons' attitudes toward theft. *Criminal Justice Behavior,* 1974, *1,* 1–8.

_____. Predicting dishonesty with the Reid Report. *Polygraph*, 1975, *5*, 139–153.

Bechtold, M.L. Validation of the KD Scale and checklist as predictors of delinquent proneness. *Journal of Experimental Education*, 1964, *32*, 413–416.

Bickman, L., Rosenbaum, D.P., Baumer, T.L., Kudel, M.R., Christenholz, C., Knight, S.L., & Berkowitz, W.T. *National evaluation program-phase I: Assessment of shoplifting and employee theft programs*. Evanston, Ill.: Westinghouse Evaluation Institute, 1979.

Bologna, J. The eight factor theory of white collar crime. *Assets Protection*, 1981, 22–25.

Bowers, K.S. Situationism in psychology: An analysis and a critique. *Psychological Review*, 1973, *80*, 307–336.

Bradley, P. *The Milby system: Validation study 1980-S*. Minneapolis: Milby Systems, 1980.

_____. *The Milby system: Adverse impact study 1981-M*. Minneapolis: Milby Systems, 1981.

Burton, R.V. Generality of honesty reconsidered. *Psychological Review*, 1963, *70*, 481–499.

Campbell, J.P., Daft, R.L., & Hulin, C.L. *What to study: Generating and developing research questions*. Beverly Hills, Calif.: Sage Publications, 1982.

Cherrington, D.J., & Cherrington, J.O. The climate of honesty in retail stores. In W. Terris (ed.), *Employee theft: Research, theory, and applications*. Park Ridge, Ill.: London House Press, 1983.

Clarke, W., & Hasler, K.R. Differentiation of criminals and non-criminals with a self-concept measure. *Psychological Reports*, 1967, *20*, 623–632.

Corey, S.M. Professed attitudes and actual behavior. *Journal of Educational Psychology*, 1937, *28*, 271–280.

Eysenck, H.J. *The structure of human personality*. New York: John Wiley and Sons, 1953.

Farrington, D.D. Experiments on deviance with special reference to dishonesty. In L. Berkowitz (ed.), *Advances in experimental psychology*, vol. 12. New York: Academic Press, 1979.

Freeman, L., & Ataov, T. Validity of indirect and direct measures of attitude toward cheating. *Journal of Personality*, 1960, *28*, 444–447.

Gerhardt, V. *Research and statistics: Pre-employment analysis questionnaire "H"*. Dallas: Psychometric Behavioral Group, undated.

Glueck, S., & Glueck, E. *Delinquents and non-delinquents in perspective*. Cambridge, Mass.: Harvard University Press, 1968.

Gough, H. Cross-cultural validation of a measure of asocial behavior. *Psychological Reports*, 1965, *17*, 379–387.

Guttman, L. A new approach to factor analysis: The radex. In P. Lazarsfeld (ed.), *Mathematical thinking in the social sciences*. Glencoe, Ill.: Free Press, 1954.

Harris, M.M. A research statement on the Reid Report. Unpublished paper available from the author, Krannunt School of Management, 1980.

Hartshorne, H., & May, M.A. *Studies in the nature of character,* I, *Studies in de-ceit.* New York: Macmillan, 1928.

Hollinger, R., & Clark, J. *Theft by employees.* Lexington, Mass.: Lexington Books, 1983.

Jones, J.W. Attitudinal correlates of emloyees' deviance: Theft, alcohol use, and nonprescribed drug use. *Psychological Reports,* 1980, *47,* 71–77.

_____. *Dishonesty, staff burnout, and employee theft.* Technical Report no. E2. Park Ridge, Ill.: London House Management Consultants, 1982. (a)

_____. Psychological predictors of employee theft. Paper presented at the 98th Annual Conference of the American Psychological Association. Washington, D.C., 1982. (b)

Jones, J., & Terris, W. Convicted felons' attitudes toward theft, violence, and il-licit drug use. Paper presented at the 7th Annual Convention of the Society of Police and Criminal Psychology. New Orleans, 1981. (a)

_____. Predictive validation of a dishonesty test that measures theft proneness. Paper presented at the XVIII Inter-American Congress of Psychology. Santo Domingo, Dominican Republic, 1981. (b)

_____. *The Employee Attitude Inventory: A validity study on theft by current employees.* Technical Report no. 33. Park Ridge, Ill.: London House Man-agement Consultants, 1982. (a)

_____. *Using the PSI to reduce employee theft in department stores: A program evaluation study.* Technical Report no. 28. Park Ridge, Ill.: London House Management Consultants, 1982. (b)

_____. Personality correlates of theft and drug abuse among job applicants. Paper presented at the 3rd International Conference on the 16-PF Test. 1983. (a)

_____. Predicting employees' theft in home improvement centers. *Psychological Reports,* 1983, *52,* 187–201. (b)

Klump, C. *The Stanton Survey manual: Description and validation.* Chicago: The Stanton Corporation, 1980.

Kochkin, S. *Some by-products associated with screening applicants with the Reid Report.* Chicago: Human Resources Department, United Airlines, 1981.

Levy, S. Lawful roles in facets in social theories. In I. Borg (ed.), *Multidimen-sional data representation.* Ann Arbor, Mich.: Mathesis Press, 1982.

Lykken, D. *A tremor in the blood.* New York: McGraw-Hill, 1981.

Moretti, D. Employee counterproductivity: Attitudinal predictors of industrial damage and waste. Paper presented at the Annual Meeting of the Society of Police and Criminal Psychology. Atlanta, 1980.

_____. *The prediction of employee counterproductivity through attitude assess-ment.* Technical Report no. 26. Park Ridge, Ill.: London House Management Consultants, 1982.

Moretti, D., Jones, J., & Terris, W. *Integrity testing in the banking industry.* Technical Report no. 34. Park Ridge, Ill.: London House Management Con-sultants, 1983.

Morey, L. *Statistical properties of the Wilkerson Pre-employment Audit*. Tulsa, Okla.: Wilkerson and Associates, 1981.

O'Grady, K.E. Measures of explained variance: Cautions and limitations. *Psychological Bulletin*, 1982, *92*, 766–777.

Personnel Security Corporation. *Survey description manual: T.A. Survey*. Oak Brook, Ill.: Personnel Security Corporation, undated.

Phase II Profile. *Adverse impact studies*. Peoria, Ill.: Lousig-Nont and Associates, 1982. (a)

_____. *Statistical validation studies*. Peoria, Ill.: Lousig-Nont and Associates, 1982. (b)

Podlesny, J.A., & Raskin, D.C. Physiological measures and the detection of deception. *Psychological Bulletin*, 1977, *84*, 782–799.

P.O.S. Corporation. *P.O.S. Pre-employment Opinion survey*. Chicago: P.O.S. Corporation, undated.

Reed, H. *The Stanton Survey: Description and validation manual*. Chicago: The Stanton Corporation, 1982.

Sackett, P.R. Honesty research and the person-situation debate. In W. Terris (ed.), *Employee theft: Research, theory, and applications*. Park Ridge, Ill.: London House Press, 1983.

Sackett, P.R., & Decker, P.J. Detection of deception in the employment context: A review and critical analysis. *Personnel Psychology*, 1979, *32*, 487–506.

Selection Research Publishing. *Development and validation of the Personal Outlook Inventory*. Chicago: Selection Research Publishing, 1983.

Shapira, Z., & Zevulun, E. On the use of facet analysis in organizational behavior research: Some conceptual considerations and an example. *Organizational Behavior and Human Performance*, 1979, *23*, 411–428.

State of Minnesota v. *Century Camera, Inc.* 309 N.W. 2d 735 (Minn. 1981).

Tampor, S. More employers attempt to catch a thief by giving job applicants honesty exams. *Wall Street Journal*, Aug. 3, 1981, sec. 2, p. 1.

Terris, W. Attitudinal correlates of theft, violence, and drug use. Paper presented at the 17th Congress of Psychology. Lima, Peru, 1979.

_____. *Attitudinal correlates of employee integrity: Theft-related admissions made in pre-employment polygraph examinations*. Technical Report no. 1. Park Ridge, Ill.: London House Management Consultants, 1982.

Terris, W., & Jones, J. *Validation of the Personnel Selection Inventory with KFC managerial and hourly job applicants*. Park Ridge, Ill.: London House Management Consultants, 1981.

_____. *Pre-employment screening to reduce employee theft in department stores: Three separate studies*. Park Ridge, Ill.: London House Management Consultants, 1982. (a)

_____. Psychological factors related to employee theft in the convenience store industry. *Psychological Reports*, 1982, *5*, 1219–1238. (b)

_____. *Attitudinal and personality correlates of theft among supermarket employees*. Park Ridge, Ill.: London House Management Consultants, undated.

U.S. News and World Report. Why employees steal: Interview with an authority on business crime. May 3, 1971, pp. 78–82.

Wickert, A.W. Attitudes v. action: The relationship of verbal and overt behavioral responses to attitude objects. *Journal of Social Issues,* 1969, *25,* 41–78.

Wilkerson, O.M. *The Wilkerson Pre-employment Audit.* Tulsa, Okla.: Wilkerson and Associates, 1980.

10

Personality Assessment
in Industry:
Theoretical Issues
and Illustrations
James Neal Butcher

The chapters in this volume are products of the times. In earlier decades organization management placed little value on personality assessment. Even when the potential value was seen, such efforts were viewed as insufficiently practical or cost-effective, or (within ethical limits) as the legal prerogative of corporations to be pursued actively.

Today, however, increasing numbers of organizations in many industrial contexts consider it desirable to employ consultants or to hire trained personnel to conduct personality testing. Many reasons can be found for this recent shift in attitude toward personality evaluation in corporate settings. First, there is an increased awareness that psychological factors may play an important role in competent performance in certain occupations. This is most obvious in occupations such as air traffic control, in which the individual is susceptible to occupational stress; in occupations that involve personal risk, such as law enforcement; and in positions that require great personal responsibility, such as nuclear power plant operator or airline pilot. Second, personality assessment technology is now available to enable the industrial psychologist or personnel manager to obtain information on "typical," normal-range personality attributes and on psychological adjustment problems quickly and at relatively low cost. Third, legal precedents have justified the use of objective personality assessment for selection in occupations for which some form of psychological evaluation is necessary to assure that emotionally unstable individuals are not placed in sensitive positions. Fourth, the "political climate" is more favorable to the use of psychological testing in government and industry. There is, at least, less concern over invasion of privacy and less objection to using psychological techniques for decision making today than there was in the 1960s. Fifth, today, there is a greater concern in many corporations for the emotional well-being of employees than there was previously. This is reflected in the widespread development of employee assistance programs, in which personality assessment may be one of the mental health services provided to employees.

This chapter explores several types of clinical assessment roles filled by psychologists who practice clinical or counseling psychology in occupational settings, and examines some of the theoretical issues raised in the practice of personality assessment in industry.

ASSUMPTIONS UNDERLYING PERSONALITY ASSESSMENT IN INDUSTRIAL SETTINGS

There are several general issues to consider before we discuss specific applications of clinical personality evaluation in the industrial context. An industrial psychological assessor makes a number of assumptions about his or her role in personality testing. The first is that the individual being assessed is a willing partner in the evaluation and stands to gain from the assessment. As we shall see, this assumption of "individual reward" in the assessment cannot always be made. For example, a psychological assessment might disclose that an individual is likely to be falsely claiming neurological or psychological problems in order to qualify for worker's compensation. The discovery of information that is detrimental to the individual's immediate goals is not unusual when the assessment is being performed at the request of the employer.

When the psychological evaluation is initiated by the corporation, and not the individual being assessed, the possibility of test-taking defensiveness must be considered. Psychological evaluations conducted with individuals who are unwilling participants may produce invalid results because of the typically defensive test-taking attitude of such a subject. The prevalence of this problem in some types of industrial assessment is an important consideration facing the psychological assessor and will be encountered several times in this chapter.

The second assumption is that the referral source (such as the employer or an insurance company) may gain from having the employee undergo psychological assessment, and has a legal right to the results of the evaluation. Such a situation, since it is prompted by the employer and may be used to the detriment of the employee, requires that the employee give permission for information to be released to the referring party.

Third, the organizational personality assessor assumes that psychological assessments, whether in the context of preemployment selection or of ongoing personality evaluation, are appropriate and ethical activities for psychologists to engage in.

The fourth assumption is that psychological assessments in the industrial context will maintain the dignity of the test subjects, and that the results of psychological studies will be treated in a professionally competent and ethical manner. Individuals undergoing such evaluations will be treated with both respect and courtesy (protecting their anonymity and confidentiality where it is appropriate).

Finally, it is assumed that the psychological procedures used in the assessment are both the most valid and the most reliable psychometric measures available, and represent the most practical means of obtaining the required information. (See Grant 1980; Dunnette & Borman 1979; Guion 1976.)

REASONS FOR CLINICAL ASSESSMENT
IN INDUSTRIAL SETTINGS

Psychological assessments in industrial settings may differ from evaluations in other settings in that the assessment study is frequently initiated at the request of a third party (such as employer or insurer) rather than of the assessed. For example, if an individual applies for a job he or she is given an ability test to determine if he or she has the requisite skills for the job; a personnel manager may request a psychological evaluation of an employee who has been on medical leave in order to determine if he or she is ready to return to work. In some industrial settings, particularly in corporations with employee assistance programs or mental health resources, psychological assessments may be used to aid employees who are experiencing psychological problems. These services resemble traditional services available at mental health centers.

A number of factors may influence the nature of the psychological examination, including the intent of the evaluation; whether the evaluation is being conducted at the request of the employer or of the employee; and whether the evaluation is designed solely to provide the employer with information that would improve the worker's employment situation, or may uncover problems that would jeopardize the employee's job.

A survey of situations in industry where personality evaluations might be used suggests that an assessment psychologist needs to weigh the intent of the examination carefully in order to determine how to interpret the test results:

- Preemployment personality appraisal.
- Evaluation for promotion.
- Performance assessment.
- Disability evaluation.
- Return-to-work evaluation.
- Assessment of clinical status of employee seeking psychological help, which may be incorporated in employee assistance programs.
- Job analysis validation research, to determine if personality or other factors are related to job success. The results of such studies do not directly affect the employees involved, but the information may be used in future preemployment assessments or promotion evaluations.
- Evaluation research to determine if employment selection procedures or training is adequate (see Bray & Howard 1983).
- Psychological evaluation as part of or in preparation for expert testimony in legal proceedings. This includes research to determine if particular products or procedures have had a negative impact on individual personality or adjustment processes—for example, determining if the presence of power lines has caused emotional problems for nearby residents.

FACTORS THAT MAY INFLUENCE PERSONALITY TEST RESULTS IN THE INDUSTRIAL SETTING

A number of important factors may bear on the validity of an individual psychological evaluation, and should be carefully examined in any industrial personality evaluation:

a.   Invalid response patterns may occur as a result of an individual's fear that management will use the test results against him or her.

b.   The attitudes of local labor organizations may affect the psychological evaluation. The union may actively protest the evaluation, encourage assessments beneficial to the employee, take a more positive, neutral, or negative position, any of which might affect the validity of the evaluation.

    c.   Management may be seeking information that is not obtainable through psychological assessment methods. For example, it may wish to eliminate candidates for promotion who may not remain in the position long. Factors other than personality variables, such as better pay elsewhere or unpleasant working conditions, may be more powerful determinants of job tenure.

    d.   The psychological tests selected should be the most valid available measures of the attributes in question.

    e.   Management may have been "oversold" on psychological techniques, and may expect easy categorical answers to complex or unanswerable questions.

    f.   The assessment questions may be inappropriate. I was once asked whether it would be possible to use psychological tests to detect the sexual preference of male candidates who would be applying for positions as airline stewards. The managers wanted to reject homosexuals, who, they believed, would "harass the male customers." Clearly, this is an inappropriate (and in many jurisdictions, unlawful) use of personality assessment.

    g.   Some aspects of the evaluation may be unwarranted violations of the individual's right to privacy. There must be valid psychological reasons for having the particular information sought in making the assessment. Butcher and Tellegen (1966) found that subjects taking the MMPI under simulated employment selection conditions were more reluctant to disclose personal information than subjects who took the test under "clinical" conditions, where they thought they would be personally helped by the testing.

    h.   The report or the recommendations from the assessment must be used properly.

THE USE OF PERSONALITY TESTS IN PERSONNEL SELECTION

The most extensive uses of psychological tests in business, industry, and government are for employee selection and for determining if an individual should be promoted. The use of psychological testing for preemployment evaluation of individuals has a long history. The first use of psychological testing as an aid in employment decisions has been traced to ancient China (DuBois 1970). The Chinese developed an extensive system of civil service examinations to determine which individuals were qualified for positions in the government.

The psychological tests used most often for preemployment screening have involved measures of general intellectual functioning and specific abilities, achievement and interest patterns, and, to some extent, attitudes and values. A very strong case can be made for the use of specific ability tests in many preemployment screening situations. For example, in selecting individuals who will work in product design in the electronics industry, it is important that the applicants have the required degree of ability in mechanical and electronic tasks. It is also easy to justify the use of intelligence and ability tests in the selection for many high-level management positions. Such tests have consistently been shown to correlate significantly with performance in a variety of management jobs.

The use of achievement tests has also gained broad acceptance as an appropriate means of assuring that candidates for positions are qualified in terms of possessing relevant basic knowledge. This applies not only to trades and crafts, but to professions as well. In most fields the use of achievement or qualifying examinations is generally accepted. Individuals applying for positions as engineers, architects, physicians, nurses, psychologists, and lawyers, as well as in other professions, demonstrate that they possess a qualifying degree of knowledge by passing a licensing examination in their specialty upon completing their training. Interest tests, used extensively in employment counseling, have also come to be used in selecting individuals for some positions. These tests enable employers to assay whether candidates have a genuine interest in and motivation for the position for which they are applying.

Personality factors have long been considered to be important in the performance of many jobs. The traditional means of evaluating prospective employees for "personality fit" has been the employment interview—a notoriously subjective device that is both highly vulnerable to error (Guion 1976) and not very cost-effective. Personality tests have been less widely used for preemployment screening than have either the selection interview or the other types of psychological measures previously discussed. A number of reasons for this can be found:

1. Personality factors may be considered less important for adequate performance in many positions than other psychological attributes. Many positions for which psychological assessment techniques are used are, perhaps, less subject to the influence of personality factors than to that of the other psychological attributes described above. For example, the intelligence of the prospective worker may be considered more crucial to adequate job performance than the individual's personality characteristics.

2. Personality factors are perhaps less "tangible," as far as their conceptualization and measurement go, than are other psychological characteristics, such as ability, achievement, and intelligence.

3. Optimal personality-job performance linkages have not been well enough established to warrant their appraisal in preemployment or promotional assessment.

4. Personality assessors have not developed their instruments and procedures well enough to generate user acceptability. Two of the reasons that intelligence is a widely used and accepted construction assessment are that several proven instruments are available with which to measure it, and that people know how to use them. This is not the case with personality tests—choice of instruments is limited and expertise in their use is not as available.

5. In the past, personnel psychologists were not as broadly trained in the use of personality assessment instruments as those in other subspecialities, such as counseling or clinical psychology. Personality assessment methods, especially those of individual assessment, usually require a great deal more time than most personnel selection situations allow (although the costs may be justified in some situations, such as selection for top managerial positions). Consequently, personality assessment methods have not been widely taught in industrial psychology training programs or used extensively in selection programs.

Measures of Normal-Range Personality Characteristics Versus Measures of Clinical Problems

An important distinction in personality tests that may be used for employment screening is that some measures focus upon characterizing an individual's personality attributes, while others aim at detecting patterns of maladjustment or psychological problems. The first type of test is used to describe personality characteristics, such as traits, motives, values, and attitudes, that are assumed to be present, to some degree, in all individuals. Tests in this category include the California Psychological Inventory, the Sixteen Personality Factor Inventory (16-PF), the Allport-Vernon-Lindzey Study of Values, the Adjective Checklist, and the Hopkins Personality Inventory. On these tests every person will obtain a "meaningful" score, since the psychological characteristics measured by the test are assumed to be found to some degree in all subjects.

Use of clinical tests, however, does not assume that the characteristics being evaluated are distributed across all subjects; rather, these characteristics represent extremes—significant adjustment difficulties that might pose problems for the individual in some occupational roles. These tests include the Minnesota Multiphasic Personality Inventory (MMPI) and the Clinical Analysis Questionnaire. In the typical personnel preemployment screening situation, use of these tests assumes that most individuals will not register in the maladjusted score range. That is, most individuals will fall within the range of scores that suggest an absence of psychological problems; score differences within this "normal" range are usually not interpretable.

Personality assessment with clinically oriented tests like the MMPI has been used in personnel selection primarily for occupations in which the personality characteristics of the individual may make him or her vulnerable to high levels of occupational stress (such as fire fighters or air traffic controllers), may cause him or her to be "flawed" in a way that could lead to abuses of power in positions of public trust (police officers), or may make him or her vulnerable to failures in judgment while in positions of public responsibility (airline flight crews or nuclear power plant operators). These occupations, which might be referred to as psychologically sensitive or stress-vulnerable positions, warrant a greater focus on adjustment factors than do other selection situations; for some occupations there have been governmental mandates to assure that the individuals chosen to fill vacancies are psychologically suited for the position.

Personality tests used to aid in the evaluation of candidates for psychologically sensitive or stress-vulnerable occupations have been used in a different way than have tests for other types of assessment in personnel selection situations. In many, if not most, personnel selection situations the psychologist determines which attributes or abilities are required by the position, then chooses a test that measures these characteristics. For example, a job analysis might be conducted to determine the skills required by a position. The psychologist would then validate the test or test components against those criteria, and develop appropriate cutoff scores to select individuals with sufficiently high levels of those skills. The use of tests to predict qualities or characteristics that match those of the criterion group is referred to as selection by the use of inclusion rules. The assessor seeks tests with components that predict known criterion characteristics. Very little research has been done using clinical tests to match "ideal types" to psychologically sensitive or stress-vulnerable positions.

Clinical assessment operates primarily by using exclusion criteria—that is, by detecting characteristics of the individual that are likely to operate against his or her success on the job. For example, it is difficult to specify the ideal level of stress tolerance that should be possessed by air traffic controllers. However, it might be possible to specify test predictors that would aid in detecting a proneness to become anxious or indecisive under stressful conditions. In these instances, individuals with a measured "likelihood" of becoming anxious would be excluded from further consideration for the position. This test practice involves the use of exclusion rules or test indices that enable the clinician to predict characteristics that would interfere with adequate job performance.

The most extensive use of clinically oriented personality tests for selection decisions has involved the assessment of police officer candidates. Many municipalities require that police department administrators use psychological screening programs to detect and eliminate from consideration those individuals whose personality maladjustments make them unsuitable for the demands of law enforcement work. Areas of such maladjustment include immature and impulsive behavior that might lead to misuse of firearms, an overly rigid and suspicious personality that might detract from objectivity in performing the job, antisocial characteristics that might lead the individual to break the law rather than enforce it, poor social skills that would impede the officer's interactions with the public, and proneness to anxiety or indecisiveness.

The most useful source of information for preemployment decisions about these stress-vulnerable occupations is, of course, personal history. That is, some types of information related to past job performance or personality difficulties can be obtained only by careful background checks, interviews, and recommendations from individuals who know the candidate well.

Personality testing can provide an informative source of hypotheses for decisions about some occupations if the tests selected have the following qualities:

1. They measure qualities or characteristics relevant to the decision.
2. They are objective, unbiased measures of personality problems.
3. They are valid indicators of personality problems.
4. They are used as sources of hypotheses rather than as the sole basis for the decision.
5. They are used by qualified test interpreters who have had substantial clinical experience with the test and are also familiar with how "normals" perform on the test.

The personality test most widely used for this type of assessment is the MMPI; over 48 percent of the police departments in the United States using psychological testing for preemployment screening use it (Murphy 1972). The success of police applicant selection with personality tests, most of which involves the MMPI, is well documented (Azen, Snibbe, & Montgomery 1973; Bernstein 1980, 1982; Blum 1964; Butcher 1979; Colarelli & Siegel 1964; Costello 1976; Costello, Schoenfeld, & Kobos 1982; Costello & Schoenfeld in press; Dunnette & Motowidlo 1975; Gottesman 1969; Hedlund 1965; Hooke & Krauss 1971; Lefkowitz 1973; Matarazzo, Allen, Saslow, & Wiens 1964; McAllister 1977; Merian, Stefan, Schoenfeld, & Kobos 1980; Murphy 1972; Naroll & Levitt 1963; Peterson & Houston 1980; Rhead, Abrams, Grossman, & Margolis 1968; Sacuzzo, Higgins, & Lewandowski 1974; Schoenfeld, Kobos, & Phinney 1980; Solway, Hays, & Zieben 1976.

The MMPI has also been used in the selection of applicants and in prediction for a number of other occupations, including physician's assistants (Crovitz, Huse, & Lewis 1973), medical assistants (Stone, Bassett, Brosseau, Demers, & Stiening 1972), psychiatric residents (Garetz & Anderson 1973), clinical psychology graduate students (Butcher 1979), nurses (Kelly 1974), business school graduates (Harrell 1972; Harrell & Harrell 1973), clergymen (Jansen & Garvey 1973), fire fighters (Arvey, Mussio, & Payne 1972), probation officers (Solway, Hays, & Zieben 1976), and government workers (Muha & May 1973).

One of the more extensive recent applications of the MMPI in personal selection involves screening for emotional problems among nuclear power plant personnel. Dunnette, Bownas, and Bosshardt (1981) studied screening for emotional problems in such workers. These investigators, using the "critical incident" technique, developed categories of job-relevant emotionally unstable behavior through workshop discussions with nuclear power plant supervisors. They identified 18 categories of behavior believed to reflect emotional problems that might adversely influence job performance. These behaviors included psychopathology, poor response to crisis, stress buildup over time, hostility toward authority, hot-temperedness, lack of a serious work attitude, impulsiveness, and alcohol and drug abuse.

Expert ratings of these 18 categories were submitted to a factor analysis, resulting in six factors: hostility to authority, irresponsibility and impulsiveness, defensive incompetence, psychopathology, compulsive incompetence, and substance abuse. The investigators then obtained expert judgments of potentially valid and appropriate methods for evaluating and detecting these problem behaviors. The authors obtained a great deal of consensus that the MMPI can be employed successfully as a screening instrument to detect many of these problem behaviors in a preemployment screening assessment.

Goals of Clinical Testing in Personnel Selection

In preemployment screening of candidates for sensitive or stress-prone occupations, the psychological assessor may approach the task in any of several ways, depending upon the amount of time available for the assessment, the nature of the decision process, and the types of tests used in the assessment. In situations where relatively few candidates are being considered and the cost of selection errors is high, the assessment task may be more extensive and elaborate. In these situations the assessor may compile results from a variety of sources of information and prepare an extensive report covering areas of psychological functioning, such as psychosocial history, general personality dynamics, defensive tactics, adjustment styles, and significant problem areas. This detailed psychological evaluation may closely resemble clinical diagnostic studies conducted in mental health settings. An example of the intensive individual study approach to personality appraisal can be found in the development of assessment centers (Bray, Campbell, & Grant 1979; Bray & Howard 1983).

In many industrial selection situations, however, limits and large numbers of candidates do not permit such an extensive individual psychological study. A more typical assessment program involves the evaluation of groups of individuals for particular positions by use of a battery of tests that is scored by machine or trained technicians. After testing, selection decisions are made with the assistance of computer-based rules, or through clinical evaluation of the test profiles. In most of these situations, the individual case is given much less attention than in the extensive individual evaluation. The use of tests to screen applicants in this way may require a simple "adjusted" versus "maladjusted" decision.

In many situations other decision processes have narrowed the field to a limited range of candidates and the psychologist simply uses the test data as a final filter to assure that individuals with abnormal profiles are not accepted, or the test results are used only to determine whether the applicant requires an extensive individual psychological interview or psychiatric evaluation.

It is not possible in this chapter to go into great detail about specific personnel assessment procedures, or to relate the specifics of how personality tests are used in personnel decisions. Screening practices vary considerably from corporation to corporation, depending upon such factors as availability of trained personnel, the ratio of candidates to jobs, the time requirements of the selection project, the judged dangers of test misprediction versus the costs of the assessments, and other factors.

Use of Electronic Computers in Personality Assessment

One of the problems inherent in the use of personality assessment in personnel selection is the large amount of time required to administer, score, and interpret many personality tests when large numbers of subjects are being screened for a given position. Additionally, as noted above, the expertise needed for interpretation of personality tests may be limited or unavailable.

Increasingly, with the advent of the electronic computer, the effort involved in processing large numbers of test protocols has been reduced considerably. The use of electronic computers to process objective psychological test data is made possible by a number of factors: the availability of self- or group-administered personality tests; the efficient operation of optical scanners and computer-interactive data entry systems to process answer sheets; the wealth of objectively established empirical scale correlates for personality tests such as the MMPI; and the wide availability of electronic computers. It is now possible to process large numbers of personality test protocols by using computer scoring and interpretation. The MMPI has a long history, both of research on objective interpretation, beginning with the pioneering work of Meehl (1954), and of computer-based interpretation procedures, beginning with Pearson and Swenson (1961). Currently there are several scoring and interpretation programs available for computer processing of the MMPI (Butcher & Keller 1984).[1]

CLINICAL ASSESSMENT IN INDUSTRIAL SETTINGS: SOME ILLUSTRATIONS FROM AN OCCUPATIONAL HEALTH CLINIC

Personality assessment in industrial settings is not limited to applicant screening or selection of managerial candidates; there are a number of other contexts in which personality assessment techniques can play an important role in personnel management. These assessment situations require the evaluation of personality functioning of current employee or individuals who are returning to work after an absence.

Psychological evaluation using ability, cognitive, and other tests has traditionally been employed in this way in industrial settings to evaluate an employee's potential effectiveness or to determine if individuals can be rehabilitated—for example, after disabling industrial accidents—to perform other occupations. The evaluation of whether an individual is able to return to work has typically included an assessment of the individual's motivation and attitudes, as well as whether he or she has regained his or her physical functioning.

In the rest of this chapter we will consider the evaluation of workers' emotional problems as they relate to adjustment to work. The case material presented in this section comes from the author's consultation practice at an occupational medical clinic. All of the cases and the assessment problems were evaluated in the context of psychological or health-related problems occurring in the work place.

Back-to-Work Evaluation

Frequently, psychological consultants working in occupational health settings must determine whether an individual, who has experienced some problem requiring an absence from work, is ready to resume his or her work responsibilities. These evaluations, like personality testing in personnel selection, tend to occur in sensitive or demanding occupations that involve great stress or responsibility. Evaluations of the individual's psychological readiness to return to work may be made following absences due to disciplinary layoff, medical absence as a result of injury, or absence resulting from acute psychological breakdown.

The scope of the evaluation and the type of procedures used will depend upon many factors, such as the nature of the problem, the extent of the disability, the complexity of the job, and the cooperativeness of the individual being assessed. In most situations the evaluation of personality or adjustment problems would not constitute the full back-to-work evaluation. Rather, other factors would need to be considered, including the "receptivity" of the work environment toward the individual's return, the possibility that a lateral transfer and a different supervisor might be necessary (for example, in cases where employee and supervisor have been unable to get along), and the need for a "work tolerance" evaluation to determine whether the individual returning to work following an injury is capable of performing the job.

In back-to-work evaluations the clinician is faced with a number of important considerations regarding the employee. In many instances the employee has been out of work for some time and may feel uncertain about being able to perform the job, physically or psychologically (for instance, a truck driver who was in a serious accident and is worried that he may not be able to control the vehicle, or an airline flight attendant who experienced an in-flight "incident" that frightened her). Other critical questions from the employee's point of view are: Is he or she psychologically able to return to the job? Does he or she want to return to work? Is he or she angry at the employer for failing to provide a "safe" working environment? Is there a worker's compensation claim involved? Are labor grievance procedures being instituted?

The other perspective to be considered is that of the employer. Questions from this vantage point include: What are the attitudes of the individual's employer or supervisor about his or her request to return to work? Is there a hidden reason for the request for a psychological evaluation? Does the employer, for example, seek psychological evidence or "justification" for not allowing the employee to return to work? Is the individual psychologically ready to return to work? Is the individual able to return to the same work environment? Would fellow employees accept his or her return to work? Would the work environment be supportive or rejecting? Would the individual be able to return to full-time work, or would a part-time arrangement with "light" duty be required?

In most occupational health consultations, even though the referral source is the employer, the individual being evaluated is considered to be the client. Consequently, the evaluation is designed as an outside, objective appraisal to help the employee arrive at the most feasible outcome under the circumstances: to return to work if the conditions allow, or to effect another desirable outcome if return to work is inadvisable. In occupational health consultation an outright release from employment is not considered a desirable outcome. In some exceptional instances, however, when the employee cannot reasonably be expected to return to the corporation, "outplacement evaluations" may be recommended. In these circumstances the employee is carefully evaluated and referred to an appropriate position in some other organization, with appropriate severance pay.

An illustrative back-to-work evaluation that involved clinical assessment is given below. In this case the MMPI was particularly valuable to the personnel staff determining whether the individual could return to work. Case 1 involved an executive who was evaluated following hospitalization for a major psychosis. (See the MMPI profile in Figure 10.1.)

Case 1: Psychotic Disorder in an Executive

Sam Z., a 32-year-old, single computer analyst was employed to manage a department in a large manufacturing firm. His job as department manager required that he move from his home in another state, where he had lived with his mother, to the city where the corporate offices were located. He had a great deal of difficulty making the move and had vacillated on his decision for weeks before he agreed to accept the position. Within three weeks after he had accepted the job and moved, Mr. Z was experiencing great psychological stress: he was avoiding other people, talking to himself, and not performing even routine tasks, such as answering telephone calls. His supervisor, concerned with his unusual behavior, referred him to a psychologist for an evaluation.

During the psychological interview Sam manifested numerous signs of an acute schizophrenic disorder; he was disoriented, was hallucinating, had delusions, and demonstrated disturbances in affect and associations. (Sam's prehospitalization profile is represented by the dotted line in Figure 10.1.)

Mr. Z. was referred and admitted to an inpatient service at a general hospital for treatment of his psychotic disorder. He remained in the hospital for six weeks and was discharged to an outpatient treatment program, in which he was receiving follow-up psychotherapy and psychopharmacologic treatment. Mr. Z asked to return to work and was referred for a psychological evaluation to determine whether he was ready to resume his duties. He was given a psychological interview and the MMPI was read-ministered.

Mr. Z appeared to be greatly improved during the interview. His retest MMPI profile reflected this apparent improvement. (The posthospitalization profile is shown by the solid line in Figure 10.1.) His schizophrenic symptoms were in remission and he appeared to have a great deal of insight into the situation that preceded his breakdown. He concluded that much of his psychological problem situation resulted from his inability to deal with the stresses of moving and meeting the demands of the new job. After reviewing his current, somewhat tenuous psychological adjustment, and the stress inherent in his position, it was agreed that a return to his managerial position would not be in his best interest. Instead, he requested, and was given, a new, less demanding, position without supervisory responsibility. He was assigned to work in the programming department, where he felt comfortable with the lower work demands and would be able to work by himself, at his own pace.

FIGURE 10.1
MMPI Profile of Sam Z.

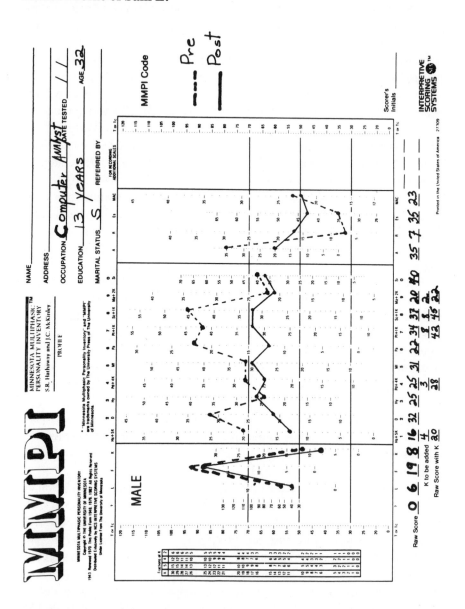

Source: Provided by author.

Worker's Compensation Evaluations

Some referrals for psychological evaluation in an occupational health setting initially begin as back-to-work evaluations but become a component in a worker's compensation claim hearing. Often the clinician does not know in advance which psychological evaluations of individuals scheduled to return to work will later become a part of an evaluation for a worker's compensation claim. The clinician should be aware of the possibility that any such evaluation might be central to such a hearing, and take appropriate care in keeping precise records of individual contacts and test protocols. The psychological assessor should also be aware that his or her evaluation may be contested by the attorneys on the opposing side and be cognizant of the possibility that contradictory psychological testimony may be forthcoming—perhaps centering on his or her own records. Psychologists testifying in court proceedings, particularly when the use of the MMPI is central to the case, should be familiar with the recommendations of Ziskin (1981a, 1981b) on the use of the MMPI in testimony.

In worker's compensation determinations, the MMPI is considered to be a laboratory procedure similar to medical laboratory tests (Shaffer 1981). As in physical medicine, disability determinations should not be made on the basis of a single finding, but should be based on an integration of all information related to the claim (Nussbaum, Shaffer, & Schneidmuhl 1969). Moreover, an instrument like the MMPI should be used only by consultants who are qualified to interpret the test findings in disability evaluation situations. Shaffer (1981) pointed out that an instrument such as the MMPI cannot appropriately be used to make a disability determination, but can appropriately be used as the basis for an opinion on a work-related disability if psychopathology is known or suspected to be involved, or the individual's physical disability is believed to be complicated by psychological factors.

In cases where an individual is seeking worker's compensation as a result of an alleged injury on the job, his or her test performance is likely to be influenced substantially by the circumstances. In these evaluations the MMPI validity indicators become a highly important component of the test report. Many individuals with questionable claims of physical disability approach the test situation in a highly defensive manner—elevations on the L (Lie) and K (Defensiveness) scales are common. They attempt to present a picture of psychological health and personal virtue, but admit to physical limitations. The resulting test patterns involve highly defensive Validity scale configurations, if not outright invalidation of the test. In addition to a defensive Validity scale configuration, their MMPI profile often reflects a neurotic pattern in which overresponding to somatic items yields highly exaggerated symptoms admission that is unlikely to result from an actual physical injury.

The typical MMPI pattern occurring among worker's compensation claimants with questionable physical injuries is usually quite different from profiles of Social Security disability claimants (see Shaffer 1981). The latter profiles typically have a different validity configuration, reflecting an exaggerated claim of mental problems. The F or Infrequency scale score is usually elevated. A number of clinical scale elevations, particularly on the D, Pt, and Sc scales, is also typical. This pattern shows an exaggerated tendency to claim extreme psychological disturbance that is manifested in an unlikely pattern of symptoms. The psychological assessor needs to be aware of the different Validity scale patterns and different validity configurations that are produced in these different disability determination situations.

The following case illustrates the worker's compensation evaluation of an individual who alleged a permanent disability as the result of a back injury that reportedly occurred on the job. Extensive medical tests produced no organic findings.

Case 2: Questionable Claim for Disability Compensation

Edna B., age 37, had been employed as an assembly line worker in a manufacturing plant for about 18 months when she injured her back on a Friday while lifting a component weighing about 37 pounds. She continued to work for the remainder of the shift, though she reportedly suffered great pain in her neck and back when she moved suddenly. She went home for the weekend and failed to report the incident to her supervisor until she returned to work the following Monday. At that time she was sent to the company doctor for evaluation and treatment. She was placed on temporary disability and treated with medication and heat for two weeks. When she reported that the pain had become worse, her physician hospitalized her and placed her in traction. She remained in the hospital for a week and was discharged as not requiring further treatment. Since her physical findings were negative, her physician recommended that she be returned to work with the restriction that she not lift anything over ten pounds and that she work only half time for the first two weeks. The first day of work, she complained of pain and was sent home with instructions to see her doctor.

Edna's physician referred her for a psychological evaluation to determine whether her physical symptoms might be stress-related and whether she might benefit from a pain treatment program. Her MMPI profile is shown in Figure 10.2. The MMPI profile reflected a highly defensive pat-

FIGURE 10.2
MMPI Profile of Edna B.

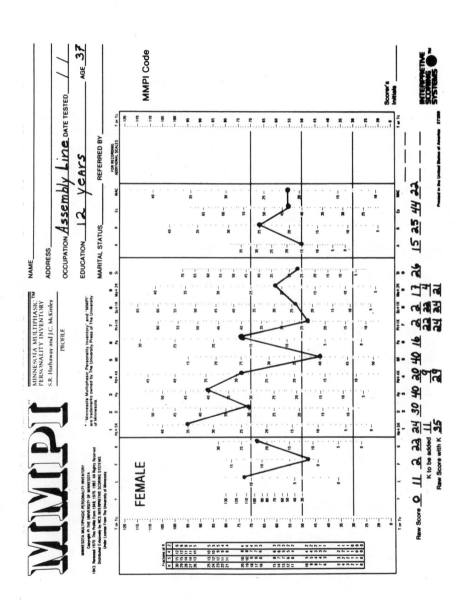

Source: Supplied by author.

tern, suggesting that she was not cooperating with the evaluation. She appeared to be attempting to present a "virtuous" image of herself while claiming that her problems were physical. Although her MMPI profile was technically invalid as a result of her L scale score, the resulting clinical profile is consistent, in that the somatic symptoms shown by the high elevations on the Hs (Hypochondriasis) scale and Hy (Hysteria) scale are unlikely to result from physical factors. Rather, the extreme elevations on these scales suggest a strong psychological component in her symptomatic pattern.

Edna was referred to a behaviorally oriented pain treatment program, which she reluctantly attended for three sessions. She refused further treatment from the company physician and indicated her unwillingness to return to work. She sought a medical evaluation from another physician who, she felt, would better appreciate the physical nature of her pain. She also filed a claim for worker's compensation.

Employer-Initiated Treatment Referral

Individuals experiencing personal problems may not be able to prevent their difficulties from adversely influencing their work. A frequent psychological referral in an occupational health setting involves problems that have been detected by supervisors who have become concerned about the employee's failure to perform satisfactorily on the job. The following case is typical of employer-initiated referrals.

Case 3: Unrecognized Alcohol Abuse

Alfred A., a 38-year-old engineer, had been absent from work for 38 days during the past year. On several occasions his supervisor had warned him that he had to be more responsible. Typically, after a weekend of heavy drinking, Alfred would miss work on Monday and, sometimes, Tuesday. On three occasions he was absent for several days after being arrested for driving under the influence of alcohol. The MMPI profile (Figure 10.3) was obtained when Alfred was told that he had to seek treatment for alcohol abuse or be fired from his job.

In the initial interview Alfred was quite reluctant to discuss his problems, and was angry at his supervisor for forcing him to see a psychologist. During the initial interview and the two sessions that followed, Alfred was given a great deal of feedback about his problem situation as reflected in the MMPI and his supervisory evaluation. At the end of the initial interview, Alfred acknowledged, albeit reluctantly, that he was in serious difficulty as

FIGURE 10.3
MMPI Profile of Alfred A.

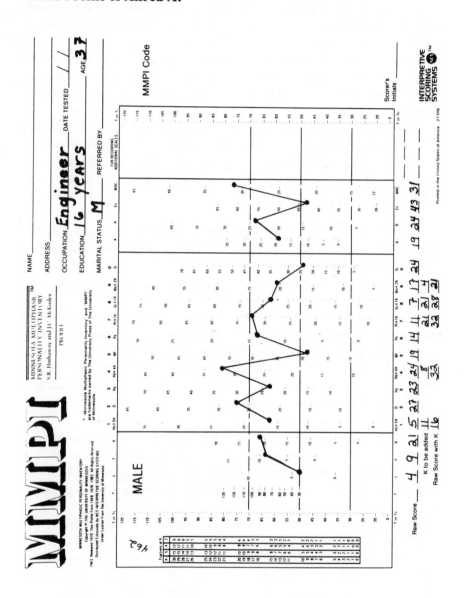

Source: Provided by author.

a result of his drinking. He came to the second interview with his wife, who expressed relief that Alfred was finally seeking professional help. She indicated that her tolerance of his behavior had run out and she had been planning to seek a divorce. Alfred admitted that he had had a serious drinking problem for some time. Even his wife was unaware of how much alcohol he consumed or that he had been missing so much work. She was aware that he had been arrested and jailed for drunk driving once but not that he had twice been arrested for driving under the influence and spent the night in jail. (She had been on business trips during the first two incarcerations.)

The MMPI interpretation was particularly valuable in convincing Alfred of his psychological and drinking problems. He acknowledged that the "objective" test information seemed to characterize his behavior pretty well. A computer-generated MMPI report[2] suggested the following problems:

Symptomatic pattern: He appears rather tense and depressed at this time, and is feeling agitated over problems in his environment. He shows a long-standing pattern of poor impulse control and lack of acceptance of societal standards. He may be experiencing a great deal of stress following a period of acting-out behavior, including possibly excessive use of alcohol and drugs. He appears to be a rather immature and impulsive individual who shows little genuine guilt over his behavior. He may be angry over his present situation, and he blames other people for his problems. He accepts little responsibiity for his present problems. He may be seeking a temporary respite from environmental stressors and may attempt to manipulate others through his symptoms in order to escape responsibility for his problems.

Interpersonal relationships: He has probably been experiencing strained interpersonal relationships. He tends to make friends easily, but his relationships are rather superficial. He appears to be quite manipulative in relationships, and may use other people for his own gratification. He is somewhat hedonistic in the way he approaches life. He tends to act out impulsively, without sufficient concern for the feelings of other people. He is likely to be experiencing marital distress.

Behavior stability: This MMPI profile reflects a long-standing personality problem; however, the subject also appears to be experiencing a substantial amount of situational distress. Even after the stress subsides and he feels more comfortable, his personality problems are likely to continue.

Diagnostic considerations: Individuals with this profile often receive a diagnosis of personality disorder with problems of substance abuse. The possibility that he is experiencing problems associated with an affective disorder should also be considered. Individuals with this profile tend to have problems with alcohol or drug abuse. Referral for a substance abuse evaluation and treatment is recommended.

Job Performance Evaluation

Psychological evaluation of currently employed individuals may be requested by employers for a number of reasons. Most frequently the referral involves the need to determine whether the individual is functioning well enough psychologically to perform critical duties in a responsible manner. The occupations of most concern in this type of evaluation are those for which psychological evaluation in initial selection is deemed important—for example, police officer, air traffic controller, nuclear power plant operator, or airline pilot. Two examples of this type of psychological diagnostic study will be provided to illustrate the job performance assessment.

Case 4: Possible Dereliction of Duty by a Police Officer

Garnet R., a 34-year-old policewoman, was referred for a psychological evaluation to determine whether her recent personal problems had adversely affected her ability to function effectively as a police officer. She was on suspension from the force until it could be determined whether she should be permitted to carry a firearm—a requirement for the performance of her job.

Officer R. was suspended from a suburban police force following an incident in which she was found sleeping on the job. Psychological evaluation was requested by her supervisor after she told him that she was under a great deal of stress and had been sleeping a great deal lately. She reported that she was experiencing a number of stresses: financial problems resulting from a three-month leave of absence without pay, worry over her health caused by the discovery of lumps in her breast (which later proved to be benign), worry over her father's health, discontent over the type of police work she was doing, and her resentment of perceived sexual harassment by senior police department personnel. Regarding her last concern, she reported that she had filed sexual harassment charges against one of her supervisors, but these were dismissed because it was her word against his. In general, she has felt that she had not been treated fairly by the department. Officer R. reported that all of these tensions had gotten to her lately, and that on the morning of the incident, she was being belittled by other officers. She said, "To hell with it," went into the ladies' room, and went to sleep for a while.

FIGURE 10.4
MMPI Profile of Garnet R.

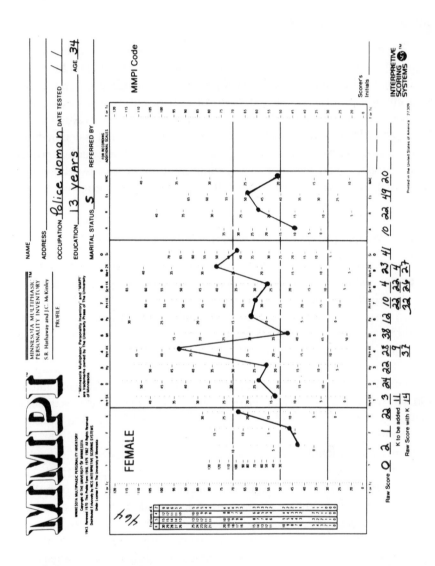

Source: Supplied by author.

Officer R. was quite defensive during the evaluation and attempted to place herself in the most favorable light possible. In the interview she sought to foster the idea that she had been depressed and under a great deal of tension. However, the computer-generated MMPI report[3] was quite helpful in putting her complaints into perspective:

Symptomatic pattern: She appears to be an extremely manipulative and somewhat impulsive person who is having a good bit of behavioral difficulties. Her tendencies to act out impulsively, in socially unacceptable ways, may get her into difficulty with authorities. She is a rather rebellious person who may assert herself in passive ways, such as procrastination, as well as in direct confrontation. She has a tendency to use poor judgment at times and to act in generally self-indulgent ways. She may appear defiant and act immaturely if her actions are frustrated. She appears to have an exaggerated sense of self-importance at times. She appears to not accept much responsibility for her own actions and blames other people for things that go wrong. There is no evidence of anxiety, depression, or psychotic thinking in her MMPI profile. She does not appear to be the type of individual who gets depressed easily but does appear to be the type of individual who discharges personal conflict by acting-out behavior.

Interpersonal relationships: Individuals with this MMPI profile tend to have generally good social skills and are usually effective in social situations. They are usually outgoing, extraverted, and able to "con" other people quite effectively. Individuals with this profile, however, tend to lack sincerity and genuine interest in other people.

Behavioral stability: This MMPI profile pattern is usually quite stable over time. Individuals with this profile tend to have long-standing personality adjustment difficulties and do not change much over time.

Diagnostic considerations: Individuals with this MMPI profile tend to have difficulties of an interpersonal nature or behavior problems resulting from authority conflicts. No depression or anxiety-based problems are reflected in this profile.

Conclusions from the diagnostic evaluation were the following: Officer R. appears to be experiencing a great deal of difficulty as a result of her lack of judgment and rebellious, impulsive behavior. She has attempted to manipulate others into excusing her behavior problems by claiming they are the result of mental health problems, specifically depression. However, she appears not to be depressed at this time. She does possess personality characteristics that make her vulnerable to behavioral or interpersonal difficulties. Her expressed psychological symptoms do not appear to be significant enough to keep her from performing her duties as an officer. She does not seem to be emotionally distraught at this time and is likely to be able to perform her duties as she has in the past. Her present psychological state appears not to require psychological intervention and her behavior should be dealt with through normal disciplinary procedures. Her long-standing personality adjustment difficulties, including immaturity and authority conflicts, could recur in situations where she becomes frustrated and angry.

Case 5: Life-style Problems in an Airline Copilot

Charles D., a 34-year-old airline copilot, was referred for a psychological evaluation following hospitalization resulting from symptoms similar to those of a heart attack. Medical tests proved negative, and Mr. D. was referred for evaluation of his "hyperventilation and anxiety as a result of fatigue and stress."

Mr. D. was seen for an extensive psychological evaluation. He was interviewed on two occasions and given a battery of psychological tests, including the MMPI and the Rorschach. Results of the evaluation were communicated over two feedback sessions.

Mr. D. was quite outgoing and friendly in the sessions. He was very talkative and seemingly open. (He usually came early to the sessions and spent time talking and joking with the secretary.) Throughout the sessions he was outwardly compliant. He talked freely about his life and his problems as he viewed them. He expressed a desire to learn why he had experienced the physical problems. Mr. D. appeared to be an intelligent individual with a broad range of interests and a high mechanical aptitude. However, he was not reflective about psychological matters and had little insight into how his behavior affected other people.

The symptoms Mr. D. experienced reportedly occurred after a period of intense stress. Mr. D. had been flying a lot recently. In addition to the flying hours on his regular job, he had reportedly spent two weeks with his National Guard unit, aiding in the evacuation of people from the Mt. St. Helen's eruption. (Actually, Mr. D. was not flying at this time, but was doing administrative work.) His "stressful situation" also involved a great deal of travel. The hospitalization occurred at the end of a three-day celebration that capped off a friend's wedding. The lengthy wedding party conflicted with a family responsibility—he was supposed to have taken his two sons to summer camp.

Mr. D. lived with his wife and two children but didn't spend much time at home. When he was not flying, he spent a lot of time with a girl friend who lived in another city. He reported that his wife was aware of his relationships with other women but did not want a divorce. He said that he did not want to get involved in a permanent relationship but liked to have affairs. He had, however, been with his present friend for three years.

In spite of his interpersonal openness and acknowledged interest in cooperating with the examination, Mr. D. produced a highly defensive MMPI. (See the profile in Figure 10.5.) He was quite reluctant to divulge personal information about himself on the MMPI. Instead, he was quite closed, probably as a result of his concern over what the test might indicate about his flight status.

The psychological tests indicated that Mr. D. appeared to be an individual who was experiencing a great deal of interpersonal conflict. He seemed to be an active and energetic person who tended to use poor social judgment at times. At the time of testing, he may have been experiencing some remorse about his behavior and his neglect of family responsibilities. He appeared to be an immature individual who was having some problems with alcohol abuse when tested. His hedonistic life-style, acting-out behavior, and alcohol abuse may have resulted in family and relationship problems that were placing great strains on him. His behavior at the time he was tested appeared to be generally sociopathic. He seemed to use denial to a great extent to deal with problems in his disruptive social life. He did not like to discuss problems or face interpersonal conflicts. When problems become intense, he was remorseful or felt the conflict in the form of physical distress.

There was a clear element of secondary gain in Mr. D's health episode. His physical "fatigue" provided excuses for his disruptive behavior, and he did not have to face the consequences of his actions. Mr. D. reacted to stress through denial and "escapist" tactics (such as running away and using alcohol). These defenses may work well enough for him much of the time, but under periods of intense stress, he appears to consume more alcohol and commit himself to things that produce further difficulties for him.

There is strong evidence in the testing that Mr. D. may be developing an alcohol addiction pattern. His alcohol abuse may be resulting in other life-style problems that are presently contributing to his high level of stress. His use of denial may prevent him from accepting his substance abuse problems at this time. Although Mr. D.'s problems are severe enough to

FIGURE 10.5
MMPI Profile of Charles D.

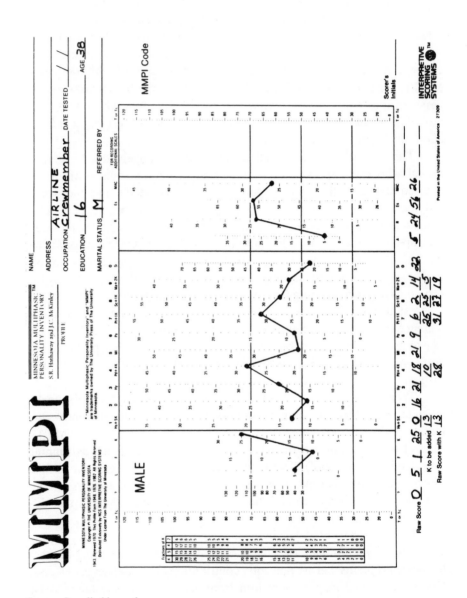

Source: Supplied by author.

warrant psychological treatment for alcohol abuse, he has not reached the point where he can accept treatment.

Further evaluation and treatment for alcohol abuse were recommended. Mr. D. agreed to accept a referral for treatment but failed to follow up on the recommendations. His FAA airman's medical certification was not renewed pending further information about his life-style problems.

SUMMARY AND CONCLUSIONS

This chapter has focused on clinical assessment of emotional problems in industrial settings. A number of conceptual issues concerning the value and appropriateness of using personality tests in industrial settings were discussed. Initially, the assumptions underlying the use of personality tests for personnel and other industrial applications were examined. A number of reasons for the broadened use of personality testing in industrial settings were found. The present use of personality testing in industry includes more extensive applications than the traditional one of personnel selection. For example, personality tests are used to evaluate individuals for promotion, for job performance assessment, in evaluations for employee assistance programs, for back-to-work evaluations, and in disability evaluations. Factors that may influence personality test results in industrial settings, such as test defensiveness, expectations of employers, and possible reactions of organized labor, were discussed.

The use of personality testing as an aid in the personnel selection process was examined. The wide use of the MMPI in selection for sensitive or stress-prone occupations was reviewed. Much of the research to date has been conducted on selection of police officer candidates, but there is some research on personality evaluation in the selection of other professional groups, including fire fighters, airline flight crews, nuclear power plant operators, clergy, mental health professionals, and medical school applicants. Research published to date supports using the MMPI as an aid in making personnel decisions. While such decisions should not be made solely on the basis of personality test information, objective test results can provide a source of hypotheses about an individual's personality functioning and adjustment, for the personnel specialist to consider in making decisions. This chapter concluded with a discussion of a number of applications of personality testing in industrial settings that differed from the traditional use in personnel selection. Several types of test applications were illustrated with case material from an occupational health setting. The cases illustrated assessment in back-to-work evaluations, worker's compensation claims evaluations, employer-referred treatment evaluations, and job performance evaluations.

NOTES

1. Information about computer scoring and interpretation of the MMPI can be obtained from the NCS Interpretive Scoring Systems, Box 1416, Minneapolis MN 55440.

2. Adapted from a "Minnesota Report" narrative report processed by the NCS Interpretive Scoring Systems.

3. Adapted from a "Minnesota Report" narrative report processed by the NCS Interpretive Scoring Systems.

REFERENCES

Arvey, R.D., Mussio, S.J., & Payne, G. Relationships between MMPI scores and job performance measures of fire fighters. *Psychological Reports*, 1972, *31*, 199–202.

Azen, R.D., Snibbe, H.M., & Montgomery, H.R. A longitudinal predictive study of success and performance of law enforcement officers. *Journal of Applied Psychology*, 1973, *57*, 190–192.

Bernstein, I.H. Security guards' MMPI profiles: Some normative data. *Journal of Personality Assessment*, 1980, *44* (4), 377–380.

_____. Truncated component regression, multicollinearity and the MMPI's use in a police officer selection setting. *Multivariate Behavioral Research*, 1982, *17*, 99–116.

Blum, R.H. *Police selection*. Springfield, Ill.: Charles C. Thomas, 1964.

Bray, D.W., Campbell, R.J., & Grant, D.L. *Formative years in business: A long term AT&T study of managerial lives*. Huntington, N.Y.: Robert E. Krieger, 1979.

Bray, D.W., & Howard, A. Personality and the assessment center method. In C.D. Spielberger and J.N. Butcher (eds.), *Advances in personality assessment*, Vol. III. Hillsdale, N.J.: Lawrence Erlbaum Associates, 1983.

Butcher, J.N. Use of the MMPI in personnel selection. In J.N. Butcher (ed)., *New developments in the use of the MMPI*. Minneapolis: University of Minnesota Press, 1979.

Butcher, J.N., & Keller, L. Objective personality assessment: Present status and future directions. In G. Goldstein and M. Hersen (eds.), *Handbook of psychological assessment*. New York: Pergamon Press, 1984.

Butcher, J.N., & Tellegen, A. Objections to MMPI items. *Journal of Consulting Psychology*, 1966, *30*, 527–534.

Colarelli, N.J., & Siegel, S.M. A method of police personnel selection. *Journal of Criminal Law, Criminology and Police Science*, 1964, *55*, 287–289.

Costello, R.M. The MMPI as an instrument in police applicant screening: An examination of method. Paper presented at the Second Annual Meeting of the Society for Police and Criminal Psychology, Long Beach, Miss., 1976.

Costello, R.M., & Schoenfeld, L.S. Time related effects on MMPI profiles of police academy recruits. *Journal of Clinical Psychology*, in press.

Costello, R.M., Schoenfeld, L.S., & Kobos, J. Police applicant screening: An analogue study. *Journal of Clinical Psychology*, 1982, *38* (1), 216–221.

Crovitz, E., Huse, M.N., & Lewis, D.E. Selection of physicians' assistants. *Journal of Medical Education*, 1973, *48*, 551–555.

DuBois, P.H. *A history of psychological testing.* Boston: Allyn & Bacon, 1970.

Dunnette, M.D., & Borman, W.C. Personnel selection and classification systems. *Annual Review of Psychology*, 1979, *30*, 477–425.

Dunnette, M.D., Bownas, D.A., & Bosshardt, M.J. *Electric power plant study: Prediction of inappropriate, unreliable or aberrant job behavior in nuclear power plant settings.* Minneapolis: Personnel Decisions Research Institute, 1981.

Dunnette, M.D., & Motowidlo, S.J. *Development of a personnel selection and career assessment system for police officers for patrol, investigative, supervisory, and command positions.* Technical report. Minneapolis: Personnel Decisions, Inc., 1975.

Garetz, F.K., & Anderson, R.W. Patterns of professional activities of psychiatrists: A follow-up of 100 psychiatric residents. *American Journal of Psychiatry*, 1973, *130*, 981–984.

Gottesman, J. *Personality patterns of urban police applicants as measured by the MMPI.* Hoboken, N.J.: Laboratory of Psychological Studies, Stevens Institute of Technology, 1969.

Grant, D.L. Issues in personnel selection. *Professional Psychology*, 1980, *11*, (3), 369–384.

Guion, R.M. Recruiting, selection and job placement. In M.D. Dunnette (ed.), *Handbook of industrial and organizational psychology.* Chicago: Rand McNally, 1976.

Harrell, T.W. High earning MBA's. *Personnel Psychology*, 1972, *25*, 523–530.

Harrell, T.W., & Harrell, M.S. The personality of MBA's who reach general management early. *Personnel Psychology*, 1973, *26*, 127–134.

Hedlund, D.E. A review of the MMPI in industry. *Psychological Reports*, 1965, *17*, 875–889.

Hooke, J.F., & Krauss, H.H. Personality characteristics of successful police sergeant candidates. *Journal of Criminal Law, Criminology and Police Science*, 1971, *62*, (1), 104–106. (a)

_____. Personality characteristics of highly rated policemen. *Personnel Psychology,* 1971, *24,* 679–686. (b)

Jansen, D.G., & Garvey, F.J. High-, average- and low-rated clergymen in a state hospital clinical program. *Journal of Clinical Psychology,* 1973, *29,* 89–92.

Kelly, W.L. Psychological prediction of leadership in nursing. *Nursing Research,* 1974, *23,* 38–42.

Lefkowitz, J. Psychological attributes of policemen: A review of research and opinion. *Journal of Social Issues,* 1975, *31* (1), 3–26.

Matarazzo, J.D., Allen, D.V., Saslow, G. & Wiens, A.N. Characteristics of successful policemen and firemen applicants. *Journal of Applied Psychology,* 1964, *48,* 123–133.

McAllister, L. The MMPI as a selection instrument for law enforcement officers in Dakota County, 1969–1977. Presentation at Police Officer Training Board Seminar, Willmar, Minn., October 12, 1977.

Meehl, P.E. *Clinical versus statistical prediction.* Minneapolis: University of Minnesota Press, 1954.

Merian, E.M., Stefan, D., Schoenfeld, L.S., & Kobos, J. Screening of MMPI applicants: A 5-item MMPI research index. *Psychological Reports,* 1980, *47,* 155–158.

Muha, T.M., & May, J.R. An employment index for identifying unfit job applicants. *Journal of Community Psychology,* 1973, *1,* 362–365.

Murphy, J.J. Current practices in the use of psychological testing by police agencies. *Journal of Criminal Law, Criminology and Police Sciences,* 1972, *63,* 570–576.

Naroll, H.G., & Levitt, E.E. Formal assessment procedures in police selection. *Psychological Reports,* 1963, *12,* 691–693.

Nussbaum, K., Shaffer, J.W., & Schneidmuhl, A.M. Psychological assessment in the Social Security program for disability insurance. *American Psychologist,* 1969, *24,* 869–872.

Pearson, J.S., Swenson, W.M., Rome, H.P., Mataya, P., & Brannick, T.L. Further experience with the automated MMPI. *Mayo Clinic Proceedings,* 1964, *39,* 823–829.

Peterson, N.G., & Houston, J.S. *The prediction of correctional officer job performance: Construct validation in an employment setting.* Technical report. Minneapolis: Personnel Decisions Research Institute, 1980.

Rhead, C., Abrams, A., Grossman, H., & Margolis, P. The psychological assessment of police candidates. *American Journal of Psychiatry,* 1968, *124,* 1575–1580.

Sacuzzo, D.P., Higgins, G., & Lewandowski, D. Program for the psychological assessment of law enforcement officers: Initial evaluation. *Psychological Reports,* 1974, *35,* 651–654.

Schoenfeld, L.S., Kobos, J.C., and Phinney, I.R. Screening police applicants: A study of reliability with the MMPI. *Psychological Reports,* 1980, *47,* 419–425.

Shaffer, J.W. Using the MMPI to evaluate mental impairment in disability deter-
mination. *Clinical Notes on the MMPI.* Minneapolis: National Computer
Systems, 1981.
Solway, K.S., Hays, J.R., & Zieben, M. Personality characteristics of juvenile
probation officers. *Journal of Community Psychology,* 1976, *4,* 152–156.
Stone, L.A., Bassett, G.R., Brosseau, J.D., Demers, J., & Stiening, J.A.
Psychological test scores for a group of MEDEX trainees. *Psychological Re-
ports,* 1972, *31,* 827–831.
Ziskin, J. *Coping with psychiatric and psychological testimony* (3rd ed.). Marina
Del Rey, Calif.: Law and Psychology Press, 1981. (a)
_____. Use of the MMPI in forensic settings. *Clinical Notes on the MMPI.* Min-
neapolis: National Computer Systems, 1981. (b)

FIGURE 10.4
MMPI Profile of Garnet R.

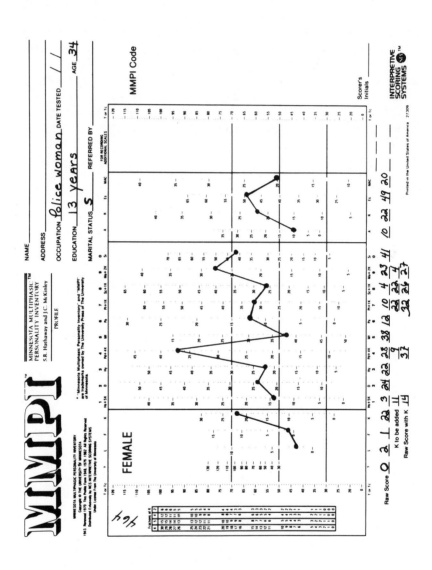

Source: Supplied by author.

Name Index

Subject Index

About the Editors and Contributors

H. JOHN BERNARDIN is professor of management and the director of research for the College of Business and Public Administration at Florida Atlantic University. He is the former director of doctoral studies in applied behavioral science at Virginia Polytechnic Institute. The author of three books and over 50 articles in industrial psychology, Dr. Bernardin serves on the editorial board of the *Academy of Management Review.*

DAVID BOWNAS is assistant manager for testing and validation at Metro-North Commuter Railroad in New York. He has performed a variety of selection validation studies employing personality and interest measures, including a project defining the concept of emotional stability in industrial settings. At the time of this symposium, he was assistant professor of psychology at Virginia Polytechnic Institute.

DR. ANNE ANASTASI is professor emeritus of psychology at Fordham University, and is internationally known in the area of applied psychological measurement. She is past president of the American Psychological Association, and of its divisions 1 (General Psychology) and 5 (Evaluation and Measurement). Her major publications include *Psychological Testing, Fields of Applied Psychology,* and *Individual Differences.*

V. JON BENTZ has been Sears Roebuck's director of psychological research and services for 30 years. In recent years he and his colleagues at Sears have developed multiple assessment techniques that use both individual and group simulations of upper-level executive tasks. His current work includes research on managerial styles, executive leadership, executive performance evaluation, and communication between executives and their managerial employees.

STEPHEN R. BRIGGS is assistant professor of psychology at the University of Tulsa. He earned his Ph.D. in personality psychology from the University of Texas at Austin. His research interests include personality measurement, applied personality research, and the self in social interaction. Recent publications have dealt with shyness, self-presentation, and the use of factor analysis in scale construction.

DR. JAMES N. BUTCHER is professor of psychology and director of graduate training in clinical psychology at the University of Minnesota. The author of 10 books and more than 50 articles dealing with personality assessment, he is especially noted for his research on the interpretation and application of the MMPI. Dr. Butcher has consulted extensively in applications of personality assessment and clinical and counseling psychology in industrial settings.

DR. DAVID CAMPBELL is Smith Richardson senior research fellow in creative leadership at the Center for Creative Leadership in Greensboro, North Carolina. Before coming to CCL, he was professor of psychology at the University of Minnesota, where he was heavily involved in research on career development, and directed the revision and publication of the Strong-Campbell Interest Inventory. In addition to numerous journal articles, he has written several popular books, including *If You Don't Know Where You're Going, You'll Probably End up Somewhere Else.*

BRUCE N. CARPENTER, who received his Ph.D. from the University of Wisconsin at Madison, is assistant professor of psychology at the University of Tulsa. Trained as a clinical psychologist, he is interested in the assessment of personality and social variables that affect functioning. He has recently been comparing processes for selecting police officers.

NICKOLAUS R. FEIMER is an assistant professor in the Department of Psychology at Virginia Polytechnic Institute and State University. His research has focused on environmental perception and cognition, assessment, and personality processes. He was coeditor of the monograph *Environmental Psychology: Directions and Perspectives* (Praeger, 1983). He has published in *Environmental Behavior, Journal of Applied Psychology, Journal of Environmental Psychology,* and *Journal of Personality and Social Psychology.*

DR. DONALD R. GOODENOUGH is currently visiting research professor in the Graduate School of Education, Rutgers University. His former positions include senior research scientist at the Educational Testing Service and professor in the Psychiatry Department of the State University of New York, Downstate Medical Center. He has conducted extensive research on sleep and dream processes and on the field dependence-independence cognitive style dimension. He is coauthor of *Cognitive Styles: Essence and Origins* and of *Psychological Differentiation.*

ROBERT O. HANSSON, is an associate professor in psychology at the University of Tulsa. He earned his MBA and a Ph.D. in social psychology from the University of Washington. Research interests include industrial gerontology, relational competence and adjustment, and personality and social influences on coping and adjustment among the elderly.

MICHAEL M. HARRIS is assistant professor of management at the Krannert Graduate School of Management at Purdue University. He received his Ph.D. in industrial-organizational psychology from the University of Illinois at Chicago. His research focuses on judgment and decision processes in the employment context. He has published in *Personnel Psychology* and presented papers at the American Psychological Association meetings.

DR. ROBERT HOGAN is university professor and chairman of the Department of Psychology at the University of Tulsa, and editor of the Personality Processes section of the *Journal of Personality and Social Psychology*. He has written more than 50 articles and a text entitled *Personality Theory*. Dr. Hogan is a fellow of APA divisions 5 and 8, and was named Behavioral Scientist of the Year for 1980 by the Washington, D.C., Academy of Sciences.

DR. JOHN B. MINER is research professor of management at Georgia State University. He has published over 60 articles and books in personnel and industrial relations, industrial psychology, and organizational behavior, dealing with such topics as personality testing, intelligence, management development, and managerial talent supplies. He is a fellow of the American Psychological Association and was editor of the *Academy of Management Journal*. He served as president of the Academy of Management in 1978.

DR. JOSEPH L. MOSES is personnel manager of research at AT&T. Active in the assessment center movement, he has directed AT&T's Advanced Management Potential Assessment Program since its inception. A fellow of the Society of Industrial-Organizational Psychology, Dr. Moses is also research professor of psychology at the New York University Graduate School. He is coauthor of *Making It Happen: Designing Research with Implementation in Mind* and of *Applying the Assessment Center Method.*

MICHAEL R. PATSFALL received his Ph.D. in psychology from Virginia Polytechnic Institute and State University. His research interests include organizational issues such as climate and development. He has published in *Journal of Environmental Psychology.*

PAUL R. SACKETT is associate professor of psychology at the University of Illinois at Chicago. He has published extensively in the areas of managerial assessment, job analysis, and employee honesty. His papers have appeared in *Journal of Applied Psychology, Organizational Behavior and Human Performance,* and *Personnel Psychology.* He is the coauthor of *Employee Staffing and Selection* (Richard D. Irwin, 1983).

DR. ELLEN VAN VELSOR, a research associate at the Center for Creative Leadership, is involved in program evaluation. Prior to joining the center, she held a post-doctoral fellowship at the Center for the Study of Aging and Human Development, Duke University. She has co-authored numerous articles in sociological journals and is a member of the American Sociological Association. She holds a Ph.D. in sociology from the University of Florida.

D

D 2010